The Old New Logic

The Old New Logic

Essays on the Philosophy of Fred Sommers

edited by David S. Oderberg
with a foreword by P. F. Strawson

A Bradford Book
The MIT Press
Cambridge, Massachusetts
London, England

MIT Press books may be purchased at special quantity discounts for business or sales promotional use. For information, please email special_sales@mitpress.mit.edu or write to Special Sales Department, The MIT Press, 5 Cambridge Center, Cambridge, MA 02142.

This book was set in Stone serif and Stone sans by SNP Best-set Typesetter Ltd., Hong Kong, and was printed and bound in the United States of America.

Library of Congress Cataloging-in-Publication Data

The old new logic : essays on the philosophy of Fred Sommers / edited by David S. Oderberg; with a foreword by P. F. Strawson.
    p.   cm.
 "A Bradford book."
 Includes bibliographical references and index.
 ISBN 0-262-15113-8 (hc : alk. paper)—ISBN 0-262-65106-8 (pbk. : alk. paper)
 1. Sommers, Frederic Tamler, 1923– . 2. Logic. I. Oderberg, David S.

B945.S7254O43 2005
160′.92—dc22

                                                                2004055165

10 9 8 7 6 5 4 3 2 1

Contents

Preface and Acknowledgments   vii

Foreword by P. F. Strawson   xi

1   **Intellectual Autobiography**   1
     Fred Sommers

2   **Trees, Terms, and Truth: The Philosophy of Fred Sommers**   25
     George Englebretsen

3   **Syntax and Ontology: Reflections on Three Logical Systems**   49
     E. J. Lowe

4   **Exploring Boundary Conditions on the Structure of Knowledge:
     Some Nonobvious Influences of Philosophy on Psychology**   67
     Frank C. Keil

5   **General Terms, Anaphora, and Rigid Designation**   85
     Alan Berger

6   **The Syntax and Semantics of English Prepositional Phrases**   101
     Patrick Suppes

7   **Modeling Anaphora in TFL**   111
     William C. Purdy

8   **An Elementary Term Logic for Physically Realizable Models of
     Information**   135
     Steven Lindell

9   **Sommers's Cancellation Technique and the Method of
     Resolution**   169
     Aris Noah

10   **Predicate Logic and Bare Particulars**   183
     David S. Oderberg

11   **Comments and Replies**   211
     Fred Sommers

Works by Fred Sommers   233
Contributors   237
Index   239

Preface and Acknowledgments

What makes a philosopher important? How can we know whether a philosopher will have a reputation that places him firmly within the lineage of figures who occupy a certain and inextinguishable place in the history of ideas? It is a sad but commonplace observation among jurists that by definition one does not become a recognized authority in legal theory until one has "gone the way of all flesh." For it is up to the historians of a discipline ultimately to determine which of its practitioners has cemented his or her place as one of the beacons who light the way for those to come. One thing of which we can be sure, however, is that there are at present names on the lips of every philosopher that one day will rarely be spoken, and yet others less often mentioned that will echo down the generations.

Without prejudging the estimation of future historians, Fred Sommers is one philosopher who has a strong claim to falling into the second category. His work, so far spanning some fifty years, ranges primarily over logic, philosophy of language and metaphysics, reaching even into philosophy of mind and scientific methodology. From papers on category theory, through logic, truth theory, realism, and related subjects, Sommers has built up an impressive body of thought notable for its originality, rigor and cohesiveness. Is originality what a philosopher should be striving for? In the common acceptation of the term, certainly not. It is not the job of the philosopher to dream up utterly new ideas and theories or to spin shiny new systems out of virgin cloth. The best philosophy, of course, is always marked by creativity and new thinking—it cannot and should not be a sterile repetition of the past. Yet that new thinking must, if it is to have any claim on our rational allegiance, build upon the wisdom and tradition of the ages, on the finest fruit of mankind's collective mental effort in penetrating the deepest and most difficult problems of meaning and existence. The kind of originality that respects the best of the past is the originality which itself deserves the respect of present and future thinkers.

Fred Sommers is among a handful of the senior philosophers of the last half-century to understand the intellectual, even moral, imperative of building on the past rather than forsaking it for new fashions and radical dead-ends. And it is in his virtually single-handed revival of the traditional Aristotelian or syllogistic logic that this sensitivity to philosophical tradition is most manifest. The logic of Aristotle, despite revisions, corrections, and additions, remained largely intact as *the* logical system taught and researched by philosophers for more than two thousand years. Its overthrow and replacement by the logic of Gottlob Frege and Bertrand Russell is the closest philosophy has ever come to a Copernican-style revolution (*pace* Kant). One cannot underestimate the sharpness of the break with the past that the development of Fregean (or "modern predicate") logic represented. If it is taught at all, Aristotelian syllogistic appears as no more than a curious footnote, perhaps a short chapter, in contemporary logic textbooks.

The opinion of most philosophers is that Aristotelian logic was good but is now as good as dead. Most of them, one suspects, would sooner see a revival of geocentrism than of syllogistic logic. Hence the vastness of the task of rehabilitating it, let alone renewing and refashioning it into a system with at least the elegance as well as the expressive and deductive power of modern predicate logic. This Sommers has done, but he could not have done it without building explicitly on the ideas not only of The Philosopher himself but of the medieval scholastic logicians, Leibniz (who himself worked hard and with ingenuity on refining and improving syllogistic logic) and the nineteenth-century algebraic logicians such as George Boole and Augustus De Morgan. His 1982 magnum opus *The Logic of Natural Language* sets out in detail the system TFL, which stands alternately (and happily) for both *term functor logic* and *traditional formal logic*. It is a dense and difficult work, and might seem quite baffling to readers not familiar with Sommers's previous writings or appreciative of the nature of the task he set himself. And yet, like all great works, with careful and patient study it yields up its secrets and rewards constant rereading. If Sommers had not written anything else, his reputation would have been assured in the eyes of all but those with an unchallengeable hostility to the very idea of his task. Will traditional formal logic as conceived by Sommers and developed by his followers, or syllogistic logic in general, ever break out of its current position as an enclave within contemporary logic and regain some of the ground lost in the previous century? Or is it doomed to remain an intellectual curiosity defended by a small number of largely traditionally minded thinkers? Again, this is for history to reflect upon, not for the current generation to predict. That Sommers has done the work of several philosophers in giving syllogistic logic its best chance of recovery since the end of the nineteenth century is beyond doubt. One cannot ask any more.

The present collection is a witness not only to the esteem in which the work of Fred Sommers—in all the areas in which he has written—is held by those who know it, but also to the influence of that work on the thinking of others. It is striking, however, in reflecting the extent of that influence on disciplines outside philosophy. For *The Old New Logic* brings together not just philosophers and logicians, but linguists, psychologists, and computer scientists who have each in their own way felt the force of Sommers's ideas. It is my profound hope that this fascinatingly diverse range of essays does its small part in bringing to the wider philosophical and intellectual community the work of the man to whom it is, in admiration, respectfully dedicated.

I would like to thank the graduate students to whom I have taught Sommers's logic in recent years, whose motivation and enthusiasm have in turn aided my own attempts better to understand his work. I am grateful also to George Englebretsen, whose unstinting support for this project has helped make it possible. He has, more than anyone, assisted myself and others in seeing the depth and importance of Fred Sommers's thought; may he continue to do so. I would like to record special thanks to everyone at the Social Philosophy and Policy Center, Bowling Green State University, Ohio, where I was a Visiting Scholar during the summer of 2003, for providing the immensely congenial conditions in which much of the editorial work was undertaken. I would also like to thank Bill Purdy for his generous technical help with last-minute preparation of the manuscript, and Judy Feldmann of The MIT Press for her expert copyediting. Finally, my gratitude goes to Tom Stone of The MIT Press for taking on this book and for his advice and encouragement.

Foreword

P. F. Strawson

It is refreshing to meet Fred Sommers, and equally refreshing to read him. He stands out among the philosophers of our time in virtue of his originality, his power and ingenuity, and his courage. I stress the last quality because it is required if one is to swim, as strenuously as he has done, against the tide of contemporary opinion or assumption.

Locke remarked that it did not need Aristotle to teach us to reason; but it certainly needed Frege and Russell to teach us to reason in the forms of modern predicate logic. Fred Sommers observed that many of the valid natural thought processes of untutored humanity seem remote indeed from these last, but conform quite closely to the forms of traditional Aristotelian logic. Admittedly, traditional formal logic as we had it seemed to suffer from an incapacity to handle types of reasoning that were easily and elegantly represented in the supplanting forms we are now familiar with. But if the logic of terms could be so adjusted as to meet this deficiency, perhaps it was due for a revival. Sommers made the adjustment and delivered the revival. He did more. He formalized the results in a quasi-algebraic mode, inspired perhaps in part by some earlier thinkers, whose efforts were made long after antiquity but well before the present. In all this he displayed a characteristic independence of mind matched by an equal resourcefulness.

The notions of category difference and category mistake were often brilliantly and even amusingly illustrated by Gilbert Ryle, and were used by him with devastating effect to dispel many insidious philosophical illusions. He never, however, succeeded in giving a systematic theoretical explanation of the ideas he so successfully exploited. His only steps toward such an account were woefully ill directed. Here again Fred Sommers took up the challenge: he was perhaps the first seriously to attempt to produce, and certainly the first to succeed in producing, a structured systematic theory of the matter.

His alethic realism, while adorned with a characteristically personal flourish, is essentially the realism of all sensible men.

This volume of essays, headed by the masterly exposition of George Englebretsen, is a fitting tribute both to Sommers's intellectual brilliance and to his strength of character.

1 Intellectual Autobiography

Fred Sommers

I did an undergraduate major in mathematics at Yeshiva College and went on to do graduate studies in philosophy at Columbia University in the 1950s. There I found that classical philosophical problems were studied as intellectual history and not as problems to be solved. That was disappointing but did not strike me as unreasonable; it seemed to me that tackling something like "the problem of free will" or "the problem of knowledge" could take up one's whole life and yield little of permanent value. I duly did a dissertation on Whitehead's process philosophy and was offered a teaching position at Columbia College. Thereafter I was free to do philosophical research of my own choosing. My instinct was to avoid the seductive, deep problems and to focus on finite projects that looked amenable to solution.

Looking back to discern some special thematic interest that may be said to characterize much of my philosophical activity, I find I was usually drawn to look for ways to explain one or another aspect of our cognitive competence. I once saw a father warn an eight-year-old boy who was approaching an aloof and unwelcoming dog not to pet him, by saying 'Not all dogs are friendly'. The boy, who did hold back, responded with 'Some dogs are unfriendly; don't you think I *know* that?' I admired how adeptly the boy had moved from 'Not all dogs are friendly' to its affirmative obverse, 'Some dogs are unfriendly'. I remember thinking that the boy certainly did not make this move by somehow translating 'Not all dogs are friendly' as something like 'Not: for every x, if x is a dog then x is friendly' and then, by (unconsciously) applying laws of "quantifier interchange" and some laws of propositional logic, quickly get to 'There is an x such that x is a dog and not: x is friendly'. I wondered how the boy actually did it. We are, generally, intuitively prompt and sure in most of our common everyday logical judgments, all of which are effected with sentences of our native language. Consider that the average, logically untutored person instantaneously recognizes inconsistency in a pair of sentences like (A) and (B):

(A) Every colt is a horse.

(B) Some owner of a colt isn't an owner of a horse.

Modern predicate logic (MPL) takes pride in its ability formally to justify such judgments—something that the older logic of terms was unable to do. But MPL's methods of justification, which involve translations into an artificial quantificational idiom, offer no clues to how the average person, knowing no logic and adhering to the vernacular, is so logically adept.

It later occurred to me that Frege's disdain of natural language as a vehicle for logical reckoning had served a strategic defensive purpose: if logic does not aim to explain how we actually think and reason with sentences of natural language—if, therefore, it is misleadingly characterized as a science that provides us with the "laws of thought"—its obvious inability to illuminate everyday deductive competence will not be deemed a defect. According to Michael Dummett, Frege's invention of the quantifier/variable notation for solving the problem of multiple generality more than compensates for the bad fit of his logical language to the language in which we actually reason. "Frege ... had solved the problem which had baffled logicians for millennia by ignoring natural language."[1] Frege's disregard of natural language was not universally praised.[2] I would later join in dissent. But in the late 1950s I was still in thrall to the Frege–Russell–Quine way of doing logic, and it did not then occur to me to look for a cognitively adequate alternative.

The Category Tree

My first attempt at illuminating a common area of cognitive competence was not concerned with our deductive abilities but with our ability to avoid grammatical nonsense of the kind known as category mistakes, a term made popular by Gilbert Ryle. I was then studying Ryle's scintillating book, *The Concept of Mind*, and it struck me that we are leading charmed conceptual lives. Sentences like 'Saturday is in bed' and 'Some prime numbers are unmarried' are easily formed, but we never actually make the mistake of using them. Indeed, the overwhelming majority of grammatical sentences are category mistakes; this was actually established by computer programs at MIT that fed random vocabulary to a computer capable of forming simple grammatical sentences, generating far more sentences like 'The accident rejected the invitation' than sentences like 'Jane rejected the invitation'. How do we avoid them? It seemed plausible to me that we must be using some strategy to stay on the straight and narrow path of category correctness. I wrote to Quine about my idea of looking for constraints on categorial predicability, and he replied that he too had tried to construct a theory of predicability and categories but had given up on it. He nevertheless approved of my efforts and encouraged them. It was, he said, the kind of problem one could "get on with."

My search was complicated by the fact that a term like 'rational' seemed equivocally predicable of things like people and numbers (for we cannot say of this person that he is more rational than that number) whereas terms like 'interesting' are univocally predicable of things in different categories (we can say that flirting with women is more interesting to Tom than mathematics). After some months of speculation and intensive trial and error, I came to see that we organize our concepts for predicability on a hierarchical tree. At the top of the tree are terms like 'interesting', 'exists', and 'talked about', which are univocally predicable of anything whatever. At the bottom are names of things we talk about. And in between, going down the hierarchal tree, are predicates like 'colored', 'factorable by 3', and 'learned' that are predicable of some things but not of others.

Aristotle had already pointed out that terms are hierarchically ordered for predicability so that some pairs (e.g., {log, white}) are naturally predicable in only one direction ('Some log is white' is a natural predication but its logical equivalent, 'Some white thing is a log', is unnatural or *accidental*). Other term pairs are reciprocally predicable, for example, {Greek, philosopher}. Still others are mutually impredicable {philosopher, factorable by 3}. Aristotle's criterion for being naturally predicable in only one direction seems to be:

If B and C are mutually impredicable, and A is predicable of both, then A is naturally predicable of B and C and B and C are not naturally predicable of A.

For example, 'white' is naturally predicable of the mutually impredicable terms 'log' and 'sky', so both 'Some white thing is a log' and 'Some white thing is the sky' are unnatural or accidental predications. Looking for a category structure, I applied the Aristotelian criterion for natural predicability. Once we have a term like 'white' that is univocally predicable of mutually impredicable terms like 'sky' and 'rational', thereby establishing that 'white' is higher than 'rational', it will not be possible to find a term like 'prime number' of which 'rational' is predicable in the sense we use it in 'rational white man'. 'Rational' has two locations on the category tree, one predicable of men (who may be white), another predicable of numbers, which may be prime but cannot be white.

Hierarchical trees have apexes and consist of one or more "∧" structures. Between any two nodes on a tree structure there is only one possible path. On a hierarchical tree, a higher term is naturally predicable of a lower term and two terms are mutually impredicable when they are connected by a path that goes both up and down. For example, to get from 'even number' to 'explosion' one may go up from 'even number' to 'interesting' and down to 'explosion' in a ∧ path. Most term pairs on a large language tree are thus mutually impredicable.

If a term (e.g., 'colored') is at a node on the tree, so is its contrary ('colorless'). The disjunctive term 'colored-or-colorless' (which I represent as '/colored/') "spans" (is truly predicable of) all things that have or fail to have some color or other, including the 'color' we call 'colorless'. Being /colored/—having Kolor (as I called it)—is an ontological attribute that raindrops and the American flag possess but things like numbers, skills, and accidents do not possess. A raindrop is colorless but a skill is neither colored nor colorless; it has no Kolor. Nor is it Kolorless. It's not as though it fails to be /colored/; there is just no procedure for testing whether a skill is orange or colorless, and so on. Nor is there any conceivable way to transform a skill into something that has Kolor. In general, if '/T/' is a category term spanning things that are or fail to be T, then /T/ *has no contrary*. Whatever has /T/ness possesses it essentially; whatever does *not* have /T/ness does not lack it. Nothing is privative with respect to a category attribute.

I used the fact that category terms have no contraries for another proof that the category structure must be a hierarchical tree. We may take it as a logical truism that if some *A* is *B* then either every *A* is *B* or some *A* is un-*B* or every *B* is *A* or some *B* is un-*A*. But where *A* and *B* are category terms, the second and fourth disjuncts are false. We are then left with the following law governing category terms:

If some /X/ is /Y/ then either every /X/ is /Y/ or every /Y/ is /X/.

This *law of category inclusion* determines that terms are distributed on a hierarchical tree for the purposes of categorially correct predication. For example, since some /red/ things /weigh five pounds/ it will either be true that all /red/ things /weigh five pounds/ or true that all things that /weigh five pounds/ are /red/. Since something like a red sky or a glow does not /weigh five pounds/ it is not true that all /red/ things /weigh five pounds/. It follows that all things that /weigh five pounds/ are /red/ so that 'red' is higher on the tree than 'weighs'.

Ontological Individuals

Ryle's book was critical of Descartes's view that a person is an ontological composite, consisting of a mind and a body. Many common things are ontological composites. We observe objects and we observe events. When we observe a flash of lightning at midnight, what we observe is not an ontological individual but an ontological composite consisting of an event (the electrical discharge) and the blue streak produced by it. We speak of Italy as a sunny democratic country but it is the Italian peninsula that is sunny and the Italian society that is democratic; Italy itself, as a society *cum* peninsula, is ontologically composite. Think of the M-shaped figure ∧∧ as a figure obtained by joining two little trees. The term 'Italy' is at the middle node at the bottom. One side predicates 'sunny' of 'peninsula' and 'Italy', while the other predicates 'democratic' of 'Italy' and 'the Labor Party'. Peninsulas are /sunny/ but not /democratic/; The Labour Party is /democratic/ but not /sunny/. There are no M shapes on the category tree. In general, there can be no three individuals, a, b, and c, and two predicates, P and Q, such that P is predicable of a and b but not of c and Q is predicable of b and c but not of a. And when we find such a configuration in natural discourse, we must either deny that b is an ontological individual or deny that P and Q are univocally predicated. In the case of sunny democratic Italy, we maintain univocity and split the figure at the bottom, recognizing that Italy is a heterotypical entity, that is to say, a category composite—a peninsula-*cum*-society—composed of entities of different types.

The Cartesian argument for psychophysical dualism uses the very same reasoning, based on the notion of a psychophysical composite rather than a sociophysical composite as in the case of countries. Assume, says the Cartesian, that a human being is an ontological individual and not a composite. Our ontology would then contain things like pure egos that /think/ but are not /tall/. It would contain things like iron gates that are /tall/ but do not /think/. And it would contain persons like Descartes himself who is /tall/ and who also /thinks/. But this would violate the law of category inclusion. Since no individual can be both /six feet tall/ and /think/, Descartes must be a category composite, consisting of a thinking substance and an extended substance.[3]

More often than not, an inadmissible configuration (one that does not fit on the category tree) serves to show that some term is equivocal. Thus Aristotle argued that 'sharp' has different senses when said of a musical note and of a knife. Skies are /gray/ but not /sharp/. Knives are /sharp/ and /gray/. Thus 'gray' is higher than 'sharp' on the category tree. Musical notes are not /gray/. So when we speak of notes as sharp, we immediately realize that we are using a sense of 'sharp' in a location on the tree that is not the same as the one we use in describing knives. A similar example is the equivocation of 'tall' when said of stories. Skies are /gray/ but not /tall/. Buildings are /tall/ and /gray/. Thus 'gray' is higher on the tree than 'tall'. Our concept of a story is not that of something /gray/. Coming across 'tall stories', we immediately recognize that this use of 'tall' is not the one in which whatever is /tall/ is /gray/.

I harvested a number of philosophical fruits of the category tree in the early 1960s. For example, I realized that category attributes like Kolor, Texture (being smooth like some stones or rough like others), and Shape (having an identifiable shape like a person or a square or being shapeless like a jellyfish or a cloud of dust)—attributes with respect to which nothing is privative—stand in the way of successfully performing the empiricist thought experiment in which we are asked to conceptually strip an object like an apple of its attributes. This we do until we are left with 'something I know not what'—a featureless substratum that empiricists and transcendental philosophers arrived at but that idealists were soon happy to remove altogether. The stripping fails because, while we can think away its redness or smoothness, we cannot coherently think away the apple's Kolor, its Texture, or any other of its ontological attributes, since such attributes "have no contrary." Since I was by temperament a realist, this Aristotelian insight was congenial to me.

Each age has its characteristic trees. Sometimes entities that do not easily fit onto the "ordinary language tree" are introduced into the ontology. 'God' creates problems when theologians insist that terms like 'merciful' and 'just' cannot have their ordinary sense when said of 'God'. This leads some to negative theology. Sometimes empirical science calls for revolutionary reconfigurations. Early in the twentieth century the newly minted notion of electrons presented difficulties directly related to the tree requirement for conceptual coherence. Electrons were an anomaly because they had features that normally applied to events and other features that normally applied to physical objects. This initially led some physicists to talk of 'wavicles' or 'event-particles', a composite category. This dualist conception of electrons was not acceptable to physicists; on the other hand, neither was it acceptable to postulate different concepts of frequency when talking of waves and electrons or different concepts of mass when talking of stars and electrons. The solution adopted by some philosophers calls for a revolutionary conceptual shift that reconstrues all physical objects as a subcategory of events. It became acceptable to affirm event predicates of physical objects. Nelson Goodman speaks somewhere of a table as a 'monotonous event'. Alfred North Whitehead built his process philosophy on this new way of talking about physical objects, calling them 'actual occasions'. The avoidance of ontological dualism for elementary particles has led to radical relocations of fundamental categories that have yet to be assimilated.

Sometimes social developments cause us to reconfigure our ontology. Since the invention of corporations as economic institutions, we are able to say of a fence and of a person that it is tall and of a person and of a corporation that it owes money. Here we face the prospect of regarding persons as an ontologically composite category, having a corporate as a well as a physical individuality (persons as fictional corporations).

In general, the tree structure provides a kind of pure cartography we can use to chart conceptual differences between contemporaneous cultures or, historically, for mapping conceptual changes over time. The category tree structure has yet to be systematically applied in doing conceptual history or comparative philosophy. Even individual persons change conceptually as they mature. As children our concept of the sky is such that we well understand Chicken Little's alarm that it is in danger of falling. As adults we find the idea of a sky falling to be a category mistake. The cognitive psychologist Frank Keil appears to have successfully applied category tree theory in his studies of the conceptual development of children.

Logic as "How We Think"

In the mid-1960s I turned to the problem of our deductive competence. How, for example, do ten-year-olds, innocent of "logic," recognize the logical equivalence of 'No archer will hit every target' and 'Every archer will miss some target'? What makes everyone instantly certain that (A) 'Every colt is a horse' and (B) 'Someone who owns a colt doesn't own a horse' are jointly inconsistent?

Modern predicate logic (MPL) formally justifies such common, intuitive logical judgments, but its justifications do not explain how we make them. In proving that (A) and (B) are inconsistent—something traditional term logic had not been able to do—MPL uses its canonical idioms of function and argument, quantifiers and bound variables, to translate (A) and (B) respectively as:

(A*) For every thing x, if x is a colt then x is a horse.

(B*) There are things x and y such that y is a colt and x owns y and such that for everything z, if z is a horse then x does not own z.

and proceeds in about twelve to fifteen carefully chosen steps to derive a contradiction from (A*) and (B*). The syntax of the canonical formulas of MPL is not that of the vernacular sentences in which we actually reason, and MPL's formal justifications of our intuitive deductive judgments cannot serve as accounts of our everyday reasoning. So I confronted the question: What would a cognitively adequate logic—a "laws-of-thought" logic that casts light on what we actually do when we use natural language in thinking deductively—be like?

Unlike MPL such a logic must, as Patrick Suppes points out, be variable-free, its syntax closely conforming to the syntax of the sentences that figure in actual reasoning. Its mode of reasoning must be transparent, since every-day reasoning is virtually instantaneous. In that respect, I realized, it would be very much like elementary algebra. A ninth grader who judges 'No archer will hit every target' to be logically equivalent to 'Every archer will miss some target' does so with the same speed and confidence that he judges '$-(a + b - c)$' to be equal to '$-a - b + c$'. Syntactic naturalness and ease of reckoning are two essential features of a cognitively adequate logic that would cast an explanatory light on the celerity with which we reason with sentences of our natural language. The logical language of a cognitively adequate logic would therefore

(i)   not radically depart from the syntax of the sentences we use in everyday reasoning;

(ii) have simple, perspicuous rules of reckoning that are instantly (if unconsciously) applicable (e.g., by older children).

Because modern predicate logic possesses neither of these necessary features, it casts no light on the way we actually reckon. And so, for all its logistical merits for grounding mathematics, I concluded that MPL cannot be regarded as the logic we use in everyday reasoning.

Seeking to learn what makes us deductively so adept, I looked at hundreds of examples of ordinary deductive judgments with special attention to the common logical words that figure in them, in the belief that words like 'not', 'every', and 'some' must somehow be treated by us in ways that make reckoning with them as easy and perspicuous as our reckoning with elementary algebraic expressions.[4] For just as a ten year old moves easily and surely from '–(a + b)' to '–a + (–b)', so she moves from 'No boy is perfect' to 'Every boy is imperfect'.[5]

The solution came to me in Tel Aviv where I was teaching in the spring of 1967. I found to my surprise that the familiar logical words 'some', 'is', 'not', 'and', 'every', and 'if', words that figure constantly in our everyday deductive judgments, behave and are treated by us as plus or minus operators. Specifically:

'Some' ('a'), 'is' ('was', 'are', etc.) and 'and' are plus-words;
'Every' ('all', 'any' . . .), 'not' ('no', 'un-' . . .), and 'if' are minus-words.

The discovery that these key natural language logical constants have a plus/minus character is an empirical one. It involves the claim that the boy who hears his father say 'Not all dogs are friendly' and recognizes it as tantamount to 'Some dogs aren't friendly' is automatically treating his father's sentence as something like:

$$-(-\text{Dog} - \text{Friendly})$$

and so instantaneously reckoning it equivalent to

$$+\text{Dog} - \text{Friendly}.$$

Two Conceptions of Predication

A standard predication in modern predicate logic consists of a singular noun-phrase subject and a verb-phrase predicate. These two constituents are not syntactically interchangeable. Nor are they mediated by any logical tie. My work in category theory had led me to adopt the classical, terminist view of predication, according to which (i) general as well as singular statements are predications; (ii) the two parties tied in predication are not a noun-phrase subject and a verb-phrase predicate but two syntactically interchangeable terms; and (iii) these constituents are connected by a predicative expression—a term connective—such as 'some . . . is' or 'all . . . are'. Aristotle often preferred to formulate predications by placing the terms at opposite ends of the sentence and joining them by a predicating expression like 'belongs-to-some' or 'belongs-to-every'. Typical examples of terms thus tied in predication are 'Some Athenian is a philosopher' [⇒ Philosopher belongs-to-some Athenian] and 'Socrates is a philosopher' [⇒ Philosopher belongs-to-every Socrates]. We may abbreviate a terminist predication by eliminating the grammatical copula, writing 'Some S is P' as 'P some S' (in scholastic notation, 'PiS') and 'Every S is P' as 'P every S' (PaS). These formulations give 'some' and 'every' pride of place as logical copulas (term connectives).

In formulating inference rules for syllogistic reasoning, Aristotle focused attention on universal propositions of the form 'P every S'. However, he gives 'some' definitional priority over 'every', defining 'P every S' as 'not: non-P some S':

We say that one term is predicated of all of another when no examples of the subject can be found of which the other term cannot be asserted.[6]

In effect, 'P every S' [PaS] is defined as 'Not: non-P some S' [$-((-P)iS)$].[7] Defining 'P every S' by taking 'some' and 'not' as the primitive logical constants is strictly analogous to taking 'and' and 'not' as primitive connectives in propositional logic and defining 'q if p' as 'not both not-q and p'. It is also analogous to taking the binary plus operator and the unary minus operator as primitive algebraic functors and then going on to define a binary subtractive operator:

$b - a =_{\text{def}} -((-b) + a)$.

Representing 'P some S' as '$P + S$' and then defining 'P every S' reveals that 'every' is a binary subtractive operator:

$$P - S =_{\text{def}} -((-P) + S)$$

In principle, 'PiS' or '$P + S$' is the primitive form of terminist predication, '$P - S$' being defined as '$-((-P) + S)$'. In practice, both 'PiS' and 'PaS' may be regarded as the two primary ways of predicating one term of another.[8]

By contrast to MPL's unmediated, nonrelational, asymmetrical version of predication, the mediating expressions in the terminist version are transparently relational. To be sure, the predicative connectives 'some' and 'every' that join the predicate term to the subject term in a monadic proposition are not dyadic relational expressions like 'taller than' or 'sibling of'; they nevertheless function as genuine relations with formal properties like symmetry, transitivity, or reflexivity. Specifically, 'every' is transitive and reflexive but not symmetrical: 'P every M and M every S' entails 'P every S', and 'S every S' is logically true, but 'P every S' is not equivalent to 'S every P'. 'Some' is symmetrical but is neither transitive nor reflexive: 'P some S' entails 'S some P', but 'P some M and M some S' does not entail 'P some S', nor is 'S some S' a logical truth.

Regarded algebraically, the symmetry of the I-functor in 'PiS' could just as well be viewed as the commutivity of the plus-functor in '$P + S$'. The general form of categorical propositions in the algebraic version of term functor logic (TFL) is:

$$\pm(P \pm S)$$

in which the outer sign represents the positive or negative quality of judgment and the inner sign represents the term connectives 'some' (+) or 'every' (–). When two propositions that have the same logical quantity (both being particular or both being universal) are algebraically equal, they are logically equivalent.

In a language like English, the predicating expressions are split in two, the word 'some' or 'all' preceding the subject term and the word 'are' or 'is' preceding the predicate term. That splitting has unfortunately obscured the unitary role of 'some . . . are' and 'all . . . are' as term connectives analogous to unitary propositional connectives like 'both . . . and' and 'if . . . then' in propositional logic. However, we get a more natural, albeit formally less elegant, term functor logic if we directly transcribe 'some X is Y' as '$+X + Y$', reading the first plus sign as 'some' and the second as 'is'. Similarly, we transcribe 'every X is Y' as '$-X + Y$'. The general form of categorical statement in TFL is an affirmation or denial that some or every X is or isn't Y:

yes/no: some/every X/non-X is/isn't Y/non-Y

$$\pm \quad (\qquad \pm \qquad \pm X \qquad \pm \qquad \pm Y)$$

Two categoricals are logically equivalent if and only if they are covalent (both being particular or both being universal) and algebraically equal. Valence for categorical propositions is determined by whether the first two signs (the judgment and quantity signs) are the same (yielding a positive valence/particular proposition) or different (yielding a negative valence/universal proposition). A term may be negative (e.g., 'noncitizen'), it may be compound (e.g., 'gentleman and scholar'), it may be relational (e.g., 'taller than every Dane'). Two compound or two relational expressions are logically equivalent if and only if they are covalent as well as equal; but here valence is determined not necessarily by the first two signs but by the overall sign of the term (every term having a positive or negative 'charge'), and the quantity sign within the term.[9]

I was enjoying the fruits of Russell's observation that a good notation is better than a live teacher. The motto of TFL is "transcription, not translation." Of course even transcription requires some "regimentation" of the vernacular. Coming across 'The whale is a mammal' we must rephrase it for algebraic transcription. Regimenting it as 'Every whale is a mammal', we transcribe it as '$-W + M$'. Regimenting 'Only mammals are whales' as 'No nonmammal is a whale' we may transcribe it as '$-(+(-M) + W)$' and show it equivalent to '$-W + M$'. The regimented forms are simple natural language sentences that contain only formatives we can algebraically transcribe.

The plus/minus character of the logical constants extends also to propositional connectives. That 'and' like 'some' is a plus word soon led to me to see that 'if' is a minus word. For we may define 'q if p' as the negation of 'not-q and p'. Transcribing 'if' as '$-$' and 'and' as '$+$':

$q - p =_{\text{def}} -((-q) + p)$

If p then $q =_{\text{def}}$ not both p and not q

$-p + q =_{\text{def}} -(+p + (-q))$

Basic inference patterns like modus ponens, modus tollens, and the hypothetical syllogism are transparent when algebraically represented:

Modus ponens	Modus tollens	Hypothetical syllogism
$-p + q$	$-p + qT$	$-p + q$
p	$-q$	$-q + r$
q	$-p$	$-p + r$

Syllogistic Reckoning and Singular Sentences

Term functor logic offers a very simple decision procedure for syllogisms. A classical syllogism has as many (recurrent) terms as it has sentences. Only two kinds of syllogism have valid moods:

(i) syllogisms all of whose sentences are universal; and

(ii) syllogisms that have a particular conclusion and exactly one particular premise.

A syllogism is valid if and only if it has a valid mood and the sum of its premises is equal to its conclusion.

In the logical language of MPL, a singular sentence like 'Socrates is an Athenian' and a general sentence like 'Some philosophers are Athenians' have different logical forms. The syntax of function and argument uses predicate letters and individual symbols (proper names and variables) that play distinct syntactic roles. In terminist logic, term letters, whether general or singular, play the same syntactic roles and may be interchanged. According to Leibniz, 'Socrates is an Athenian' is elliptical for either 'Some Socrates is an Athenian' or 'Every Socrates is an Athenian'. Because 'Socrates' is a uniquely denoting term (UDT), we are free to assign either quantity to 'Socrates is an Athenian'. In general, where '$X*$' is a singular term, '$X*$ is Y' has *wild quantity*. Since either quantity may be assigned, ordinary language does not specify a quantity for singular statements.

For logical purposes, however, it is often necessary to assign one or the other quantity. For example, in the inference 'Socrates is an Athenian; therefore no non-Athenian is Socrates', we must assign universal quantity to the premise, thereby regarding the inference as 'Every Socrates* is Athenian; therefore no non-Athenian is Socrates*'. By contrast, in the inference 'Socrates is an Athenian; therefore some Athenian is Socrates', the premise must be particular: 'Some Socrates is an Athenian'. Because singular propositions have wild quantity, term logic can syllogistically derive the conclusion 'Some Athenian is wise' from the two singular premises 'Socrates is wise' and 'Socrates is an Athenian': +S* + W; −S* + A; ∴ + A + W. (The same inference in MPL invokes a special principle, namely existential generalization.)

TFL's singular advantage over MPL is particularly evident in the way the two logics deal with the kind of singular predications we call identities. For the terminist logician an identity is a monadic categorical proposition distinguished from other categoricals only in having uniquely denoting terms in *both* subject and predicate positions. For example, 'Tully is Cicero' is a monadic categorical statement of form 'C*iT*' (+T* + C*) or 'C*aT*' (−T* + C*). In MPL, by contrast, 'Tully is Cicero' is represented as 'I(t,c)' or 'T = C'. Because MPL construes all identities dyadically, its account of inferences involving identity propositions must appeal to special principles, known as laws or axioms of identity, explicitly asserting that the dyadic relation in '$x = y$' possesses the formal properties of symmetry, reflexivity, and transitivity. In term logic these are properties that routinely characterize the predicative relations that mediate the terms of I or A monadic categorical propositions, general as well as singular, nonidentities as well as identities. I-forms are symmetrical, A-forms are reflexive and transitive; because identity statements in TFL involve wild quantity for both terms, they come out reflexive, symmetrical, *and* transitive. Thus term logic has all the inference power it needs for dealing with identity propositions. For example, the indiscernibility of identicals is demonstrated by ordinary syllogistic reasoning. The following argument shows that since Tully is Cicero, whatever is true of Tully (e.g., that he is a senator) is true of Cicero:

Tully is Cicero	Some T* is C*
Tully is *P*	Every T* is *P*
Cicero is *P*.	Some C* is *P*.

Multiply General Sentences

Traditional term logic was inferentially weak in being unable to cope with relational arguments. MPL replaced traditional term logic in the twentieth century because, in Dummett's words, "[i]t stands in contrast to all the great logical systems of the past . . . in being able to give an account of sentences involving multiple generality, an account which depends upon the mechanism of quantifiers and bound variables."[10]

Term functor logic, however, has no problem with multiple generality. Following a suggestion of Leibniz, TFL treats the relational term in 'some boy loves some girl' as a Janus-faced expression '$_1L_2$' that turns one face to 'some boy' as 'lover' and the other to 'some girl' as 'loved'. According to Leibniz, such a sentence contains 'some boy loves' and 'some girl is loved' as subsentences. One may transcribe the sentence as '$+B_1 + L_{12} + G_2$', which indeed entails '$+B_1 + L_{12}$' (some boy loves) and '$+G_2 + L_{12}$' (some girl is loved).[11] Note that the common numerical index shows how terms are paired for predication. Thus 'Paris$_1$ is a lover$_1$' and 'Helen$_2$ is loved$_2$' are two subsentences of 'Paris loves Helen' ($\Rightarrow$'$P^*_1 + L_{12} + H^*_2$'). Terms that have no index in common cannot properly be paired. Thus 'P_1, H_2' is not a proper term pair and 'Paris is Helen' is not an implicit subsentence of 'Paris loves Helen'. Transcribing 'Paris loves Helen' as '$+P^*_1 + L_{12} + H^*_2$' and 'Helen is loved by Paris' as '$+H^*_2 + L_{12} + P^*_1$', term functor logic (which I sometimes call *algebraic* term logic) can express the equivalence of 'Paris loves Helen' to 'Helen is loved by Paris' as

$$+P^*_1 + L_{12} + H^*_2 = +H^*_2 + L_{12} + P^*_1$$

TFL copes with relational as well as classically syllogistic arguments by applying Aristotle's *Dictum de Omni* as the basic rule of inference:

Whatever is true of every X is true of any (thing that is an) X

The dictum validates any argument of the form:

$P(-M)$
$\underline{\dots M \dots}$
$\dots P \dots$

whose "donor" premise, $P(-M)$, asserts or implies that being P is true of every M, and whose "host" premise contains an algebraically positive ("undistributed") occurrence of the middle term, M. Given two such premises, we may adduce a conclusion by adding the donor to the host, thereby replacing the host's middle term by P, the expression the donor claims is true of every M. For example:

(1) Some boy envies every astronaut	$(+B_1 + E_{12}) - A_2$	$+B_1 + E_{12}(-A_2)$
(2) Some astronaut is a woman	$+A_2 + W_2$	$\dots A_2 \dots$
(3) Someone some boy envies is a woman	$+(+B_1 + E_{12}) + W_2$	$\dots (+B_1 + E_{12}) \dots$

The conclusion (3) is formed by adding (1) to (2) and replacing 'astronaut' by 'some boy envies' ($+B_1 + E_{12}$), which (1) claims is true of every astronaut.

In a TFL argument middle terms cancel out algebraically. A monadic sentence like 'Some astronaut is a woman' is not normally given pairing subscripts since its two terms are obviously paired with one another. We may, however, arbitrarily use any number as a pairing index for the two terms of a monadic sentence. When one of the terms is a middle term in an argument that has a relational premise, we assign both middles the same number, so that they will be uniformly represented for cancellation.

My explanation of why we intuitively and instantly judge that (A) 'Every colt is a horse' and (B) 'Some owner of a colt is not an owner of a horse' are jointly inconsistent assumed that we intuitively apply the dictum in everyday reasoning. We see immediately that adding (A) and (B) together entail 'Some owner of a horse isn't an owner of a horse':

(A) Every colt is a horse	$-C_2 + H_2$	$H_2(-C_2)$
(B) Some owner of a colt is not an owner of a horse	$+(O_{12} + C_2) - (O_{12} + H_2)$	$\ldots C_2 \ldots$
(C) Some owner of a horse is not an owner of a horse	$+(O_{12} + H_2) - (O_{12} + H_2)$	$\ldots H_2 \ldots$

By contrast, any MPL proof that (A) and (B) lead to self-contradiction requires quantificational translation and many further steps; no such proof casts light on why we instantly see inconsistency in (A) and (B).

Reference

A central aspect of my work on term logic concerned reference.[12] In MPL, definite reference by proper names is the primary and sole form of reference. In TFL, by contrast, indefinite reference by subjects of form 'some S' is primary reference and definite reference (e.g., by 'the S' or by a proper name) must be construed as a variant of the primary form. The doctrine I presented in *The Logic of Natural Language* was that definite referring subjects are pronominal in character, borrowing their reference from antecedent indefinite subjects. The logical form of a pronominal sentence is 'Some S* is P', in which 'S*' is a UDT introduced to denote 'the thing (e.g., person, place) in question' originally referred to by an indefinite subject (such as 'an infant', 'a king', 'a lake', etc.) of the anaphoric background proposition.

Strawson had persuasively argued that 'The present king of France is bald' implicitly harks back to an antecedent proposition like 'France has a king'. He was in effect pointing to a sequence like 'France has a king . . . the present king of France is bald'—a pronominalization of form 'An S is P; it is Q'. The falsity of the antecedent sentence should not, however, lead us to deny a truth value to a pronominal sentence like 'He is bald' or 'The king is bald'. Both antecedent and pronominal sentence should then be regarded as false. *The Logic of Natural Language* extended the pronominal account of definite reference to proper names. The origin of a proper name harks back to contexts like 'We have a wonderful baby', moving on to 'The baby is healthy', 'It is asleep', and so on, and later on settling on a fixed way of referring to the baby by replacing 'it' and 'the baby' with a special-duty pronoun such as 'Eloise' or Richard'.

Realism and Truth

With the publication of *The Logic of Natural Language* in 1982, I felt I had gone a long way to reconstituting the old logic of terms as a viable "laws-of-thought" (cognitively adequate) alternative to modern predicate logic. My dissatisfaction with MPL had increased with my growing suspicion that it was inadequate as an organon for general philosophy. I am an unregenerate metaphysical realist—the kind Hilary Putnam is always inveighing against and allegedly refuting. For Putnam, a belief in correspondence is integral to being a metaphysical realist.[13] I believed (and still do) that true statements correspond to facts that make them true. We may refer to any fact by means of a phrase of the form 'the existence of x' or 'the nonexistence of x'. For example, 'Some horses are white' and 'Every U.S. senator is a U.S. citizen' are made true by the existence of white horses and the nonexistence of U.S. senators who are not U.S. citizens (the respective facts to which these statements are said to correspond).

Unfortunately for the fate of realist philosophy in the twentieth century, modern logic's treatment of 'exists' is resolutely inhospitable to facts as referents of phrases of the form 'the (non-)existence of φ'. Frege regarded the existence of horses as a property of the concept *horse*. Citing Kant, Frege says, "Because existence is a property of concepts, the ontological argument for the existence of God breaks down."[14] I accepted Kant's negative thesis that existence is not a property of anything that is said to exist, but could not accept Frege's positive thesis that the existence, say, of the Earth's moon is a property of the concept *terrestrial satellite*, namely, its having an instance. Russell has a similar view of what existence comes to: to say that horses exist is to say that '*x* is a horse' is sometimes true. These ways of construing existence seemed to me badly deficient in that 'robust sense of reality' demanded of an acceptable logical theory. The existence of the moon or of horses and the nonexistence of Twin Earth are characteristics of reality, not characteristics of concepts or open sentences. In any case, such ways of construing existence cannot give us the truth-making facts. (That '*x* is a horse' is sometimes true cannot serve as the fact that makes 'There are horses' true.) Along with truth-making facts, Frege rejected the correspondence theory of truth. These negative views were endorsed by the majority of Anglo-American analytic philosophers including, notably, Quine, Strawson, Davidson, and Putnam (for whom facts are just true statements).[15]

Hence facts as objective, truth-making correlates of true statements were metaphysical orphans in twentieth-century analytical philosophy. Davidson's view is typical: "The realist view of truth, if it has any content, must be based on the idea of correspondence . . . and such correspondence cannot be made intelligible. . . . [I]t is futile either to reject or to accept the slogan that the real and the true are 'independent of our beliefs.' The only evident positive sense we can make of this phrase, the only use that consorts with the intentions of those who prize it, derives from the idea of correspondence, and this is an idea without content."[16] This strong doctrine—that the very idea of truth-making facts is *incoherent*—should have aroused more suspicion: I wondered about the cogency of a challenge to produce X followed by the communiqué that X is not the sort of thing that could possibly be produced. The rejection of metaphysical realism left American philosophers in thrall to an unattractive pragmatism of the kind I had had my fill of at Columbia. It reopened the road back to John Dewey's and Richard Rorty's view that knowledge is not "a matter of getting reality right, but rather . . . a matter of acquiring habits of action for coping with reality."[17]

Strawson, more cautiously, had denied that there are any such things as facts *in the world*, saying: "It is evident that there is nothing else in the world for the statement itself to be related to. . . . The only plausible candidate for the position of what (in the world) makes the statement true is the fact it states; but the fact it states is not something in the world."[18]

Unlike Davidson, Strawson had left it open that a true statement like 'Some cats are mangy' may correspond to a feature of reality that is not, strictly speaking, "in the world."[19] I would later avail myself of this opening and say the existence of mangy cats—the fact that makes 'There are mangy cats' true—though not a property of anything *in* the world, is nevertheless a real property.

Of What Existence Is a Property

In the 1990s I wrote several papers[20] explicating a notion of existence needed for a realist notion of (truth-making) facts to which true statements correspond. Any statement is a claim of φ-existence or ψ-nonexistence made about some domain under consideration (DC). A world or domain is a totality of things characterized by the presence of certain things and by the absence of certain things. The contemporary world is positively characterized by the existence of mangy cats and lifeless planets and characterized negatively by the nonexistence of saber-toothed tigers and Santa Claus (facts that make 'Some planets are devoid of life' and 'Saber-toothed tigers are extinct' true). The domain of natural numbers is characterized by such facts as the existence of an even prime number and the nonexistence of a greatest prime number. Very often the domain of the truth claim consists of objects in one's field of vision, as when I point to a bird and say 'That's a cardinal'. Any φ-presence or ψ-absence that characterizes the DC is a property of that domain. The DC may be quite circumscribed, as when I say 'There is no hammer' when looking in a drawer; the absence of a hammer is a negative existential property of the totality of objects in the drawer that constitutes the DC of my assertion.

Suppose there are K things in the DC but no J things. Such a domain is '{K}ish' but 'un{J}ish.' By construing the existence of K-things ({K}ishness) and the nonexistence of J-things (un{J}ishness) as attributes of the domain under consideration, one takes the decisive step in demystifying truth-making facts.[21] A fact is an existential characteristic *of* the domain; it is not something *in* the domain. To search for truth-making facts *in* the world is indeed futile.[22] The presence of Tony Blair in the world (its {Tony Blair}ishness) is a truth-making fact, but while *Blair* is present in the world, (the fact of) his *presence* is not, no more so than the fact of Santa's absence. Neither fact is an item in the real world (in that sense neither fact exists) but both are existential properties *of* the real world (in that sense both facts obtain and are real). Nothing in the world is a fact. But facts as positive or negative properties of the world are the correspondents of truth-bearers in a realist metaphysics.[23]

Modern logic's powerful influence is not always progressive. If the above views on existence, facts, and propositional contents have not (yet) attracted much attention, this may be because they do not readily comport with the Frege–Russell view of existence suggested by the role of the existential quantifier in modern predicate logic. Similarly, because TFL challenges the currently accepted dogma that genuine logic is a matter of quantifiers and bound variables, the discovery—now more than three decades old—that 'some' is a *plus* word and 'every' a *minus* word (and the associated claim that the +/– character of the natural logical constants is the key to explaining how we actually reason with the sentences of our native language) tends to be dismissed or ignored. The sentences that figure in everyday reasoning are largely variable-free. That several generations of philosophers should so easily have jettisoned the classical conception of logic as the science of how we think and reason with such sentences shows that the revolution in logic has made MPL the only game in town.

MPL holds some very good thinkers in thrall. Noam Chomsky famously demands of any adequate theory of our use of language that it account for the extraordinary linguistic competence of native speakers, including, presumably, their deductive competence. Chomsky never questions the authoritative status of quantificational logic, so we find him saying that "the familiar quantifier-variable notation would in some sense be more natural for humans than a variable-free notation for logic."[24] At one point he claims that "there is now some empirical evidence that it [the brain] uses quantifier-variable rather than quantifier-free notation."[25] This fanciful and baseless bit of speculative neuroscience is forced on him because he is in the grip of two dogmas, one correct and one incorrect. He rightly believes that deductive competence is an innate endowment. But because he wrongly believes that MPL is *the* canonical human logic, he would account for our competence in everyday reasoning by postulating a "module" in the brain with the syntactic structure of the quantifier-variable language of modern predicate logic.

A Pedagogical Note

MPL replaced the older term logic because the latter could not cope with such phenomena as relational inferences, for example the valid inference of 'Every horse is an animal, so every owner of a horse is an owner of an animal'. I believe, however, that term logic will once again become "the logic of the schools." For I expect that twenty years from now, many students will know that 'Every horse is an animal' reckons like '−H + A'; they will know that if they conjoin (add) '−H + A' to a tautological premise, '−(O + H) + (O + H)' (Every owner of a horse is an owner of a horse), they can cancel and replace the positive middle term H with A, thereby immediately deriving '−(O + H) + (O + A)' (Every owner of a horse is an owner of an animal). It will not be easy to persuade such students that it is vital for them to learn the language of quantifiers and bound variables and to apply rules of propositional and predicate logic in a lengthy and intricate proof that '$(\forall x)(Hx \supset Ax)$' entails '$(\forall x)((\exists y)(Hy\&Oxy) \supset (\exists z)(Az\&Oxz))$'.

Although the short-term prospects for reviving term logic in the universities are admittedly not bright, the continued preeminence of predicate logic is by no means assured.

Notes

1. M. Dummett, *Frege: Philosophy of Language* (Cambridge, Mass.: Harvard University Press, 1981), p. 20.

2. Here is one complaint: "How did it come to be that logic which, at least in the views of some people 2,300 years ago, was supposed to deal with evaluation of argumentation in natural languages, has done a lot of extremely interesting and important things, but not this?" (Yehoshua Bar-Hillel in J. F. Staal, ed., "Formal and Natural Languages: A Symposium," *Foundations of Language* 5 [1969]: 256–284).

3. Nondualists avoided Descartes's conclusion by denying the possibility of a pure (bodiless) ego.

4. Because the way these logical words figure in natural syntax is lost in canonical (MPL) translation (which translates 'Every colt is a horse' as a conditional formula involving two atomic sentences 'x is a colt' and 'x is a horse') I reverted back to the logic of terms, which, whatever its shortcomings, did not move away from the syntax of the sentences with which we reckon in everyday reasoning.

5. I was trying to devise a formal, terminist logical language that would transcribe sentences of natural language as algebraic formulas. I had, in 1967, proposed an algebraic algorithm for syllogistic reasoning that represented 'Every M is P' as a fraction 'M/P' and 'Some M is P' as $(M/P^{-1})^{-1}$ (not every M is not-P). BARBARA syllogisms were represented as deriving the conclusion 'S/P' from 'M/P x S/M'. The fraction algorithm proved of limited value for handling relations. Nor did it cast much light on how we actually reckon, since we do not reckon 'Every M is P and every S is M, hence every S is P' by thinking in terms of fractions and reciprocals. I was nevertheless convinced that our intuitive way of reasoning was probably algebraic in nature. See "On a Fregean Dogma," in I. Lakatos (ed.), *Problems in the Philosophy of Mathematics* (Amsterdam: North-Holland, 1967), pp. 47–62.

6. *Prior Analytics*, 24b29–30.

7. The range of the definition is limited to the case where there are S things. If neither 'P some S' nor 'non-P some S' is true, then both 'P every S' and 'non-P every S' are undefined. For Aristotle, 'some' is primitive, 'every' is defined. By contrast, Frege takes the universal quantifier as primitive and uses '$-(\forall x)-$' where we use '$\exists x$'.

8. I regarded the negative forms 'PeS' ($\Rightarrow$ 'No S is P') and 'PoS' ($\Rightarrow$ 'Some S is not P') as derivative, 'PeS' (e.g., 'No creature was stirring') being construed as 'not(PiS)' or '$-(P + S)$' ('Not: a creature was stirring') and 'PoS' as '(not-P)iS' or '$(-P) + S$'.

9. For example, 'hit every target' ($\Rightarrow +(H_{12} - T_2)$) is equivalent to 'did not miss a target' ($\Rightarrow -((-H_{12}) + T_2)]$, but not to the divalent term 'hit some nontarget' ($\Rightarrow +(H_{12} + (-T_2))$). The first two terms both have negative valence (an overall + and a – sign of quantity in the first; an overall – and a + sign of quantity in the second), whereas the third term has a positive valence (an overall + and a + sign of quantity, 'some nontarget').

10. *Frege: Philosophy of Language,* pp. xxxi–xxxii.

11. See "Predication in the Logic of Terms," *Notre Dame Journal of Formal Logic* 31 (1990): 106–126.

12. See *The Logic of Natural Language* (Oxford: Clarendon Press, 1982), chapters 3, 4, 5, and 11.

13. Thus he says of Quine that he cannot be a metaphysical realist in my sense since he does not accept the correspondence theory of truth; see *The Many Faces of Realism* (La Salle: Open Court, 1987), p. 31.

14. Gottlob Frege, *Die Grundlagen der Arithmetik* 53 (trans. Austin, *The Foundations of Arithmetic* [Oxford: Basil Blackwell, 1952]). For an excellent discussion of the doctrine that existence is an attribute of concepts, see C. J. F. Williams, *What Is Existence?* (Oxford: Clarendon Press, 1981), chs. 2–3.

15. See, for example, W. V. O. Quine, *Word and Object* (Cambridge, Mass.: The MIT Press, 1960), p. 247; P. F. Strawson, "Truth," in his *Logico-Linguistic Papers* (London: Methuen, 1971), pp. 194–195.

16. "The Structure and Content of Truth," *Journal of Philosophy* 87 (1990): 279–328, at 304–305.

17. Richard Rorty, *Objectivism, Relativism, and Truth* (Cambridge: Cambridge University Press, 1991), p. 1.

18. P. F. Strawson, "Truth," pp. 194–195.

19. Strawson's purpose, in which he succeeded, was to refute Austin's version of the correspondence theory in which true statements correspond to situations locatable in the world. Like Kant, Strawson left us the question: To what, if not to something in the world, does a statement asserting the existence of a mangy cat correspond?

20. See: "'The Enemy Is Us': Objectivity and Its Philosophical Detractors," in H. Dickman (ed.), *The Imperiled Academy* (New Brunswick: Transaction, 1993); "Naturalism and Realism," *Midwest Studies in Philosophy* 19 (1994): 22–38; "Existence and Correspondence to Facts," in R. Poli and P. Simons (eds.), *Formal Ontology* (Dordrecht: Kluwer, 1996), pp. 131–158; "Putnam's Born-Again Realism," *Journal of Philosophy* 94 (1997): 453–471.

21. Nontrivial existence as an attribute of the world is always specified presence (elk-existence); nontrivial nonexistence is specified absence (elf-nonexistence). Anything in a world under consideration is a thing, a mere "existent," in the uninformative sense that Kant derided. In the *informative* sense, to exist or to fail to exist is to characterize the world by *specified* presence or absence.

22. Austin's version of truth-making facts, which located them in the world, was thus rightly rejected by Strawson.

23. Compare, by contrast, Davidson's view: "the real objection [to correspondence theories] is rather that such theories fail to provide entities to which truth vehicles (whether we take these to be statements, sentences or utterances) can be said to correspond" ("The Structure and Content of Truth," p. 304).

24. Noam Chomsky, *Rules and Representations* (New York: Columbia University Press, 1980), p. 165.

25. Chomsky, *Lectures on Government and Binding* (Dordrecht and Cinnaminson: Foris, 1981), p. 35.

2 Trees, Terms, and Truth: The Philosophy of Fred Sommers

George Englebretsen

1 Preliminary Remarks

My personal debt to the man whom this festschrift honors is enormous. He has been the source or inspiration for much of my work for a very long time. It is only his generosity, modesty, and tolerance (perhaps his humor, as well) that have prevented him from calling me to account for what I have done to the many fine ideas I have purloined from him. This essay is only a small attempt at repaying my debt. For his philosophy, and so much else, I thank him.

Nearly forty years ago I read a paper in *Mind* entitled "The Ordinary Language Tree." It was by Fred Sommers, a philosopher of whom I had never heard. I hated it. Having recently extracted myself from the mathematical and logical formalism in which I had been trained, I had thrown away my *Tractatus* and begun the *Investigations*. I thought of myself as an "ordinary language" philosopher but found this "ordinary language tree" quite extraordinary. Nonetheless, I continued to read Sommers. With a small degree of understanding the hatred soon evaporated, to be replaced eventually by admiration. Sommers has led me on a merry chase these past four decades. I've stumbled along trying to keep up with him as he turned from his work on the language tree to new work on logic and, in recent years, to the topic of truth. Sommers's work in each of these areas, especially the first two, has attracted both other followers as well as critics. But most readers of Sommers limit their interest to just one of the three. The topics appear at first to have little internal connection. Yet I believe that a careful consideration shows that all of Sommers's philosophical work—his building of the tree theory, his formulation of a revitalized term logic, and his proposal for a renewed version of a theory of truth by correspondence to facts—constitutes a unified whole. In short, Sommers's work can be seen as constituting a single overall philosophical program, one that amounts to a large, coherent, multifaceted account of language, the world, and mind.

2 The Tree Theory

"Why with an M?" said Alice.
"Why not?" said the March Hare.
—Lewis Carroll, *Alice's Adventures in Wonderland*

If there is one idea that is the keystone of the edifice that constitutes Sommers's united philosophy it is that *terms* are the linguistic entities subject to negation in the most basic sense. It is a very old idea, one that has tended to be rejected in recent times. Sommers articulated it more clearly and exploited it more fully than anyone else. He exploited the idea first in a series of papers published between 1959 and 1971. There Sommers proposed, formulated, explicated, and explored the consequences of a theory of language structure and ontological structure, where these turn out to be isomorphic. In accounting for the structure of language he took the "predicable" terms of any language (terms that could be used to characterize any subject, whether truly or falsely) to come in logically charged (positive or negative) pairs. English examples might be 'red'/'nonred', 'massive'/'massless', 'tied'/'untied', 'in the house'/'not in the house'. The recognition of charged term pairing was essential to the proposed theory of language. And the idea that terms can be negated (have negative charge) was essential for such pairing.

The predication of a term to some subject might result in either a true proposition, a false proposition, or a senseless proposition (what Sommers, following Ryle, called a *category mistake*). A term that can be predicated sensibly (truly or falsely but not categorically mistakenly) of some given individual is said to *span* that individual. Thus, for example, 'red' spans Socrates, the apple in my lunch, and the moon; it does not span the number 42, my fear of falling, or the moon's orbit. Moreover, if a term spans any individual so does its oppositely charged partner. This means that 'nonred' spans (can be predicated truly or falsely, i.e., sensibly, of) whatever 'red' spans, and it fails to span whatever 'red' fails to span. In particular, the number 42 cannot sensibly be said to be either red or nonred. If our concern, then, is with the semantic relation of spanning, we can ignore the charge on a term; we can attend to its *absolute value* (as mathematicians talk about the absolute value of a given number). So '/red/' (absolute 'red') would be either 'red' (positive) or 'nonred' (negative).

The set of individuals, all of which are spanned by a given term, is a *category*. Whatever is red or nonred (including: Socrates, my apple, and the moon, but not: 42, my fear of falling, or the moon's orbit) constitutes the category of individuals with respect to '/red/'. Let '*P*' be any term; then '/*P*/' will stand for either the absolute value of the term or for the category of individuals with respect to that term, the set of individuals spanned by that term.

Given a language with a finite vocabulary of terms (and thus of absolute terms), one could ask after the semantic relations that hold among them, over and above the semantic relation of spanning, which holds between terms and individuals—between linguistic items and ontological items. As it happens, speakers can form sensible propositions by using two terms, one as the subject term, the other as the predicate term. In each such case the result will be either true or false or category mistaken. For example, one might say, 'Some people are red', 'No people are nonred', 'All material objects are massive', 'No material objects are massless', 'Some number is prime', 'No number is nonprime', and so on, where terms such as 'red' or 'nonred' are joined with terms such as 'people', 'prime' and 'nonprime' with 'number', and so on, to form sensible propositions. By contrast, some term pairs cannot be joined to form a sensible proposition. 'Some number is massless', 'All numbers are nonred', 'These people are prime', and the like, are all category mistakes. Notice that whenever a term can be joined sensibly or nonsensibly to another term the same will hold for its oppositely charged partner. Again we can ignore for now the charge of a term and take it absolutely. Now, pairs of (absolute) terms that can be joined to form a sensible subject-predicate proposition are said to be *U-related* ("U" is for "use" since the terms can be used sensibly together). Pairs of terms that cannot be so joined are *N-related* ("N" for "nonsense"). Every possible pair of terms in a language, then, will either be U-related or N-related. The U and N relations are symmetric (and reflexive, but not, it turns out, transitive). In principle, one could draw a diagram of all the "sense" relations (U or N) that hold among all the terms of a finite language, drawing straight line segments only between pairs of absolute terms that are U-related. The result would be the sense-structure of the language. The genius of Sommers's theory is its ability to show that there is a small number of simple rules governing this structure and guaranteeing that it has the form of a binary, reticulating, single-apex tree—thus the tree theory.

Two terms are *connected* if and only if they are in the same language. Two conditions of connectedness hold: any two terms U-related to a third term are connected; any two terms connected to a third term are connected. A language, then, will be the largest set of mutually connected terms. Any two terms that are connected on a language tree such that a continuous upward or downward path of line segments leads from one to the other are themselves U-related. It might be thought from this that a structural requirement would be the *transitivity* rule: any two terms U-related to a third must be U-related to each other. But this rule does not hold. An English counterexample would be 'person' and 'prime', both of which are U-related to 'interesting' but are not U-related to each other. What *is* the structural principle governing the sense structure of a language is what Sommers calls the *law of category inclusion*, which he formulated in a number of equivalent ways. When read as a rule governing the sense relations among terms it says that, given two N-related terms that are U-related to a third term, there can be no other term that is U-related to one of the first two but N-related to the third. Suppose the first two terms are the N-related pair, '/P/' and '/R/', and the third term, to which they are both U-related, is '/Q/'. This can be diagramed on a tree segment as follows (from now on, for convenience, we will assume the terms on a diagram are absolute):

Now let '/S/' be the fourth term. Since it is U-related to one of the first two terms (say, '/P/') but N-related to '/Q/', there must be some fifth term that is U-related to '/S/' but not to '/Q/'. In other words:

This is the M configuration, and the law forbids it. As a consequence, no path of sense relations can change its upward or downward progression; once a path of U-relations begins to descend it continues downward—no

M shapes. Given that the language is finite, a further consequence is that there will be a single top node on the tree and a finite number of bottom nodes.

The law is the law of *category* inclusion. Recall that a category is a set of individuals all of which are spanned by a given term. Moreover, letters on a tree diagram can represent either terms or the categories relative to those terms. Reading a diagram as a *language* tree, the letters represent terms; reading it as an *ontological* tree, the letters represent the categories relative to those terms. The line segments of a language tree represent U-relations; they represent *inclusion* relations on an ontological tree. Thus, the law of category inclusion holds that if two categories (represented by '*P*' and '*R*') are included in a third category, '*Q*', but not in each other, then there can be no fourth category, '*S*', that includes one of the first two (say, '*P*') but does not include the other ('*Q*'). In other words, if two categories share any member in common, then at least one of them must be included in the other. Categories can be mutually exclusive or one can include the other; but they cannot overlap. The salient feature of terms at the bottom nodes of a tree is that they are U-related to every term that is above them on the path they terminate. This means that the category determined by a bottom term is included in each of the categories determined by the terms to which that term is U-related. Such bottom node categories are *types*. While my apple and Socrates both belong to the category with respect to '/red/' (and to a number of others as well), they do not belong to the same type. If two individuals belong to the same type, then *any* term that spans one will span the other. In other words, all members of a given type are spanned by all of the same terms. Just as categories constitute a subset of sets (their differentia being that they never merely overlap), types constitute a subset of categories—types never include one another.

Tree rules, rules governing the tree structure, are of three kinds. *Language-* tree rules govern the sense relations among terms. The first version above of the law of category inclusion was such a rule. *Ontological*-tree rules govern the inclusion relations among categories. The second version of the law was such a rule. The language tree and the ontological tree are isomorphic. There is a one-to-one correspondence between the elements of one and the elements of the other, and the relations (U and inclusion) represented in one are parallel to those represented in the other. A third kind of rule is a *translation* rule. Such rules allow the translation between reading a tree as linguistic and reading it as ontological. They rest on the relation of spanning that holds (or not) between a term and an individual. The prohibition against the dreaded M configuration is both linguistic and ontological, but it is in its translational guise that its philosophical import is seen most vividly. In its translational version it is the *rule for enforcing ambiguity*. What it says is that no two terms that are such that each spans an individual not spanned by the other can both span some other individual. Letting uppercase letters again represent (absolute) terms, lowercase letters individuals, and line segments spanning relations, the rule enjoins against the following:

Again, no M structure allowed.

The rule for enforcing ambiguity, along with the complete mutual exclusivity of types, provides insights into a number of philosophical problems, giving the tree theory an unexpected and enviable power as a tool of philosophical analysis. Here is how the rule applies in practice. In effect, the rule is an adequacy condition on any theory. It says that no theory is "categorially coherent" if it allows the M structure. Further, theories that avoid the M structure may falter on other grounds, but they are at least categorially coherent. A categorially incoherent theory can be rendered coherent, submitted to the rule, in a number of alternative ways. Consider the M structure above. It can be avoided by: (1) denying that 'P' is a single, univocal term (i.e., rendering 'P' ambiguous as it applies to a and to b); (2) denying the univocity of 'Q'; (3) denying that a is spanned by 'P'; (4) denying that c is spanned by 'Q'; (5) claiming that a is spanned by 'Q'; (6) claiming that c is spanned by 'P'; (7) denying that 'P' spans b; (8) denying that 'Q' spans b; (9) denying that b is an individual, that is, taking b to be a composite of two individuals, one spanned by 'P' and the other spanned by 'Q'; (10) denying the existence of a altogether; (11) denying the existence of c altogether; or (12) any combination of (1)–(11).

Alternatives (1) and (2) give the rule its name. Enforcing ambiguity was foremost in Sommers's mind when he formulated the rule because he intended to use it to replace a rule found to be implicit in Ryle's work on categories and category mistakes. Ryle's rule prohibits any univocal term from applying sensibly to two individuals belonging to different categories (in Ryle's sense of "category"). Ryle's famous application of his rule was to Descartes's theory of mind–body dualism. Since, on any understanding of categories—and certainly on Descartes's own—minds and bodies belong necessarily to different categories, any term ('exists' or 'causes', for example) that applies to both a mind and a body must be ambiguous. Considerations of Ryle's rule (*inter alia*) and counterexamples to it led Sommers to formulate his rule for enforcing ambiguity—a key element of the tree theory. A few examples show how Sommers's rule applies to a theory. Strawson's theory of persons, when disembodied spirits ("former persons") are allowed, reveals the M configuration. Strawsonian P-predicates apply both to Kant's disembodied spirit and to Tony Blair but not to the moon. Strawsonian M-predicates apply to Tony Blair and to the moon but not to Kant's disembodied spirit. Such a theory is categorially incoherent. Some coherent and well-known alternatives are those that enforce ambiguity on the P-predicate (Aquinas's theology of analogy, for example), those dualist theories that deny that Tony Blair is an individual (instead he is a composite of two individuals, one to which the P-predicate applies—a mind, and the other to which the M-predicate applies—a body), and those theories that deny disembodied spirits altogether (probably Ryle's own theory).

The phenomenalist theories of perception that allow both material objects and the immediate objects of (each mode of) perception are categorially incoherent—they allow the M structure into their theories. According to such theories, a term such as 'seen' applies to both the skunk and the visual phenomena, such as its color; 'smelled' likewise applies to the skunk and to its odor. However, 'seen' cannot apply to the odor, nor can 'smelled' apply to the color. Thus the rule is broken. Materialists avoid this incoherence by denying phenomenal objects; idealists achieve the same end by denying that the skunk is an individual (it is just a bundle of ideas—immediate objects of perception, as Berkeley would have it). As a final example, consider the two terms 'true' and 'French'. The first seems to span both sentences and propositions but not words; the second seems to span sentences and words but not propositions. The result is, once more, an M structure. Categorial coherence is usually gained either by denying propositions, identifying propositions with sentences, or enforcing ambiguity on 'true' (and thus on 'false' as well)—making 'true' apply to propositions in a primary sense and to sentences in a secondary sense.

As a tool for philosophical analysis the tree theory has proved its worth. But it has also generated a great deal of attention and debate among cognitive psychologists, linguists, and philosophers who are interested in semantic and conceptual development and the notion of natural kinds. Frank Keil's work (with both adults and English- and Spanish-speaking children) beginning in the late 1970s was the impetus for much subsequent work establishing the *psychological reality* of Sommers's theory. It turns out that speakers tend to share a common set of intuitions concerning the sense or senselessness of given propositions. In other words, language users, even at a fairly early age, make the same sorts of judgments concerning sense (U-/N-relatedness, category inclusion/exclusion, and spanning). Moreover, these judgments are in remarkable conformity with what one might predict on the basis of the tree theory. Furthermore, speakers tend to apply the injunction against the M configuration, usually enforcing ambiguity on a term in order to avoid it.

One of the ideas crucial to the tree theory was the notion of term negation. The ancient, and still commonsense, notion that terms can be negated, that terms come in logically incompatible (i.e., oppositely charged) pairs, found an important place in Sommers's account of sense and categories. A concomitant idea is that there is a crucial distinction to be drawn between affirming a negated predicate term of some subject and *denying* the unnegated version of that term of that same subject. In other words, one must take care to distinguish between a proposition of the form '*X* is non-*P*' and '*X* is not *P*'. Term negation and sentence negation (denial) are different operations. As well, the tree theory assumes that propositions can be analyzed as pairs of terms joined by some kind of predicational glue. These three ideas—that terms can be negated, that such negation is distinguishable from denial, and that propositions can be construed syntactically as predicationally tied pairs of terms—turn out to be not only important underlying elements of the tree theory but of Sommers's new term logic as well.

3   Term Logic

"... but as it isn't, it ain't. That's logic."
—Lewis Carroll, *Through the Looking-Glass*

Today's standard first-order calculus takes singular sentences such as 'Socrates is wise' and 'Plato taught Aristotle' as fundamental. These are so-called atomic sentences, containing no formative elements. Molecular sentences are formed, ultimately, from these atoms by the application of logical formatives. An atomic sentence with a monadic predicate is (syntactically) the simplest kind of sentence. It consists of just two words. These do not form the sentence by being predicationally tied. They form a sentence, a single syntactical unit, simply by being fit for each other. For they differ radically in their semantics. The subject (now called *argument*) is a singular term, used to name or refer to a single individual; the predicate (or *function expression*) is a general term, used to characterize that individual. This difference in semantic roles is reflected in the standard formal language by a difference in symbols: lowercase letters for subjects, uppercase for predicates.

The asymmetry here is fundamental (despite Ramsey's early doubts) to this kind of logic. The view is that many things that can be done to general terms cannot be done to singulars. The former, but not the latter, can be negated, conjoined, and disjoined with one another. By contrast, singular terms, unlike general terms, can be quantified over. Doing any of these things results, of course, in a new, syntactically more complex molecular sentence. An important instance is the negation of a general term. The standard logic recognizes only one kind of negation: sentential negation. Sentences are the only kinds of expression properly subject to negation. Consequently, negation of a general term/predicate always amounts to negation of the entire sentence. Sentences such as 'Socrates is unwise' and 'Socrates isn't wise' are always construed as 'It is not the case that Socrates is wise'. This point highlights another important feature of the logic: ultimately, anything done to a term (singular or general) amounts to the application of some function to the entire sentence. For sentences, not terms, are the basic linguistic expressions of a language (one arrives at terms only by the analysis of sentences). This priority of sentences to terms means that the logic of sentences (*sentential logic*) is more basic than the logic of terms (*predicate logic*).

A logic of terms rejects all of these ideas. Nearly all logic before Frege was a logic of terms. This "traditional" logic, initiated by Aristotle, had the advantage of being both natural (in that it could be applied directly to natural language sentences and that it embodied some natural logical intuitions) and relatively simple. But it was not logically powerful. There were several kinds of inferences whose logic could not be easily or systematically accounted for. The new, "mathematical" logic embodied in the first-order calculus does have such logical power. What it lacks is naturalness and simplicity. Sommers's term logic is the result of his program, executed in a number of papers and books beginning in the mid-'60s, to build and defend a "logic of natural language."

Term logic does not recognize the asymmetry alluded to above. In term logic the two terms that enter into the making of a sentence are on a syntactic par. Any term can be in any position. The modern logician achieves sentential unity (at least for atomic sentences) by treating singular terms and general terms differently, construing them as semantically fit beforehand for the task of uniting to form a sentence. Term logicians achieve this unity without relying on such prior semantic distinctions by recognizing a formative element in every sentence (consequently, no sentence is atomic, or devoid of formatives), an element whose job is to bind or tie the two terms into a united sentence. For Aristotle there were four such formatives. English versions are 'belongs to some', 'belongs to every', 'belongs to no' (equivalently: 'does not belong to some'), and 'does not belong to every'. They are, quite literally, logical *copulae*. Aristotle would have written, 'Wise belongs to some man'. The Latin-speaking Scholastic logicians would render this more natural by splitting up the copula (into a quantifier for one term and a qualifier for the other), rearranging the term order, and adjusting the grammar to yield something familiar: 'Some man is wise'. This *subject-predicate* sentence consists of a quantified term (the subject) and a qualified term (the predicate).

But it is important to see that the quantifier and the qualifier are not two formative elements—they are two parts of a single formative expression. They are a *split* logical copula. Important as this insight is, few traditional logicians saw it. Sommers saw it, highlighted it, and exploited it in his term logic. The "categorical" sentences of traditional logic are, of course, amenable to analysis into pairs of copulated terms. What the tradition could not do was incorporate into the logic singular sentences, relational sentences, and compound sentences. Aristotle, the Scholastics, the Port Royal logicians, Leibniz, the nineteenth-century British algebraists all had a go at one or more of these—with no lasting or satisfying results. Sommers's term logic, consistently and rigorously applying the idea that every sentence—of any sort—is the result of a copulated pair of terms and that singular terms, general terms, relational expressions, and entire sentences are all *terms*, incorporates all those recalcitrant sentences in a principled way into a single calculus of terms.

There is one area in which the modern logician might claim to have the advantage in terms of naturalness. Consider the fact that for a term logic any term is fit for any position in a sentence. Among other things, that means that the term logician can accept, say, 'Some wise (person) is Socrates'. This sentence happens to be true (or, as Sommers would eventually say, it can be used to express a true proposition). After all, it is equivalent to 'Socrates is wise'. But the original, unlike its equivalent, is fairly unnatural. The mathematical logician can claim that this is a result of the unnatural and unnecessary injection of a formative element (copula) or elements (quantifier and qualifier) into an atomic sentence, where only nonformative expressions are required or permitted. Singular terms, such as 'Socrates', and general terms, such as '. . . is wise', cannot (logically or grammatically) change places (a favorite theme of both Geach and Strawson). Any inference of 'Some wise (person) is Socrates' from 'Socrates is wise' is either a simple reiteration of the premise or involves the introduction of the apparatus of quantifiers binding individual variables, sentential connectives, and a special identity relation. By contrast, the term logician accounts for the inference as a simple case of conversion on a particular affirmation. Still, the original sentence, 'Some wise (person) is Socrates', is not "what we would normally say." And it is just here, in accounting for why this is so, that Sommers's term logic is once again informed by elements of his tree theory.

In *Posterior Analytics* (81b22–23), after briefly reviewing formal inference via syllogisms, Aristotle wrote: "If, however, one is aiming at truth, one must be guided by the real connexions of subjects and attributes." He went on then in the next few pages to distinguish between on the one hand *natural* and on the other *coincidental* (or *accidental*), that is, nonnatural, predication, giving 'That white (thing) is a man' as an example of the latter. Its natural equivalent would be 'That man is white'. Though both are true (and equivalent), only one is natural. Only the latter reveals the "real connexion" (i.e., the proper order of connexion) between the two terms. Surely Aristotle was right about this. Only one of the sentences is natural in the sense that it is the member of this equivalent pair that ordinary speakers would naturally use. Moreover, he suggested a principle of language structure to account for this. According to Aristotle, the terms of a language form a finite hierarchy, where higher terms are predicable of more things than are lower terms. A term's position in the hierarchy is determined by what terms it can be sensibly paired with and by the extent of the set of things to which it applies, relative to those other terms. Terms that apply to just one thing—singular terms like 'Socrates'—are at the bottom of the hierarchy. Natural predication occurs only when the subject term of a sentence is lower than the predicate term. The extension of 'Socrates' is just Socrates; the extension of 'wise' includes Socrates and much more. The naturalness of 'Socrates is wise' relative to 'Some wise (person) is Socrates' has nothing to do with atomicity, asymmetry, and the like. It is simply a semantic (thus nonsyntactical) matter of location of terms in a structure of sense. The details of such a theory were not finally worked out and understood until Sommers built his Tree Theory.

Standard mathematical logic is simply not very natural. And most logicians today accept this. The naturalness of Sommers's term logic rests primarily on the fact that it makes use of a logical syntax (terms copulated pairwise to form sentences and other more complex terms) that is very close to the syntax of natural language. Little, if any, regimentation into the formal language is required of most natural language sentences. But the mathematical logician would argue that the inferential power gained by first-order logic is well worth the price paid in losing large degrees of naturalness (not to mention simplicity). But, as indicated earlier, Sommers's new terminist version of logic enjoys at least as much power. That such power can be demonstrated easily is owing to the symbolic algorithm forged by Sommers. Leibniz had made many starts at formalizing logic in mathematical terms. And the nineteenth-century logicians had debated whether logic should, after all, be treated simply as a branch of mathematics, so that mathematical expressions and principles could be applied to it (Boole, De Morgan, Peirce), or whether mathematics should be treated as a branch of logic, so that no mathematical expressions or principles could be used in formulating a logical language (Frege, Russell).

After some initial attempts at alternatives, Sommers eventually devised his "calculus of terms," whose language consists essentially of term-variables and signs of opposition (pluses and minuses). Logical inference is then simply algebraic. Deciding the validity of any inference is generally just a matter of determining whether the premises add up to the conclusion and whether the number of particular premises equals the number of particular conclusions (viz., one or zero). Proof proceeds by application of the standard, traditional rules of immediate and syllogistic inference (e.g., conversion, obversion, the *dictum de omni et nullo*, etc.), all of which satisfy the validity conditions.

It must be noted again that traditional logic was unable to deal adequately with inferences involving three kinds of terms: singulars, relationals, and sentences. Sommers's term logic incorporates them in a simple and principled way. The only difference between singular terms and general terms is that the former are known to have but a single individual in their denotation (they are UDTs—*uniquely denoting terms*). Denotation is a semantic rather than syntactic feature of terms. In a formal language both singular and general terms can be treated alike. Nonetheless, given that the denotation of a singular is *known*, inferences involving singular sentences can be made on the basis of this extralogical, semantic information. Consequently UDTs are given a special mark to remind one of this. Sometimes Sommers has marked all such terms with a '$\wedge$'. Other times he has simply allowed the quantity on such terms, when quantified, to do the job. For it turns out, as Leibniz first showed, that a quantified singular term can be either universal or particular (it is our special extralogical knowledge of the term's denotation that gives us the freedom of choice). After all, every Socrates is Socrates and so is some Socrates. Singular terms have what Sommers calls 'wild' quantity (which he usually marks with a '$*$'). Since singular terms are on a logical par with general terms (enjoying only the semantic advantage of known denotation) they can, just like general terms, be both quantified (wildly) and qualified (i.e., predicated, be predicate terms). This means that there is no need in term logic for a special 'identity' relation and the additional entourage it requires. There is no 'is' marking just an 'identity relation' (as Wittgenstein had pointed out). From a terminist point of view, every 'is' is an 'is' of predication—a qualifier.

The greatest challenge for traditional term logicians was the proper formulation and treatment of relational expressions. Sommers's ingenious insight was that all syntactical complexity was the result of pairs of terms tied together by a (split or unsplit) logical copula. The resulting complex terms are themselves fit for term-positions within still more complex terms. Compound (conjoined or disjoined) terms, relational terms, and entire sentences are then viewed as complex terms. A sentence such as 'Some politician is kissing every baby' would be parsed as having the two terms 'politician' and 'kissing every baby', with the first particularly quantified and the second positively qualified. In turn, the predicate term is itself complex, consisting of the two terms 'kissing' and 'baby' tied together by the unsplit universal affirmative copula (in this case, the English word 'every'). In the symbolic algorithm, both adicity (the number of places in the relation) and the order of subjects and objects are indicated by the appropriate use of numerical subscripts. Thus the relation indicated by 'loves' (L) in the two sentences 'Abelard loves Heloise' and 'Heloise is loved by Abelard' could be given pairs of subscripts in reverse order: '$A_1L_{12}H_2$' and '$H_1L_{21}A_2$'. Inference via passive transformation is, then, simply a matter of reordering subscripts. Complex relational terms are terms; they can be quantified or qualified. Thus the qualified relational term in 'Some politician is kissing every baby' can be the subject term in a different sentence: 'Whoever is kissing every baby is insincere'.

In spite of its inferential power (especially when it comes to relationals), modern logic is surprisingly unable to offer any genuine logical insight into a number of kinds of inferences also beyond the range of traditional logic. Yet, it turns out, such inferences are easily accounted for by term logic. First-order logic cannot offer much explanation of inferences involving relationals with singular subject- and object-terms (e.g., 'Abelard loves Heloise') when passive transformation is applied. The best the standard logic can do is mere repetition. But there are other inferences involving relationals and singulars that are also left in the dark by the standard logic. Consider: 'Abelard was mutilated by an uncle of Heloise'. From it anyone can validly infer 'Something Abelard was mutilated by was an uncle of Heloise'. The best standard logic can do to exhibit the form of this inference is again mere repetition: $(\exists x)(Mxa \ \& \ Uxh) \ / \ (\exists x)(Mxa \ \& \ Uxh)$. Term logic reveals that the inference proceeds not by mere repetition but by a rule of association: $+A_1 + (M_{21} + (U_{23} + H_3)) \ / + (+A_1 + M_{21}) + (U_{23} + H_3)$.

Finally, consider: 'Abelard wooed Heloise with logic'. One valid conclusion that can immediately be drawn is 'Abelard wooed Heloise'. Yet again, first-order logic offers no help. In fact, in such cases as this, it cannot even fall back on mere repetition. For the standard logic demands that the adicity of any relational term must remain constant throughout a given inferential context. In other words, the number of gaps (fit for filling by singulars) in a function expression must remain fixed. Such a restriction does not apply to a natural language such as English (witness the obvious acceptability of the inference above), nor does it apply to term logic. (Note that an alternative, and still controversial, extension of first-order logic is due to Donald Davidson, who allows for quantification over events [a move with ontological consequences not generally favored by standard logicians who prefer a starker, more minimalist ontology]. The result of following Davidson, however, is that our 'Abelard wooed Heloise' example would be analyzed as follows: 'There is an event of wooing by Abelard of Heloise with logic' entails 'There is an event of wooing by Abelard of Heloise'.)

First-order predicate calculus rests on the foundation of the logic of sentences. Sommers was able to show that from a terminist point of view sentences are simply complex terms. As such, they are fit for any term position. Since all logical formatives can be viewed as signs of opposition (thus the pluses and minuses of the formal language), sentential connectives are on a logical par with the formatives found in any complex term. Indeed, he was able to show that the logic of sentences is simply a special branch of the logic of terms. And the salient feature of the logic of sentences making it a *special* branch of term logic is the singularity of sentential terms. In term logic conditional sentences share a common form with universally quantified sentences, while conjunctions share the form of particulars (thus Peirce insisted on the isomorphism of term and sentential logic). There are, however, some crucial disanalogies between the two, and only Sommers has been able to account for them. There are two obvious ones. First, whereas a conjunction entails its corresponding conditional, a particular does not entail its corresponding universal. Second, although an I categorical is logically compatible with its corresponding O categorical, a conjunction of a sentence with a second sentence is not logically compatible with a conjunction of the first sentence with the *negation* of that second sentence. It is the recognition of the fact that sentences (*qua* complex terms) are singular terms that accounts for such disanalogies and permits the inclusion of sentential logic as a special branch of term logic. The insight required to see this concerns the semantics of terms (and thus sentences) in general.

Every term, when used in a statement-making sentence, normally has a denotation. So sentences themselves, when used to make statements, have denotations. Sommers's insight is that since every sentence so used is used relative to a specifiable 'domain', 'universe of discourse', or 'world' (viz., a totality of individual objects), what a statement-making sentence denotes is that world. Thus sentences denote just one thing—the world relative to which they are used to make a statement. For sentential logic, sentences are taken to be used to make statements about a single world—*the* actual world. So the sentences formulated in such a logic are all singular terms and all denote the same thing (the actual world). It is this singularity of sentences that accounts for the disanalogies. For singular terms, when used as subject terms (in sentential logic this means they are the first conjuncts of conjunctions or the antecedents of conditionals), have wild quantity. And one way of construing wild quantity is to say that the universal is a (nonformal, semantic) consequence of its corresponding particular. Thus, one cannot infer 'Every philosopher is a logician' from 'Some philosopher is a logician', but one *can* infer '(Every) Frege is a logician' from '(Some) Frege is a logician'. In the same way, one can infer 'If there are dogs then there are fleas' from 'There are dogs and there are fleas', where these are read 'terminally' as 'Every world in which there are dogs is a world in which there are fleas' and 'Some world in which there are dogs is a world in which there are fleas'. Knowing that there is but one world (like knowing that there is but one Frege) is what permits the inference. That same extralogical knowledge accounts for the incompatibility between 'There are dogs and there are fleas' and 'There are dogs and there are no fleas' even though 'Some philosopher is a logician' and 'Some philosopher is not a logician' can both be true. Since there is only one actual world, and since nothing can share incompatible properties, the world can have dogs but it cannot both have and not have fleas. The logic of sentences is the logic of terms. The former is a special branch of the latter only on extralogical grounds.

4 Truth and Facts

"What I tell you three times is true."
—Lewis Carroll, *The Hunting of the Snark*

Sommers's account of the semantics of terms is far more extensive than just a story about wild quantity, sentence logic, and so on. Although he had written about the concept of truth from time to time, since the late 1980s he has devoted much attention to the formulation of a theory of truth. Sommers's particular truth theory is a revitalized correspondence theory of truth.

Over the last quarter of a century or so truth has become one of the hottest topics of discussion and investigation among philosophers of logic, language, and mind. Traditionally, truth had been considered by the vast majority of philosophers to be a substantial concept, one that can be analyzed and even defined. The most common definitions of truth were in terms of correspondence. A statement (sometimes: sentence, or proposition, even belief or judgment) was taken to be true just in case it corresponded to a fact (state of affairs, situation), otherwise it was said to be false. This "correspondence theory" of truth was taken to reflect our unschooled intuitions concerning truth and became something of a default theory. It was also generally taken to be integral to modern science. Alternative theories of truth, such as coherence theories and pragmatic theories, enjoyed the support of significant numbers of philosophers, but they were never supported by a majority. Nonetheless, what all traditional theories of truth shared was the conviction that truth is a substantial property of whatever is true, that truth is definable. While early analytic philosophers such as Moore, Russell, and Austin were ready to accept and even defend some version of the correspondence theory, in recent years a very large number of philosophers, both analytic and not, have challenged the notion that truth is even substantial. They have either argued that the concept of truth essentially contains an epistemic element, or that there is virtually no substance to the concept at all. This latter, deflationist view comes in several varieties (e.g., Quine's disquotationalism, Horwich's minimalism), which have received wide acceptance in much of the philosophical community.

In the 1940s, Tarski offered his semantic theory of truth as a more rigorous formulation of traditional correspondence. As it happened, many later philosophers chose to interpret that work as providing the foundations for deflationism. A decade later Strawson attacked Austin's version of correspondence in particular and all versions in general. Schematically, a correspondence theory of truth says that a truth-bearer is made true by its correspondence with a truth-maker. Defenders of such a theory were, in effect, challenged to give an adequate account of each of these: truth-bearers, truth-makers, and the relation of correspondence between them. Strawson, Quine, Davidson, and many others have persuasively argued that if there are such things as truth-makers (facts), they are not to be found in the world. As Strawson would say to Austin: there is the cat, there is the mat, but where in the world is the *fact* that the cat is on the mat? Without facts (or some other sort of truth-maker) both truth-bearers and correspondence are left dangling. For many today truth simply applies to sentences (or at least to "eternal sentences") and is either redundant, disquotational, or (for Rorty) merely rhetorical.

Still, the demand for a clear account of truth-makers, truth-bearers, and correspondence is a legitimate challenge to any defender of a correspondence theory of truth. If sentences are not the primary bearers of truth, then what are? If facts, unlike cats, are not to be met with in the world, then either there are none or some special (and satisfactory) account of them is required. If truth is indeed a matter of correspondence between truths and facts, just what is the nature of this correspondence? Sommers outlined a rich theory of the semantics of terms consonant with his term logic. In doing so he was able to meet these challenges to a correspondence theory and to build his own truth theory.

Any term, when used, *expresses* a *concept*. From an epistemic point of view a concept is what is grasped when a term is understood; viewed purely semantically, a concept is the *sense* of a term. As well, any term normally *signifies* a *property* and *denotes* whatever has that property. Consider the term 'wise'. It signifies the property of being wise (wisdom) and denotes whatever has that property (Socrates, Confucius, etc.). Suppose no one or no thing is wise. Then nothing is denoted by 'wise' and no property is signified by 'wise' (there are no unhad properties). The term 'wise', then, would be denotationally and significationally *vacuous*. As it turns out, 'wise' is not vacuous in these ways. But some terms are. For example, 'unicorn' and perhaps 'perfect' can be taken to be vacuous. Assume that nothing is perfect. It will follow that 'perfect' is denotationally vacuous, and, since no properties are unhad, there is no property of perfection (so it is also significationally vacuous). Still one wants to say that 'perfect' is not totally meaningless; it has some sense (otherwise one could not say, for example, 'My friend is not perfect' or 'She thought her children were perfect'). And one is right to want this. Whenever a speaker uses a term he or she expresses a concept, and that concept may or may not correspond to a property had by some individual objects. Thus 'perfect' expresses the concept of perfection, has a sense, even though no object has the property of perfection.

For the term logician, statements (i.e., sentences used to make truth claims) are (complex) terms. So statements have the same threefold semantics shared by all (used) terms. The sense of a statement, what it expresses, is a *proposition*. Propositions are the proper bearers of truth. Statements are true just in the sense that they are used to express true propositions. What a statement signifies (if anything) is a *fact*. Facts are truth-makers. *A proposition expressed by a given statement is true if and only if it corresponds to the fact signified by that statement.* But what are facts? Critics of correspondence, such as Strawson, assume that facts must be construed as nonlinguistic, abstract objects somehow denoted, referred to, named by true statements—going on then to point out that no such objects are to be found in the world. On Sommers's truth theory, since facts are what statements signify, and since statements are merely a species of terms, and since what terms signify are properties, facts must be a species of property. Sommers's insight is the recognition that facts must be viewed as properties *of the world*—not as things *in the world*.

The (actual) world is a totality of individual objects. The world has many properties, some of which it has simply by virtue of what objects it has or lacks. The soup in my lunch is hot and nutritious, but it is also salty and meatless. These last two properties it has just because salt is one of its ingredients and meat is not. Properties that totalities have by virtue of the objects they have or lack (what are and what are not their constituents) are *constitutive properties*. Having a constituent is a *positive* constitutive property; lacking a constituent is a *negative* constitutive property. The world contains dogs; the presence of dogs in the world is a positive constitutive property of the world. The world contains no unicorns; this absence is a negative constitutive property of the world. (The world does contain nonunicorns, but this is a positive constitutive property—in spite of the 'non'.) Thus existence and nonexistence are not primarily properties of individual objects (dogs, unicorns), but of totalities. To say that some object exists is just to say that it is a constituent of the world, which, in turn, is a characterization of the world, not the object. Hume and Kant were right to deny existence as a property of objects.

In the normal, nonvacuous case, statements, like terms in general, express, signify, and denote. What a term denotes are the objects having the property it signifies. What a statement denotes is the world, that which has the (constitutive) property it signifies. The logic of statements is incorporated into term logic and its disanalogies accounted for by virtue of the singularity (denotation of just one thing) of statements. When a term denotes nothing (and thus signifies no property—since, again, there are no unhad properties) it is vacuous (both significationally and denotationally). A statement that is vacuous in this way, not denoting the world, not signifying any fact (constitutive property of the world), expresses a proposition that is *false*. Thus a false proposition is not made false by anything like a "falsifying" fact. A false proposition simply fails to be made true by *any* fact. A true proposition is expressed by a statement that signifies a property (fact) of what the statement denotes (the world). In such cases the proposition *corresponds* to the fact. Facts are truth-makers; they make true the propositions, truth-bearers, to which they correspond. 'Some dogs have fleas' expresses a true proposition because there are flea-bitten dogs in the world. 'Every elephant has a trunk' expresses a true proposition because there are no trunkless elephants in the world. 'The present king of France is bald' expresses a false proposition because no fact makes it true, there being no present king of France (in the world). Truth is correspondence. A true proposition corresponds to a fact. Just as a portrait may correspond to a specified person (say, Queen Elizabeth), it might just as well correspond to no particular person at all. Trying to "make our statements fit the facts" is like trying to make the portrait we are painting fit the features of our model. We might fail, in which case we speak falsely—correspondence fails to hold. But if what we say is true then there is something corresponding to what we say—a fact; the world is as we say it is. In other words, the proposition we express corresponds to *how* the world is, to a (constitutive) property of it.

Sommers's truth theory is a powerful version of the correspondence theory. It is defensible against the standard attacks on correspondence, and Sommers has made those defenses. But it also has a number of far-reaching consequences, which can be deployed in addressing some old philosophical problems. Much of ontology is illuminated not only by the tree theory but by Sommers's idea that the attribution of existence or nonexistence to objects is always analyzable into a positive or negative characterization of the world. The truth theory can also shed light on some problems in epistemology and the philosophy of mind involving the notion of belief.

Just as terms can be said to express concepts (epistemically) or senses (semantically), what statements express can likewise be viewed either epistemically or semantically. Viewed semantically, statements express propositions; viewed epistemically, statements express *beliefs*. One way of

looking at beliefs is as dispositions to assent to the truth of certain propositions. From this point of view beliefs are propositional, *de dicto*. There is
little doubt that many of our beliefs are propositional. But as often as not
beliefs are grounded in perception. We perceive objects. But we also perceive the environments in which those objects are found. Such environments are either the world or some salient, perceived part thereof. In
perceiving an environment as the background for the perception of a given
object, one perceives that environment as having a given constitutive
property, namely the property of having that object in it. In general, to
perceive an object relative to an environment is not only to perceive that
object but to perceive the environment (the world or part of the world) as
having that object as a constituent. Naturally such perceptions bring about
beliefs. The perception (or misperception) of a flea-bitten dog yields the
belief that there are flea-bitten dogs, that the world has such things. Those
who see ghosts believe the world is ghostly, has ghosts. To believe in God
is to take the world to have God as a constituent.

Beliefs that the world (or at least an important part of it) is characterized by the presence or absence of some thing are *de mundo* beliefs. Often
de mundo beliefs serve as grounds for *de dicto* beliefs. To hold a *de dicto* belief
is to be prepared to assent to some specifiable proposition, to accept it as
true. Taking the world to have ghosts in it (having seen or hallucinated
one) would likely ready one for assent to the proposition that there are
ghosts. But the step from a *de mundo* belief to a *de dicto* belief requires the
ability to assent to a given proposition, which requires the ability to *express*
a proposition. And that ability, in turn, requires the ability to produce a
statement. Thus, a necessary condition for holding *de dicto* beliefs (but not
for holding *de mundo* beliefs) is the possession of language. This difference
accounts in a simple, natural way for the fact that very young children, as
well as animals, do not have *de dicto* beliefs, but do have *de mundo* beliefs.
Seeing its mother the young child takes its world to have her as a constituent. Unable to find its kittens, the mother cat takes its small piece of
the world to lack her kittens. Such beliefs require no language.

The account of propositions as senses expressed by statements is an
essential part of the truth theory. It has been used by Sommers to manage
semantic paradoxes such as that of the Liar. The distinction between
sentences and propositions is crucial. Yet one can talk about either. Sentences can be mentioned and characterized in various ways. Examples are

' "Socrates is wise" is English' or 'There are three words in "Socrates is wise" '. Quoting or mentioning a sentence yields a name of that sentence, a singular term denoting it. Terms denoting propositions can also be formed, and permit a speaker to characterize those propositions in various ways. Consider 'Socrates is wise': one can denote the proposition expressed by the use of that sentence by such terms as 'the proposition expressed by "Socrates is wise" ', 'what so-and-so said', or simply, 'that Socrates is wise'. Whereas 'Socrates is wise' denotes a sentence, 'that Socrates is wise' denotes a proposition. Sentences can be (or fail to be) spoken, written, English, three-worded, long, and so on. Propositions can be (or fail to be) true, believable, understood, shocking, and so on. Given the tree theory, then, sentences and propositions belong to different types. Nevertheless, it must be kept in mind that (as the above examples illustrate) proposition-denoting terms always "embed"—explicitly (e.g., 'that Socrates is wise') or implicitly ('what his teacher told him')—the sentences used to express those propositions. More important, sentences using propositional terms can be said to embed those sentences embedded in such terms. Let 's' be a sentence and '$[s]$' be the proposition expressed by it. One can see that 's' is embedded in '$[s]$'; also that 's' is embedded in any sentence about $[s]$, such as '$[s]$ is shocking'. Suppose 's' is 'Socrates is wise'. To make a statement with 's' is to say something about Socrates. To say, however, that it is true that Socrates is wise (i.e., '$[s]$ is true') is to say something not about Socrates but about '$[s]$', the proposition expressed by the statement about Socrates. Now '$[s]$ is true' is a sentence (which embeds the sentence 's') being used to express a new proposition. Suppose one says of this new proposition that it is doubtful; then the proposition being expressed is $[[[s]$ is true] is doubtful].

This embedding of 's' is, theoretically, unlimited in depth. Nonetheless, there are restrictions on such embedding. Any sentence expressing a proposition must have a determinate 'propositional depth'. The propositional depth of 's', 'Socrates is wise', is zero; it embeds no sentence at all, it makes no use of propositional terms. The depth of '$[s]$ is true' is one. The depth of '$[[s]$ is true] is doubtful' is two. To see why depth must be determinate, consider the Liar paradox. Let 'L' be the Liar sentence. Taken in its strengthened form, it seems to express the proposition that it is not true, i.e. $[[L]$ is not true]. Because this sentence is about a proposition it must have a depth greater than zero; call its depth x. But 'L' just is '$[L]$ is not true', so the embedded sentence must have a depth less than x. However, since [L] = [[L] is not true], the depth of the proposition is both x and less than x. In other words, the Liar sentence has no determinate propositional depth. In general, the restriction means that a statement can never be about the proposition it expresses. Such statements are not to be confused with statements that are just about themselves, not about what they purport to express. Thus the statement made by the use of 'This sentence is English' is about this sentence, not about the (true) proposition it expresses. Self-referential statements that refer to what they purport to express cannot be true (so they are significationally and denotationally vacuous), but they are also *expressively* vacuous—they fail to express a proposition at all.

5 A United Philosophy

Seen as a unified whole, Sommers's philosophical work sheds much-needed light on the nature of language, the world, and mind. In particular, it gives a rich account of both the underlying logical syntax of natural language and the structure of semantic (sense) relations that hold among the terms of natural language. It shows how the natural categories of individuals are arranged in a hierarchy of inclusion relations that is isomorphic with the linguistic semantic structure. These are tasks that have been pursued by philosophers since ancient times, but Sommers has carried them out in a clear, systematic, intuitively appealing way that is unprecedented. His work shows how ordinary language users' instincts, their easy avoidance of category mistakes, are in conformity with the semantic structure of language, and how the underlying logical syntax of language, which is close to the surface syntax of ordinary language, is reflected in the ways ordinary speakers make inferences in everyday life. Both the world and speakers determine, in their ways, the overall nature of language. Thus, inevitably, any investigation of language, if pushed far enough, will open paths into both ontology and the philosophy of mind. An important aspect of Sommers's truth theory is that it show ways in which speakers (*qua* believers and truth-claimers) are related to the world.

In summary, the world is a totality of individual objects; the presences in, or absences from, that totality determine the worlds' positive, or negative, constitutive properties. Those properties are the facts that account for the truth of true propositions expressed by speakers' statements.

Propositions, whether true or not, are the proper bearers of truth and the proper objects of belief (for a belief about the world is a belief that the world has some constitutive property). Moreover, the individual objects that constitute the world belong to exclusive types, which in turn constitute categories in a hierarchical structure isomorphic with the structure of senses of the terms of the language.

The three theories that together provide this unified picture of language, the world, and mind are tied together by a number of common theses. Primary among these is the recognition of term negation. The idea that terms come in logically charged, positive or negative, pairs is a key element in Sommers's tree theory, term logic, and truth theory. The old Aristotelian idea that the semantic structure of language reflects a hierarchy, accounting for the commonsense recognition of a distinction between natural and nonnatural predications, is a common element in both the tree theory and term logic. Indeed, the idea that the syntax of ordinary language sentences can be simply accounted for by the notion of pairs of terms tied together predicationally (via a split or unsplit logical copula) is an important feature of all three parts of Sommers's unified theory. Finally, term logic and the truth theory both embody the idea that statements signify constitutive properties of the world, so that the logic of statements is a logic of claims about the world and the propositions expressed by truth-claims are made true by their correspondence with properties of that world.

Other contributions to this volume probe deeply into some of the details of Sommers's work that are only alluded to above. Other writers advance that work in various directions. The effort spent in a critical but open-minded exploration of these studies, and especially Sommers's own work, will pay valuable dividends in terms of an understanding of a powerful philosophical theory, a well-articulated one rich in implications, insights, and suggestions for a very wide range of philosophical issues. It might very well be that such understanding does not culminate in acceptance of some, or any, of the theory. But the best way to honor a thinker is to listen carefully.

3 Syntax and Ontology: Reflections on Three Logical Systems

E. J. Lowe

[I]f objects and concepts are as different as Frege says they are, then it would seem entirely reasonable to hold that object-words and concept-words are as syntactically different as Frege makes them and the prohibition against predicating object-words is then also reasonable. I do not find much in this . . . [T]o anyone who finds an alternative to the atomicity thesis, the object-concept distinction loses its syntactical authority and becomes a metaphysical distinction of no great interest to the logician or the grammarian. The strength of the object-concept distinction is precisely the strength of Frege's logical syntax; the former is dependent on the latter and not vice versa.[1]

How far should logical syntax be expected to reflect ontology? And which, if either, is explanatorily prior to the other? The passage just quoted from Fred Sommers's book would suggest that he, at least, thinks that it is wrong-headed to attempt to make our logical syntax conform to our ontological preconceptions and, indeed, that some of these preconceptions may in any case be rooted in antecedently assumed syntactical distinctions which possess little merit in themselves. The "atomicity thesis" of which he speaks in that passage is the assumption, central to the first-order quantified predicate logic of Frege and Russell, that the most basic form of elementary proposition is 'Fa', where 'a' is a proper name of a particular object and 'F' expresses a concept under which that object is said to fall (or, in another idiom, a property it is said to exemplify). For such logicians, more complex propositions can then be formed by means of truth-functional operations or by quantifying into positions capable of being occupied by names of objects. Thus we obtain propositions of such forms as '$(\forall x)(Fx \rightarrow Gx)$' and '$(\exists x)(Fx \ \& \ Gx)$', which are standardly construed as being the logical forms of such natural language sentences as 'All men are mortal' and 'Some philosophers are wise', respectively.

Traditional formal logic, championed by Sommers himself, holds on the contrary that the logical forms of the latter two sentences are, respectively, 'Every F is G' and 'Some F is G' and takes these forms to be logically basic, along with such forms as 'No F is G' and 'Some F is non-G'. Such sentences are said to have subject-predicate form—that is, the form 'S is P'—with terms symbolized as 'F' and 'G' taken as being capable of occupying either subject or predicate position. (Note here that such terms do not, in general, constitute *in their entirety* either the subject or the predicate of a sentence with subject-predicate form, according to traditional formal logic, because they need to be supplemented by logical particles such as 'every', 'some', and 'non'; I shall return to this important point in a moment.) By contrast, it is central to Frege–Russell logic that while atomic propositions may legitimately be said to have subject-predicate form, in them only a *proper name* can occupy subject position. Correlatively, it is built into this conception of logical syntax that a proper name can never occupy *predicate position*, because according to it a predicate just *is* what remains when one or more proper names is deleted from a sentence—and a proper name alone can never be all that remains when one or more other proper names is deleted from a sentence. As a consequence, Frege–Russell logic absorbs the 'is' of predication into the predicate, treating 'is wise' in 'Socrates is wise' on a par with 'thinks' in 'Socrates thinks'. In contrast, traditional formal logic does quite the reverse, reformulating the latter sentence so as to include explicitly a copula: 'Socrates is a thinking thing'.

Whereas for Frege and Russell elementary propositions are "atomic," having such forms as 'Fa' or (in the case of relational propositions) 'Rab', and thus contain no logical particles, for Sommers all elementary propositions contain, in addition to nonlogical terms, logical particles expressive of *quantity* or *quality*, which are taken to be syncategorematic parts of the subjects and predicates, respectively, of those propositions (as was mentioned above). For example, 'some' is expressive of quantity and 'non' of quality in 'Some F is non-G'. The distinction between sentence negation and predicate negation is correspondingly crucial for Sommers—'It is not the case that some F is G' is not logically equivalent to 'Some F is non-G'—whereas it is entirely repudiated by Frege–Russell logic, for which sentence negation alone has any significance.

Frege and Russell disagree among themselves, of course, concerning the membership of the class of proper names—Russell restricting it to what he calls "logically" proper names, while Frege is much more liberal, including even so-called definite descriptions. But this difference between them is minor in comparison with the doctrines that they hold in common and in opposition to those of traditional formal logic. One vital feature of Sommers's defense of traditional formal logic against the current Frege–Russell orthodoxy is his contention that proper names are themselves just terms, capable of occupying either subject or predicate position in elementary propositions as conceived by traditional formal logic—their only distinctive peculiarity being that, because such a name (unlike a so-called common name) is understood to be applicable to only one thing, it is a matter of indifference whether 'every' or 'some' is prefixed to such a name when it is in subject position. Thus, on Sommers's account, 'Socrates is a thinking thing' can indifferently be understood as saying either 'Every Socrates is a thinking thing' or 'Some Socrates is a thinking thing': a proper name has, as Sommers puts it, "wild" quantity (by analogy with the notion of a "wild card" in certain card games).[2]

Sommers holds that the Fregean notion of a distinctive 'is' of *identity* is just an artifact of Fregean logical syntax, without independent motivation.[3] The argument is that it is only because Frege insists that proper names (at least, when they are being used as such) cannot occupy predicate position in a subject-predicate sentence, and recognizes no logical role for 'is' as a copula, that he is compelled to postulate an 'is' of identity. (Frege himself famously cites the sentence 'Trieste is no Vienna' as a case in which 'Vienna' is *not* being used as a proper name.[4]) For consider the sentence 'Cicero is Tully', which contains two proper names. Because 'Tully' is the name of an object and so, according to Frege, cannot occupy predicate position, 'is Tully' cannot be treated by him as a simple monadic predicate on a par with 'is wise', in which the 'is' of predication has, allegedly, no genuine logical role. On the other hand, 'Cicero is Tully' cannot simply be treated as the juxtaposition of two proper names, with the logical form '*ab*', for no proposition can have that form. Hence the 'is' in 'Cicero is Tully' cannot be regarded as being, like the 'is' of predication, logically redundant: rather, it must express a *relational* concept, on a par with 'loves' in 'John loves Mary'. In accordance with the Fregean doctrine that a predicate is what remains when one or more proper names is deleted from a sentence, the 'is' in 'Cicero is Tully'—given that it must genuinely *remain* when both 'Cicero' and 'Tully' are deleted from that sentence—

must be regarded as being quite as much a genuine predicate as the 'loves' in 'John loves Mary'.

For Sommers, as I say, Frege's need to recognize a distinctive 'is' of identity is merely an artifact of his doctrines concerning logical syntax. According to traditional formal logic as interpreted by Sommers, 'Cicero is Tully' has the form 'Every/some F is G', with 'Cicero' occupying subject position and 'Tully' occupying predicate position, while the 'is' is just the familiar logical copula that traditional formal logic regards as indispensable. So, although Sommers agrees with Frege that the 'is' in 'Cicero is Tully' is not logically redundant, he thinks that this is so because this 'is' is just the familiar copula that traditional formal logic always takes to be nonredundant: whereas Frege, who quite generally recognizes no genuine logical role for an 'is' of predication, is forced in this special case to recognize such a role for 'is', which thereby becomes elevated by him into a supposedly distinctive 'is' of identity. Sommers presses home his objection to this Fregean doctrine of identity by pointing out that Frege is obliged to postulate distinct and irreducible laws of identity to govern the logical behavior of identity statements, whereas such laws appear to be immediate consequences of more general logical principles according to traditional formal logic. In particular, the laws of the reflexivity and substitutivity of identity (the latter being one construal of Leibniz's law) seem to be straightforwardly derivable: a fact of considerable significance, given that in modern quantified predicate logic the remaining laws of identity—the laws of symmetry and transitivity—are derivable from these two. For example, that 'Cicero is Cicero' is a logical truth seems just to be a special case of the logical truth of statements of the form 'Every F is F' and 'Some F is F' (assuming that 'Cicero' is not an empty name and remembering that 'Cicero' in subject position is supposed to have wild quantity). And that 'Tully is wise' follows from 'Cicero is Tully' and 'Cicero is wise' seems just to be a special case of the fact that 'Some F is G' follows from 'Every H is F' and 'Some H is G'.[5]

While Sommers is critical of the claim promoted by many of Frege's latter-day devotees, such as Geach and Dummett, that Fregean logical syntax constitutes a momentous and irreversible advance over what they see as the benighted syntactical doctrines of traditional formal logic, he is more charitable regarding the merits of modern first-order quantified predicate logic with identity than most modern logicians are regarding traditional formal logic. In fact, he is at pains to argue that traditional formal logic is at no expressive disadvantage with respect to quantified predicate logic, in that the formulas of each can be translated into corresponding formulas of the other.[6] It would seem that the main advantage he claims for traditional formal logic is that its syntax is much closer to that of natural language and consequently easier for people to manipulate and understand. It does not appear that he thinks it makes much sense to ask which of these logical systems is "correct," given that their formulas are intertranslatable—any more than, say, it makes sense to ask whether an axiomatic or a natural deduction formulation of quantified predicate logic is "correct," even though each may have distinct practical advantages.

On the other hand, Sommers's criticisms of the Fregean doctrine of identity would suggest that he is in fact committed to a somewhat less ecumenical position. As we saw in the passage quoted from Sommers's book at the outset, it seems that Sommers favors—there, at least—the view that the logician's conception of syntactical structure should float free of ontological considerations.[7] However, it is difficult to see how one could accept Sommers's own complaint that Frege's doctrine of identity is merely an artifact of his views about logical syntax without rejecting, as a consequence, Frege's belief—which is clearly ontological in character—that there is such a relation as the relation of identity. More generally, it seems that we cannot entirely divorce Frege's syntactical doctrines from his ontological views. His distinction between object and concept may well be at least partly syntactical in origin, but it is indubitably ontological in import. And while we may very reasonably have doubts about the legitimacy of attempting to *found* ontological distinctions on syntactical ones—if that is indeed what Frege attempted to do—it is open to us to agree with certain of Frege's ontological insights and to concur with him on the relevance of those insights to questions of logical syntax.

Suppose we agree with Frege in advocating something like his object–concept distinction, construed as capturing—or perhaps, rather, as conflating—aspects of two more familiar distinctions of traditional metaphysics: the distinction between *substance* and *property* and the distinction between *particular* and *universal*. (Frege himself no doubt thought that he was improving upon these older distinctions, by drawing on the mathematical distinction between function and argument, but we need not concur with him in this opinion.) Would it not then be reasonable to expect this distinction to be reflected in a perspicuous logical syntax? Logic is the science of reasoning, and what we reason *about* are possible states of affairs and their relationships of mutual inclusion and exclusion.[8] We reason about them by representing them propositionally and reflecting on relations of mutual consistency and entailment among propositions. That being so, should we not aim to make logical syntax ontologically perspicuous by articulating or regimenting propositions in forms that reflect the constituent structure of the possible states of affairs that we are attempting to reason about? Suppose, for instance, that a certain possible state of affairs consists in some particular object's possessing some property, or exemplifying a certain universal. In that case, it seems that the state of affairs in question contains just two constituents—the particular object and the property or universal—which belong to fundamentally distinct ontological categories.[9] Would it not then be reasonable to represent this state of affairs by a proposition that likewise contains just two constituents of formally distinct types—by, indeed, an "atomic" proposition of the classic Frege–Russell form 'Fa'?

Here, however, we may be beset by doubts of the sort famously raised by Frank Ramsey concerning the origins and legitimacy of the particular–universal distinction—doubts with which Sommers himself clearly has some sympathy.[10] Ramsey suggested that this supposed ontological distinction is a spurious one founded on a superficial understanding of the subject–predicate distinction. He pointed out that if we think of the proposition 'Socrates is wise' as somehow implicitly differentiating between Socrates conceived as being a "particular" and wisdom conceived as being a "universal" that characterizes that particular, then we should observe that we can restate the proposition in the equivalent form 'Wisdom is a characteristic of Socrates', in which 'wisdom' rather than 'Socrates' is now the subject of which something is said by means of the proposition's predicate.[11] (To emphasize the parallel between the two equivalent formulations, we could even contract the second to something like 'Wisdom is Socratic', without loss of significant content.) The suggestion, then, is that the entities picked out by the subject terms of either of these equivalent sentences—Socrates and wisdom—do not really belong to distinct ontological categories in any intelligible sense. Each is just whatever it is, and either can be truly and equivalently predicated of the other. My answer to such doubts is that it would indeed be mistaken to think that insight into the ontological distinction between particular and universal could be gained simply by reflection on the subject–predicate distinction—and even more seriously mistaken to suppose that the latter distinction could provide the foundation of the former. The lesson is that if the particular–universal distinction is a proper one to make, it must be one that it is made on wholly ontological, not syntactical, grounds. More specifically, the only legitimate way to found the particular–universal distinction—or any other putative distinction between ontological categories—is, I consider, to provide a well-motivated account of how the existence and identity conditions of putative members of the one category differ quite generally from those of putative members of the other. And I believe that this can in fact be done in the case of the particular–universal distinction, as I shall explain later. But first I need to provide a fuller picture of the system of ontological categories that I am inclined to favor.

To begin with, let me return to a suggestion that I made in passing a little while ago, namely, that Frege's distinction between object and concept unhelpfully conflates two traditional metaphysical distinctions—the distinction between substance and property and the distinction between particular and universal. It is my view that we do indeed need to endorse both of these distinctions and that they should both be reflected in a perspicuous logical syntax. I consider that the two distinctions cut across one another, serving to generate *four* fundamental ontological categories: the category of particular substances, the category of particular properties (and relations), the category of substantial universals, and the category of property- (and relational) universals. This is precisely the *four-category ontology* (as I call it) that we find hinted at in the beginning of Aristotle's *Categories*, perhaps the most important single text in the history of ontology.[12] An example of a particular substance would be a certain particular dog, Fido. An example of a substantial universal would be the species or kind *dog* of which Fido is a particular instance. An example of a property-universal would be the color—say, whiteness—which Fido has in common with other white things. And an example of a particular property would be the particular whiteness of Fido, which is necessarily unique to that particular dog and which is a particular instance of whiteness, the property-universal. This is not the place to attempt to justify the four-category ontology—something that I have tried to do at length in other places.[13] I do, however, believe that we need to find room in our ontology for entities belonging to each of these categories, and that in no case are the entities belonging to one of them wholly explicable in terms of, reducible to, or eliminable in favor of entities belonging to one or more other categories. This is what it means, in my usage, to say that these categories are *fundamental*. Moreover, I am not denying—any more than Aristotle did—that there are other ontological categories besides these four (for instance, it may be contended that there is a distinct ontological category of *events*): I am committed only to the view that any such further categories are not fundamental in my sense.

As well as recognizing these four fundamental ontological categories, we need to recognize two fundamental ontological relations in which entities belonging to these categories stand to one another: I call these relations *instantiation* and *characterization*. Instantiation is the relation in which a particular instance of a universal stands to that universal: so, for example, it is the relation in which Fido stands to the kind *dog*, and it is the relation in which Fido's particular whiteness stands to whiteness the property-universal. Characterization is the relation in which properties stand to the substantial entities of which they are predicable. So, for example, Fido's particular whiteness characterizes—is a characteristic of—Fido. Analogously, whiteness the property-universal characterizes certain substantial universals or kinds, such as the kind *polar bear*. It does not characterize the kind *dog* as such, because not every kind of dog is white, just as not every kind of bear is white. What I have just said concerning characterization may be extended from the case of properties to the case of relations and the substantial entities that stand in those relations to one another. Thus, the particular relation of loving in which John stands to Mary characterizes John and Mary, taken in that order. Analogously, the relational universal of loving characterizes, perhaps, the human kinds *mother* and *child*, taken in that order. But I should emphasize that these putative examples are for illustrative purposes only, since not every relational expression should be assumed to denote a genuine relation, any more than every monadic predicate should be assumed to denote a genuine property. *That* we should include in our ontology properties and relations—both as particulars and as universals—I am now taking as given: but *which* properties and relations we should include is another question, to be settled by further discussion and argument, in which considerations of ontological economy and explanatory power will have an important and perhaps decisive role to play. This question is not one that concerns me at present, however.

I have spoken of instantiation and characterization as being fundamental ontological relations. But now I must qualify what I have just said, because in an important sense I do not think that they really are *relations*, that is, entities belonging either to the category of nonsubstantial universals or to the category of nonsubstantial particulars. In fact, I do not think that instantiation and characterization are *entities*—elements of being—at all. The fact that Fido instantiates the kind *dog* is not a *relational fact*, in the way that the fact that John loves Mary is. To put it another way, instantiation is not a *constituent* of the fact that Fido instantiates the kind *dog* in addition to its constituents Fido and the kind *dog*, in the way that their particular relation of loving is a constituent of the fact that John loves Mary in addition to its constituents John and Mary. One plausible way to account for this difference is to classify instantiation and characterization as so-called *internal* relations and to urge that such "relations" are, in David Armstrong's useful phrase, "no addition of being."[14] An internal relation, in the sense now at issue, is one in which its relata *must* stand, of logical or metaphysical necessity, given merely that they themselves exist and have the intrinsic properties or natures that they do. Perhaps the paradigm examples of internal relations in this sense are identity and distinctness. This, however, is not the place to pursue this important issue further. The crucial point is that we should *not* include instantiation and characterization amongst the relational entities belonging to either of our two fundamental categories of nonsubstantial beings. I like to register this point by calling instantiation and characterization purely *formal* relations—but we could equally if more grandiloquently call them *transcendental* relations in order to register the same point.[15]

We may conveniently represent the ontological scheme that I have just sketched by means of a diagram, as shown in figure 3.1, which I call *the ontological square*. One aspect of this scheme may seem puzzling, namely, that I speak of substantial particulars as being characterized by nonsubstantial particulars and as instantiating substantial universals—that is,

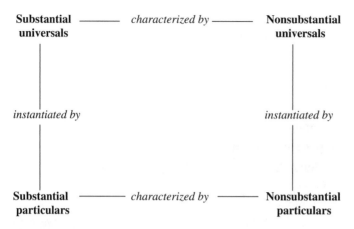

Figure 3.1
The ontological square.

kinds—but have said nothing explicitly so far about any relationship between substantial particulars and *nonsubstantial* universals, that is, between an entity such as Fido, a particular dog, and an entity such as whiteness, the property-universal. However, it should be evident from the ontological square that there are in fact two different ways in which such entities may be related. On the one hand, a substantial particular may instantiate a kind that is characterized by a certain property-universal, while on the other a substantial particular may be characterized by a particular property that instantiates a certain property-universal. Thus, for example, on the one hand Fido instantiates the kind *dog* and the kind *dog* is characterized by the property-universal carnivorousness, while on the other hand Fido is characterized by a certain particular whiteness and this particular whiteness instantiates whiteness the property-universal.

My view is that it is this ontological distinction that underlies the semantic distinction between dispositional and categorical—or, as I prefer to call the latter, *occurrent*—predicates. In effect, to say that a substantial particular is *disposed* to be *F* (or is "potentially" *F*) is to imply that it is a thing of a *kind* which has *F*-ness as a general feature, whereas to say that it is *occurrently* *F* (or is "actually" *F*) is to imply that an instance of *F*-ness is one of *its* particular features. Clearly, something may be disposed to be *F* even though it is not occurrently or actually *F*: for example, a crystal may be disposed to dissolve in water even though it is not actually dissolving in water. By my account, it has this disposition in virtue of being an instance of some chemical kind—such as the kind *sodium chloride crystal*—of which the property of dissolving in water is a characteristic. That the kind *sodium chloride crystal* has this characteristic is, however, nothing less than a *natural law*, most naturally expressible in English by the sentence 'Sodium chloride crystals dissolve in water', or, equivalently, 'Sodium chloride crystals are water-soluble'. So, in effect, my account of dispositionality may be summed up by saying that, according to it, a substantial particular, *a*, has a disposition to be *F* just in case there is a law connecting *F*-ness with the kind of thing that *a* is.[16]

I do not expect this ontological scheme to seem entirely compelling simply on the basis of the very sketchy account of it that I have been able to provide here, but it is not vital for my present purposes that I should be able to convince the reader of its correctness. My current purpose, rather, is to persuade the reader that it is legitimate and indeed desirable to tailor one's theory of logical syntax to one's ontological convictions. For this purpose, I need nothing more than the reader's concurrence that the four-category ontology as I have sketched it is at least coherent and worthy of consideration. From this point on, then, I shall take the ontology to be as I have described it and attempt to show how our account of logical syntax needs to be adapted in order to accommodate that ontology in a perspicuous fashion. But before doing so I must redeem a promise made earlier, to indicate how the categorial distinctions that I have invoked may be explicated in terms of the distinctive existence and identity conditions of the members of the categories concerned.

Very briefly, then, what I have to say on this matter is as follows.[17] Nonsubstantial particulars depend for their existence and identity on the substantial particulars they characterize. For example, Fido's particular whiteness exists only because Fido does and is distinguished from other particular whitenesses precisely in being *Fido's*. In contrast, Fido depends neither for his existence nor for his identity on his particular whiteness, since he could exist without it (if, for example, he were to change color). We may summarize this sort of ontological asymmetry between substantial and nonsubstantial particulars by saying that the former are *independent* and the latter *dependent* particulars. As for universals, whether substantial or nonsubstantial, they are dependent entities in another sense, at least according to the sort of immanent or "Aristotelian" realism concerning universals that I favor, for they are "generically" existentially dependent on their particular instances. That is to say, according to this immanent realist view, a universal can exist only if it has *some* particular instances: there are and can be no uninstantiated universals. But a universal is not dependent for its *identity* on its particular instances: the very same universal could have had different particular instances from those that it actually has. Finally, we need to say something about the distinction between substantial and nonsubstantial universals. The plausible thing to say here is this. First, nonsubstantial universals depend for their existence but not for their identity on substantial universals. For instance, whiteness the property-universal plausibly would not exist if no *kind* of thing had the characteristic of being white, but whiteness is not the very property that it is in virtue of the kinds of things that it characterizes—for it could have characterized quite other kinds of things. Second, substantial universals depend for their identity—and hence also for their existence—on at least some nonsubstantial universals. Thus, the kind *dog* depends for its identity on a number of property-universals—its "essential" characteristics—which include, for example, the properties of warm-bloodedness and carnivorousness. I would be the first to acknowledge that this account of the matter in hand involves a considerable amount of oversimplification, but it should at least suffice to give a reasonably accurate idea of the lines along which a fuller and more adequate account could be expected to proceed.

Now let us return to the question of logical syntax. The first thing to observe here is that modern first-order predicate logic with identity—the logic of Frege and Russell—is patently inadequate to the representational requirements of the four-category ontology. In effect, this logic is tailored to the needs of a *two*-category ontology, which includes only the category of substantial particulars (in Fregean terms, "objects") and the category of nonsubstantial universals (in Fregean terms, "concepts"). This limitation imposes a number of syntactical distortions from the perspective of the four-category ontology. One such distortion is the inability of Frege–Russell logic to distinguish syntactically between a proposition affirming that a substantial particular instantiates a certain substantial kind and a proposition affirming that a substantial particular exemplifies a certain property—between, for instance, 'Fido is a dog' and 'Fido is white'. Both propositions are represented in Frege–Russell logic as having the form '*Fa*'. Another such distortion is the inability of Frege–Russell logic to distinguish syntactically between a proposition affirming that a certain substantial kind is characterized by a certain property and a proposition affirming that some or all of the substantial particulars that instantiate that kind exemplify that property—between, for instance, 'Polar bears are white' (or 'The polar bear is white') and either 'Some polar bears are white' or 'All polar bears are white'. Both propositions are represented in Frege–Russell logic as having either the form '$(\exists x)(Fx \,\&\, Gx)$' or the form '$(\forall x)(Fx \to Gx)$'. A third example is the inability of Frege–Russell logic to distinguish syntactically between a proposition affirming that a substantial particular is disposed to be F and a proposition affirming that a substantial particular is occurrently F—between, for instance, 'Fido growls' or 'Fido eats meat' and 'Fido is growling' or 'Fido is eating meat'. Both propositions are again represented in Frege–Russell logic as having the form '*Fa*'.

All of these distortions can be eliminated by means of some simple syntactical amendments to Frege–Russell logic.[18] First, we can include two different types of individual constants and variables, one to name and range over substantial particulars and one to name and range over substantial universals—$a, b, c, \ldots x, y, z$ on the one hand and $\alpha, \beta, \gamma, \ldots \phi, \chi, \psi$ on the other. Next, we can include, in addition to the identity sign, '=', a sign for instantiation, '/'. Finally, we can adopt the convention that when individual constants and variables are written *after* a predicate or relation symbol *occurrent* predication is intended, whereas when they are written *before* a predicate or relation symbol *dispositional* predication is intended. The modifications can be illustrated using the examples deployed earlier. First, then, 'Fido is a dog' will be symbolized in the form 'a/β', whereas 'Fido is white' (assuming that the predication is intended to be occurrent) will be symbolized in the form '*Fa*'. Next, 'Polar bears are white' will be symbolized in the form 'γF' (with the predication taken to be dispositional in intent), whereas 'Some polar bears are white' and 'All polar bears are white' will be symbolized in the forms, respectively, '$(\exists x)(x/\gamma \,\&\, xF)$' and '$(\forall x)(x/\gamma \to xF)$' (again assuming that the predication is intended to be dispositional).[19] Finally, 'Fido growls', taking the predication here to be dispositional in intent, will be symbolized in the form 'aG', whereas 'Fido is growling' will be symbolized in the form 'Ga'. Moreover, if the account of dispositionality advanced earlier is correct, our extended logical syntax allows us to represent that fact by affirming the logical equivalence of a proposition of the form 'aG' with one of the form '$(\exists\phi)(a/\phi$ & $\phi G)$'.[20]

It will be noted that the extensions we have so far made to the syntax of Frege–Russell logic do not yet fully accommodate the representational requirements of the four-category ontology, because we have as yet made no provision for quantification over *nonsubstantial entities*. However, this limitation could easily be overcome in obvious ways. The important point is to see that one's ontology really does impose some constraints on what will serve as a perspicuous logical syntax, in which necessary connections internal to that ontology may be reflected adequately in formal relations between propositions.

Elsewhere, I have called the kind of logic for which this extended logical syntax is designed *sortal* logic.[21] Sortal logic is "first-order" logic in the sense that it does not, as we have just noted, involve any quantification over *properties or relations*. But a logician of the Frege–Russell school could not see it in this light, because sortal logic does involve reference to and quantification over *substantial universals*, which such a logician—being wedded to a two-category ontology—is unwilling to distinguish from properties. On the other hand, from the point of view of the traditional formal logician, it looks as though sortal logic agrees with his system—in opposition to modern predicate logic—in allowing general terms to occupy both subject and predicate position in elementary sentences, because it recognizes sentences both of the form 'a/β' and of the form 'βF'—for example, both 'Fido is a dog' and 'A dog eats meat' (understanding the latter as a variant form of 'Dogs eat meat'). However, this is in fact a somewhat misleading way of representing the situation, because sortal logic does not really treat 'Fido is a dog' as a subject-predicate sentence, on a par with, say, 'Fido growls' or 'Fido eats meat'. According to sortal logic, the 'is' in 'Fido is a dog' is not the 'is' of predication, which, in common with Frege–Russell logic, it regards as being logically redundant. In fact, sortal logic goes further than Frege–Russell logic in including *two* logical relation symbols, rather than just one: the sign of instantiation as well as the sign of identity, with the former appearing in 'Fido is a dog' and the latter appearing in, say, 'Fido is Rover'. (However, it is technically feasible in sortal logic to define identity in terms of instantiation, if it is allowed that every substantial entity trivially instantiates *itself*: for then we can say that $a = b =_{df} a/b$ & b/a and $\alpha = \beta =_{df} \alpha/\beta$ & β/α.[22]) Finally—although this is something that I have not alluded to until now—it seems that sortal logic, unlike Frege–Russell logic but once again like traditional formal logic, has need of a distinction between predicate negation and sentence negation. This arises from its recognition of a distinction between dispositional and occurrent predication, because it seems clear that there is a difference between affirming that *a* is disposed to be non-*F* and denying that *a* is disposed to be *F*—between, for example, saying 'Fido *doesn't* growl' and saying '*It's not the case that* Fido growls'.[23]

No doubt Sommers would object to my recognition of a distinctive 'is' of instantiation quite as strongly as he objects to Frege's recognition of a distinctive 'is' of identity.[24] In reply, I would say, for reasons that should by now be clear, that without recognizing such a distinctive 'is' we cannot perspicuously reflect, in our propositional representation of many of the possible states of affairs that we need to reason about, the constituent structure of those states of affairs—on the assumption, of course, that the four-category ontology is correct. It is my opinion, in opposition it seems to Sommers, that the theory of logical syntax should not and indeed cannot be ontologically neutral. It may be that logic should be free of existential commitments, but it cannot, I think, be profitably regarded as metaphysically innocent. Sommers's critique of modern predicate logic and the hegemony of the Frege–Russell legacy is entirely to be welcomed for helping to open our eyes to the distortions which that legacy has imposed on prevailing conceptions of logical syntax. But rather than seeking the remedy in an attempt to eschew ontological considerations altogether where questions of logical syntax are concerned, I prefer to look for the remedy in a reformation of ontology and a renovation of logical syntax in alignment with it.

Notes

1. Fred Sommers, *The Logic of Natural Language* (Oxford: Clarendon Press, 1982)—hereafter *LNL*—p. 125.

2. *LNL*, p. 15.

3. *LNL*, ch. 6.

4. See "On Concept and Object," in *Translations from the Philosophical Writings of Gottlob Frege*, Second ed., trans. P. Geach and M. Black, (Oxford: Blackwell, 1960), p. 50.

5. See *LNL*, p. 129.

6. See *LNL*, appendix A. See also Fred Sommers and George Englebretsen, *An Invitation to Formal Reasoning: The Logic of Terms* (Aldershot: Ashgate, 2000).

7. But see also the contrasting remarks at p. 305 of *LNL*.

8. It would seem that Sommers himself is not unsympathetic to this sort of view: see *LNL*, ch. 8.

9. This, certainly, would be David Armstrong's verdict: see his *A World of States of Affairs* (Cambridge: Cambridge University Press, 1997).

10. See *LNL*, pp. 41ff.

11. See F. P. Ramsey, "Universals," in his *The Foundations of Mathematics and Other Essays* (London: Kegan Paul, 1931).

12. See further my *The Possibility of Metaphysics: Substance, Identity, and Time* (Oxford: Clarendon Press, 1998), pp. 203ff. Here I should acknowledge that Sommers himself has important things to say about categories and is, of course, very sympathetic to Aristotle—see *LNL*, ch. 13. However, Sommers's approach to the theory of categories is very different from mine, according a central place to the notion of a "category mistake" in the Rylean sense.

13. See, for example, my "A Defence of the Four-Category Ontology," in C. U. Moulines and K. G. Niebergall, eds., *Argument und Analyse* (Paderborn: Mentis, 2002), pp. 225–240.

14. See Armstrong, *A World of States of Affairs*, pp. 116ff.

15. See further my "Some Formal Ontological Relations," *Dialectica*, forthcoming.

16. See further my *Kinds of Being: A Study of Individuation, Identity, and the Logic of Sortal Terms* (Oxford: Blackwell, 1989), ch. 8, and my "Dispositions and Laws," *Metaphysica* 2 (2001): 5–23.

17. For a much fuller discussion of the issues, see my *The Possibility of Metaphysics*, ch. 6.

18. For more details, see my *Kinds of Being*, ch. 9.

19. That even color predicates exhibit the dispositional–occurrent distinction is argued for in my *Kinds of Being*, ch. 8.

20. See my *Kinds of Being*, p. 170.

21. See my *Kinds of Being*, ch. 9.

22. See my *Kinds of Being*, pp. 39–40 and 183–184.

23. See my *Kinds of Being*, pp. 191ff., where it is argued more generally that we need to distinguish between compound sentences and compound predicates.

24. Such an objection is indeed raised by George Englebretsen in his thoughtful review of my *Kinds of Being*: see *Iyyun, The Jerusalem Philosophical Quarterly* 40 (1991): 100–105. In that review, Englebretsen takes me to task for "put[ting] the ontological cart before the logical horse" (p. 103). I accept the charge, but disagree about which should be described as the horse and which as the cart.

4   Exploring Boundary Conditions on the Structure of Knowledge: Some Nonobvious Influences of Philosophy on Psychology

Frank C. Keil

1   Introduction

It might seem from a distance that the primary way in which philosophy would inform psychology, and for that matter much of the rest of cognitive science, is by helping to clarify what fundamental issues researchers should be addressing, such as the problems and pitfalls of dualism, the paradoxes of consciousness, the possibility of a subsymbolic computational mind, and the nature of thought without language. These and many other similar topics are indeed relevant to psychology and have been discussed extensively in the cognitive science literature, but they do not necessarily provide the best route to empirical research projects.

A second sphere of influence between philosophers and psychologists is found where philosophers explore the implications of experimental research conducted by psychologists. For example, when preverbal human infants are shown to engage in forms of addition and subtraction, philosophers consider the implications for the relations between language and thought. When studies suggest that young preschoolers cannot understand how false beliefs in other minds influence the behaviors of those individuals, philosophers ask how a folk psychology might work without the normal belief-desire calculus. This form of influence, however, is largely unidirectional, where philosophers examine the results of psychological research, and, much of the time, their examinations have relatively little impact back on the research.

There is, however, a third way in which philosophy and psychology interact that has often been a more direct source of inspiration for experimental researchers, and which has been the primary way in which my own research has been influenced by philosophy. That form of influence comes from philosophical analyses that do not make any explicit predictions for, or interpretations of, psychological phenomena, but which nonetheless do have strong implications for experimental studies of the structure of human knowledge and how it might change over time. In my own research early on, the writings of Fred Sommers suggested a new way of experimentally exploring possible constraints on semantic and conceptual structure. In these cases the philosopher's work may not mention psychological research at all, but rather consist of a detailed proposal concerning the structure of knowledge. When those proposals are sufficiently detailed as to allow precise characterizations of some aspect of knowledge, that structural description often carries with it an implicit experimental research program.

The main point of this essay is to illustrate some ways in which philosophers have inspired psychological research as a result of clarifying philosophical questions in their own right and not by trying to make psychological predictions. It is particularly appropriate to make this point in a volume dedicated to Fred Sommers, whose foundational work in the philosophy of logic and language has had a profound influence on psychological research. I will consider how a series of papers by Sommers led to a set of experimental studies on children and adults, studies that were heavily aided by a model for research that had emerged from the interactions between advances in linguistic theory and developmental psychology. I will then consider some other examples of how basic work in philosophy has influenced psychology, examples where the philosophical work is not even about knowledge at all but rather about proposed abstract regularities in the world, and examples where the philosophical proposals about what is not part of knowledge led to psychological research on how humans deal with those gaps. In all cases the message is similar: although it might seem that work in the philosophy of mind should have the most direct link to psychological research, in fact work in the philosophy of logic, of science, and metaphysics has often had a more fruitful albeit unintended influence.

2 Patterns of Predicability

It is obvious, with a little introspection, that not all properties and relations can apply to all things. Certain propositions are category mistakes that are not evaluable in terms of truth value because the juxtaposition of a particular predicate and subject is nonsensical. This phenomenon was of interest to Aristotle (1963) and many others over the years and was discussed by Russell (1924) and Ryle (1938); but those earlier analyses led to many indeterminate cases and it remained difficult to see any large scale patterns to category mistakes until Sommers wrote a landmark paper on predicability (Sommers 1959). Russell had focused on the idea that terms that take the same predicates are of the same kind while Ryle focused on the idea that predicates that take the same terms were of the same type, but neither put the two together in a manner that explained the entire system of relations. Sommers solved the problem by introducing the notion of predicates *spanning* terms, where a predicate spanned a term if either it or its negation was potentially true. For example, 'is a predator' is predicable of all mammals even if it is not true of all of them because it or its negation is plausibly true. By contrast, there is no truth of the matter as to whether a chair is a predator or not. Such a question is a category mistake.

Sommers's use of spanning to explore patterns of predicability, as opposed to patterns of truth or falsehood of predicates, offered the potential to come up with profoundly different principles about categories and their relations. Sommers saw this potential and offered a number of observations that help us better understand how to explore those relations. Most critical for my research is the claim that predicates and terms are related to each other in a hierarchical manner and that there can be no downwardly converging branches. Consider the example shown in figure 4.1. Predicates such as 'is alive' and 'is heavy' apply to nested sets of kinds such that a pure hierarchy is preserved. Thus, 'is heavy' spans all physical objects while 'is alive' spans all living kinds. Hence, 'is heavy' must apply also to all living kinds and 'is alive' cannot apply to any nonliving kinds. Predicability relations are nested hierarchically and correspond to a nested set of ontological categories (in this case, physical objects dominate the mutually exclusive categories of furniture and animals).

When there are apparent exceptions to this downward nonconvergence rule, an ambiguity lurks beneath the surface. Consider for example the case of 'bat'. 'Is a predator' is predicable of all mammals and not of artifacts. It is therefore also predicable of bats. 'Is made of wood' is predicable of all artifacts and not of mammals, yet it also seems to be predicable of the word

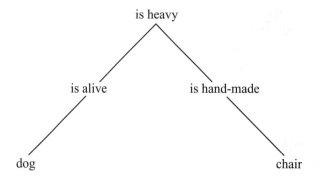

Figure 4.1

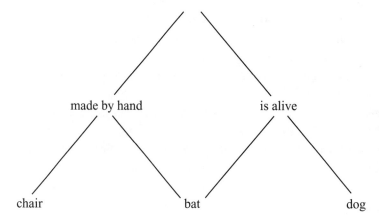

Figure 4.2

'bat' as shown in figure 4.2, creating a downward convergence. The solution is to stipulate that all such cases of apparent downward convergences are only illusory and arise from a lexical ambiguity in one of the words in the set of predicability relations. In this case, the ambiguity is particularly blatant. 'Bat' has two distinct meanings referring to two different sorts of things. If we think of these two senses of 'bat' as really two different terms, the downward convergence disappears, as shown in figure 4.3. In contrast, trees composed of truth-dependent relations show all sorts of downward convergences. Thus, if a predicate dominates a term in a tree if and only if it is truly applicable to a term, as has often been the case in traditional attempts to model semantic memory, the clean hierarchy becomes tangled.

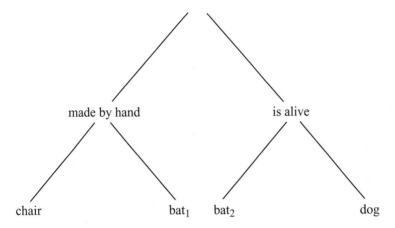

Figure 4.3

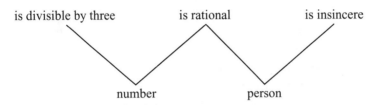

Figure 4.4

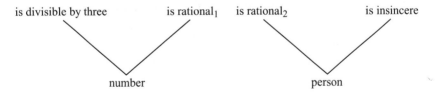

Figure 4.5

For example, in such a tree, the predicate 'is red' might dominate a 'fire hydrant' and 'cardinal' and not 'tire' and 'crow', while 'is manufactured' would dominate 'fire hydrant' and 'tire' but not 'cardinal' and 'crow'. Sommers illustrated how the ambiguities occurred not only in terms but also in predicates, as shown in figures 4.4 and 4.5.

In his papers, Sommers develops a series of compelling arguments for how and why predicability relations should have this property of pure hierarchies that honor what he called an *M rule* (Sommers 1959, 1963, 1964, 1965, 1971, 1973). When I first encountered these papers in 1975, I was struck by how these patterns might illuminate principles about how we represent some of the most fundamental categories of existence. Sommers had demonstrated that patterns of predicability seem to bring into relief ontological categories, those broad categories representing truly distinct domains of discourse. Shortly before reading those papers I had also read some arguments by Chomsky on the importance of constraints on linguistic structure in models of language acquisition (Chomsky 1965, 1975). Chomsky argued in his famous discussions of different forms of adequacy that the formal constraints on grammar as discovered by linguists and philosophers achieve explanatory adequacy, as opposed to merely descriptive adequacy, only when those constraints also explain ow the emergence of language in a child is guided by them. From my perspective, Chomsky was suggesting that formal structural analyses of the products of human cognition such as language would yield powerful insights into how knowledge emerges in the developing human. In particular, those analyses might provide constraints on the space of possibilities that would otherwise overwhelm a learner. The learning of language would be immensely simplified if the child were to come to that situation with an implicit knowledge of some of the same constraints that were being discovered in formal analyses of language.

The juxtaposition of these two sets of arguments by Sommers and by Chomsky suggested to me that Sommers's proposals about predicability might be understood as proposals not just about the interface of logic and language but about constraints on the structure of knowledge, constraints that should be operative in the course of development and indeed which might greatly help the child figure out the fundamental categories of existence and what properties could be applied to what sorts of entities. Using the linguistic notion of constraints on syntactic structure, one can describe Sommers's M rule principle of no downward convergence as the *M constraint*, namely, that predicability relations cannot make structural patterns that resemble an M shape. In this way, a fascinating claim about structural ontology started to suggest experimental research on human intuitions. Because any one set of intuitions might be confounded with other factors irrelevant to predicability, four different converging sets of intuitions were developed, all of which were designed to get at implicit notions of predicability (Keil 1979): intuitions about anomaly, similarity, copredication, and naturalness of classes. It was possible to demonstrate that the same set of hierarchical relations among types and properties keeps occurring, a pattern that indeed seems to honor the M constraint. In this way it was possible to show that adult intuitions about predicates and kinds could be used to reveal a structural ontology of the sort that Sommers had proposed, one that results in a multilayered hierarchy.

The critical question, however, was whether the M constraint holds in cases where the hierarchical structure varies, just as linguistic constraints stay constant when grammatical structures vary across development. To address this question, the task was modified in a manner that made it possible to ask children as young as five years of age about whether predicates could be sensibly applied to terms. The major challenge was to make sure that children understood that the questions were about the sense of applying a predicate to a kind and not about the truth of that predication. By developing a set of questions that ask about a property and its antonym, it was possible to explore predicability, and not truth judgments, in young children. It might seem to have been easier to ask about p and not-p rather than about p and the lexical antonym for p, but young children can have great difficulties understanding explicit negation and the antonyms therefore provided a more sensitive measure.

The results, across several studies, were striking. Children at all ages showed a strong tendency to honor the M constraint even as their actual ontological trees were markedly different, usually by being much less differentiated (Keil 1979, 1981, 1983). As these trees "grew" over time, they continued to honor the constraint. We were able to show that conceptions of properties and of the sorts of things that they could potentially describe were powerfully constrained throughout development even as there was dramatic change. It was also possible to show that when a child did form a new branch in her ontological tree, it tended to happen all at once such that all the relevant predicates and terms would sort themselves out at the same time. For example, it was common for younger children to collapse together nodes for sentient creatures and all other animals, while older children and adults made predicability judgments that clearly kept them apart. Once they saw the distinction for some terms and predicates, however, they tended to see them for all other terms that were relevant to that distinction (Keil 1983). In this way a deep conceptual insight was mirrored almost immediately with all relevant terms and predicates.

This initial line of research had a profound effect on how I have done work ever since. Because of the wonderfully explicit and careful description of structural relations offered by Sommers, I was able to see the potential for a set of psychological predictions and experiments. More importantly, I realized that some of the most useful ways in which philosophy influences psychology are not by looking at philosophers' direct predictions about psychological processes or suggestions for experiments, but rather by at looking philosophical discoveries in a more abstract and formal realm that might then have implications for experimental research.

I have not worked on the M constraint and intuitions about structural ontology for more than twenty years, but the usefulness of that approach has inspired me ever since. As is always the case, the M constraint story has become more complex. Ambiguity is not always easy to tell apart from vagueness or metaphor (e.g., is the term 'country' ambiguous when it is said to be mountainous and democratic?). In addition, finer-grained categories seem to involve spanning relations that are somewhat like predicability but that do not represent ontological categories understood as fundamental categories of existence. For example, 'is touchtone' could be said to be predicable of all telephones (which are either dial or touchtone) and of nothing else, implying that telephones are their own ontological kind since it seems to be a category mistake to apply the predicate 'is touchtone' to other artifacts (e.g., 'touchtone sofa', 'touchtone toaster'). But these complications do not detract from the great value of Sommers's original idea. Moreover, it has served as an illustration of how basic work in analytic philosophy can lead to psychological research in the same manner that formal linguistic theory has led to a vast array of research on language processing and acquisition.

3 Essences and Kinds

It is useful to consider more broadly some other examples of how basic work in philosophy has had implications for psychology. A different sort of example comes from work on the causal theory of reference developed by Putnam and by Kripke (Kripke 1980; Putnam 1975). Although the primary discussions in those early papers were about meaning and reference, there were other important ideas that led to psychological research. One was the idea that natural kinds might have a radically different structure from artifacts, such that the act of referring to natural kinds was not the same process as that of referring to artifacts (Schwartz 1977). In particular, natural kinds were thought to have essences, which language users might not know but assumed were the basis of reference. Artifacts by contrast did not have essences in that sense of the word at all; their meanings derived from the intended functions of their creators. (See, however, Bloom 1996, which argues for intended functions as a kind of essence in their own right.)

The consideration, in the philosophical study of meaning and reference, of essence in general and of the contrast between artifacts and natural kinds in particular, led to a series of experimental studies in psychology. Two psychological proposals emerged: that people might be constrained to assume and search out the presence of essences, often in ways that go far beyond the available data; and that the different causal structural principles underlying natural kinds and artifacts would cause differences in how they are learned and mentally represented. More specifically, the following questions were posed: do people in fact assume a hidden essence for natural kinds but not for artifacts? If so, is that essentialist bias an early emerging and organizing principle for natural kind concepts and perhaps one that formed a kind of constraint in its own right on conceptual structure? Does the acquisition of knowledge about artifacts and natural kinds show different patterns of development? Are people's beliefs about the causal processes responsible for the existence of artifacts and natural kinds related to these judgments? Can people be shown to be irrational essentialists in come cases?

A flurry of research over the past fifteen years has uncovered several patterns. There does indeed seem to be an essentialist bias (Medin and Ortony 1989; Keil 1989; Gelman 2003). Moreover, the bias appears very early in development (ibid.) and seems to continue into adulthood. It may also lead to some distortions where things are "essentialized" as natural kinds that really should not be, perhaps most tragically in false assumptions about "essences" for various racial groups of humans (Hirschfeld 1996). Thus, philosophical considerations about the role of essences in fixing reference for natural kind terms did not directly suggest any psychological exploration of essences, but they raised the question of how people who often do not know the essences of things, as so clearly pointed out by Locke, can nonetheless operate in a manner that seems to depend on essences. The answer was the discovery of a strong and early emerging human cognitive bias to think that things must have essences.

A critical question remains concerning essences and their causal connections to surface properties. Indeed, one recent analysis of natural kinds as patterns of causal homeostasis has raised a whole new set of psychological questions about essences (Boyd 1999). For many phenomena, such as living kinds, the essence may not be a fixed entity but rather a relatively stable set of causal relations among basic properties that creates a stable kind. Thus, certain properties tend to support the presence of other properties in a mutually reinforcing manner that results in property clusters being stable over time. A key research question is whether laypersons have some sense of such causal homeostatic clusters or whether they tend to think of fixed single-entity essences for natural kinds. The contrasting ideas of homeostatic causal clusters and single originating essences are not in themselves psychological proposals, but they lead naturally to questions about the potential psychological consequences of such a contrast.

Whether or not people appreciate that the essences of natural kinds can be a causal network of properties, they do have a strong sense that the essences of natural kinds are strikingly different from the factors behind the origin and stability of artifact kinds. It is obvious to adults that some aspect of superficially invisible microstructure or microstructural relations is often at the core of what it means to be a tiger or gold and that such a principle does not hold for the basis of what it means to be a chair or a coffeepot. Again this idea originated in philosophical discussions of how reference is determined for natural kinds and artifacts (e.g., Putnam 1975; Schwartz 1977, 1978). It is obvious that we do not have sciences of artifacts in the sense that researchers probe the chemical makeup of chairs and coffeepots or try to discover laws governing the behavior of their parts.

This artifact–natural kind contrast is highly influential on our understanding of how we learn the meanings of words; but it also suggests that if there are profound differences between the causal forces responsible for the existence of artifacts and of natural kinds, people might apprehend them quite differently as well. To explore this possibility a variety of studies have asked adults and children to judge whether or not an entity remains a member of the same kind after various sorts of transformation of its properties. For example, adults and young children often regard changes in surface parts to be enough to change the kind of artifact involved while rejecting such changes as relevant for animals (Keil 1989). Still other studies have suggested that preschoolers sense some critical differences between natural kinds and artifacts in terms of how they initially come into existence and in terms of their ability to support inductions (ibid.; Gelman 1988, 2003).

In short, adults and children at least as young as five see a profound difference between artifacts and natural kinds. How they learn this contrast and what they sense as critically different between natural kinds and artifacts awaits further exploration, but the difference between the two and the involvement of notions of essence is clear and owes its impetus to work done by philosophers. Of course, it has been obvious for thousands of years that the natural and artificial worlds are different, but it was not until more careful analytic attempts to describe natural kinds, essences, and their causal relations that psychologists began to see implications for research. More broadly, just as researchers in perception have guided their studies by assuming that dramatically different information patterns probably have psychological consequences for how they are learned and represented, psychologists have benefited immensely from discussions by philosophers as to how less visible but equally important differences in causal relational patterns might exist between different domains in the world. Metaphysical discussions have revealed kinds of information contrast that, though not as immediately obvious to the layperson as perceptual contrasts, have just as important psychological consequences.

One intriguing recent finding is that people may think they know far more about essences and their causal consequences than they really do. There is now strong evidence for an illusion of explanatory depth in which a wide range of adults and children think they understand the causal structure of the world in far more detail than is actually the case (Rozenblit and Keil 2002). As a result, the extent to which we believe in essences largely on the grounds of blind faith is far larger than we might assume.

4 Divisions of Linguistic and Cognitive Labor

One other example serves to illustrate some nonobvious links between philosophy and psychology, namely the idea of division of cognitive labor. The notion was first introduced by Putnam as a division of "linguistic labor" to describe how laypersons must in some sense defer to experts to ground their assumptions about essences for things like gold and tigers (Putnam 1975). Few laypersons would know how to tell whether something had the right atomic structure to be gold or the right genetic structure to be a tiger, but most laypersons sense that there are experts who could make such a decision and are ready to defer to such experts. Philosophers made a compelling case for the powerful limits of causal explanatory knowledge in any one mind and then explained how individuals with large gaps in their understanding could nonetheless get by through deference to experts. In a sense the only direct psychological proposal here was a negative one: that people do not know many sets of causal relations that are nonetheless essential for grounding reference (Wilson and Keil 1998).

This claim about the division of labor also indirectly raises several fascinating psychological questions that, though not part of the original philosophical discussions, are powerfully prompted by them. The notion of division of linguistic labor has broadened to one of the division of cognitive labor (Hardwig 1985; Kitcher 1990; Goldman 1999, 2001, 2002) and has become a central theme in the philosophy of science. But consider some of the psychological questions that it raises: How does one know when one needs to defer? How does one decide whom to defer to and how much deference to allow? How much does one need to know already to be able even to capitalize on the division of cognitive labor that occurs in all cultures? Thus, as psychologists we do not seek to verify that a division of cognitive labor exists, this being the most straightforward consequence of the philosophical proposals. Instead, we take for granted that such a division exists and ask how it might actually work and develop. What means might we use to infer the boundaries and depth of knowledge in other minds?

It is incontestable that all cultures have divisions of cognitive labor just as much as they do divisions of physical labor. The critical questions all arise concerning how we are able profit from the division of labor and not be excessively misled by it. This is a relatively recent area of research, but already some of the results are quite surprising. There are in fact several distinct ways of understanding the clustering of knowledge in other minds: by common disciplinary principles, by common goals, by favored access to information, and by surface topic. Each of these has tradeoffs, but only the first, by disciplinary principles, is the sense originally intended by

Putnam. In a series of studies in our lab we have been able to ask which ways of clustering are normally used and at what ages.

We can assess how people understand the division of cognitive labor by using a "triad task" in which we state that a person knows a good deal about 'why X', where X is some sort of phenomenon. We then ask what else the person is likely to know by virtue of knowing that first piece of information, for example Y or Z, where Y and Z compete on different dimensions. Consider the following triad:

John knows a great deal about why big boats take a very long time to stop.

Because he knows a lot about this, what else is he likely to know?

Why ice cream cones cost more in the summer?

or

Why basketballs bounce better on the sidewalk than on the grass?

Most adults will put the basketball-bouncing and big-boat-stopping expertise together, often citing them to be part of the domain of physics. Impressively, even five-year-olds tend to see such relations at above-chance levels with examples of the sort just provided. They sense the clusters of causal phenomena corresponding roughly to the large divisions of the natural and social sciences within the university. At the same time, they are usually completely unable to articulate why.

In other respects, however, the younger children are quite different. Consider a case where there is a common topic involved, as in:

John knows a great deal about why big boats take a very long time to stop.

Because he knows a lot about this, what else is he likely to know?

Why big boats are mostly made in Asia?

or

Why basketballs bounce better on the sidewalk than on the grass?

In these cases, many of the younger children put together the two kinds of big-boat expertise while adults continue to see expertise as clustered more in the area of a sort of naive mechanics. Across several studies, a pattern emerges in which even preschoolers have some sense of the causal patterns in the world that cluster in ways corresponding to broad disciplines of knowledge; but an awareness of this form of knowledge as somehow privileged or more generative than other forms of knowledge takes many years to develop. Other ways of clustering knowledge, such as by common topic (e.g., big-boat expertise), common goals (e.g., knowing about all factors that will help support attainment of a goal such as selling shoes), or by favored access (e.g., things that a typical college student would know more than average about) all compete in the early years with the discipline-based form of viewing the terrain of knowledge. Moreover, much later in life, these other ways of knowledge still have important roles and must be continuously kept in mind as well.

The concept of division of linguistic labor was developed in philosophy to explain how certain issues in meaning and reference could be handled without requiring a language-user to have immediate knowledge of the basis for reference to members of various natural kinds. It did not make an explicitly psychological proposal; but the need for such a division was so compelling in the philosophical arguments that they naturally raised questions for psychologists about how individuals actually could be aware of and use the division of expertise around them. Research in this area is relatively new, but it is now obvious that many different lines of work lie ahead, all of which have been inspired by the original philosophical work.

5 Conclusion

I have argued that philosophical work over the past fifty years has had a profound influence on psychological research on both adults and children. But the pattern of influence has not been that which would have seemed most likely at first glance. It might have seemed that work in epistemology and the philosophy of mind would lead most naturally to psychological research, and in some cases it has, with studies in the theory of mind, consciousness, and qualia perhaps being the most obvious. But in a large number of cases some of the most dramatic influences have come from other areas of philosophy where specific psychological claims have only been implicit. In the philosophy of science, of language, and in logic and metaphysics, we have seen some of the most interesting connections. I see three large classes of influences.

First, work in philosophy may provide a highly explicit structural description of some aspect of knowledge, a description that may be interpreted as positing constraints on the structure of knowledge analogous to those found in linguistic theory. The philosopher often may not see the structural pattern as a cognitive constraint, but being highly explicit about a description or pattern does enable it to be tested as such.

Second, work in philosophy may suggest informational patterns in the world that indicate contrasts in terms of how information might be acquired, mentally represented, and used. In perception, we often get insights along these lines from natural scientists who tell us how patterns of sound or light cluster and thereby enable psychologists to explore the extent to which people track those patterns and how they might distort them to represent them in a more efficient manner. Other patterns are not part of perception but rather of cognition, such as patterns of causation that might be different for natural kinds and for artifacts. A philosopher, for example, who discusses how patterns of causal homeostasis organize many natural kinds is not making a proposal about knowledge or about any psychological processes. Yet the idea that a certain pattern of causality for natural kinds might be sharply different from that for artifact kinds suggests in turn studies to see whether such a difference is reflected in differences as to how those kinds are learned, understood, and reasoned about.

Third, work in philosophy might presuppose a psychological process that has not been considered before as such. The philosopher might presuppose a division of linguistic and cognitive labor and, through a series of arguments, show how that division might be essential to explaining a number of nonpsychological problems. But once that process is stated, psychologists may then ask how it could possibly work, and a cascade of studies can thereby emerge.

It is also striking that so many of the influences of philosophy on psychology have been on developmental themes. Thus, questions about how knowledge emerges often seem to link more directly to basic philosophical questions than questions about the state of that knowledge in adults. The reasons for this developmental bias are complex, but one major factor may be that patterns of change help highlight more clearly the boundary conditions of systems. Thus, if one sees in a discussion of predicability the possibility of a constraint on semantic and conceptual structure, one might find the strongest test of that constraint to be its continued presence across otherwise dramatic cases of change. Similarly, if one thinks that the causal patterns associated with natural kinds and artifacts are profoundly different, one might well suspect that the differences should be manifested in some of the earliest attempts of children to learn about the two kinds of thing.

In my own research I owe a special debt to Fred Sommers for providing one of the clearest and most compelling accounts of the relations between language and knowledge in structural formal terms, an account that bears a strong analogy with linguistic theory. The moral for psychologists, at least, is not primarily to expect inspiration for research to come from philosophers who make predictions about behavior. It will come equally if not more often from philosophers who reveal in highly explicit and detailed ways structural principles that seem to govern some bounded aspect of knowledge or who point out qualitative and structural differences between sorts of things in the world. Through their careful and systematic analyses they revealed patterns that afforded a research strategy used by the earliest psychologists who emerged out of philosophy to study perception. Just as one can look at the physical variables that specify depth and then ask which ones human use especially in their perceptual development, philosophers enable us to see higher-order, nonperceptual abstract patterns and to ask which ones humans use to make sense of the world around them, and how they acquire them over the course of their cognitive development.

It is far less obvious to me what we as psychologists in recent years have been able to offer the philosophers. Is it the case that psychological research has had more of an impact in those areas of philosophy that are directly concerned with the philosophy of mind and language, or has the impact been much more diverse such as on the philosophy of science and mathematics? It may still be too early to tell, but my hunch is that here, too, the most fertile areas of influence may not always be those that connect to the ostensibly most closely related areas of philosophy.

Acknowledgments

Preparation of this essay was supported by National Institutes of Health grant R-37-HD023922 to Frank Keil.

References

Aristotle. 1963. *Categories.* Translated with notes by J. L. Ackrill. Oxford: Oxford University Press.

Bloom, P. 1996. "Intention, History, and Artifact Concepts." *Cognition* 60: 1–29.

Boyd, R. 1999. "Homeostasis, Species, and Higher Taxa." In R. Wilson (ed.), *Species: New Interdisciplinary Studies.* Cambridge, Mass.: The MIT Press.

Chomsky, N. 1965. *Aspects of the Theory of Syntax.* Cambridge, Mass: The MIT Press.

Chomsky, N. 1975. *Reflections on Language.* New York: Pantheon Books.

Gelman, S. A. 1988. "The Development of Induction within Natural Kind and Artifact Categories." *Cognitive Psychology* 20: 65–95.

Gelman, S. A. 2003. *The Essential Child: Origins of Essentialism in Everyday Thought.* New York: Oxford University Press.

Goldman, Alvin. 1999. *Knowledge in a Social World.* Oxford: Clarendon Press.

Goldman, A. 2001. "Experts: Which Ones Should You Trust?" *Philosophy and Phenomenological Research* 63: 85–109. Reprinted in Goldman 2002.

Goldman, A. 2002. *Pathways to Knowledge: Private and Public.* New York: Oxford University Press.

Hardwig, J. 1985. "Epistemic Dependence." *Journal of Philosophy* 82: 335–349.

Hirschfeld, L. A. 1996. *Race in the Making: Cognition, Culture, and the Child's Construction of Human Kinds.* Cambridge, Mass.: The MIT Press.

Keil, F. C. 1979. *Semantic and Conceptual Development: An Ontological Perspective.* Cambridge, Mass.: Harvard University Press.

Keil, F. C. 1981. "Constraints on Knowledge and Cognitive Development." *Psychological Review* 88: 197–227.

Keil, F. C. 1983. "On the Emergence of Semantic and Conceptual Distinctions." *Journal of Experimental Psychology: General* 112: 357–389.

Keil, F. C. 1989. *Concepts, Kinds, and Cognitive Development.* Cambridge, Mass.: The MIT Press.

Keil, F. C. 1995. "The Growth of Causal Understandings of Natural Kinds." In Sperber et al. 1995: 234–267.

Kitcher, P. 1990. "The Division of Cognitive Labor." *Journal of Philosophy* 87: 5–22.

Kripke, S. A. 1980. *Naming and Necessity.* Oxford: Blackwell.

Lutz, D. R., and Keil, F. C. 2002. "Early Understanding of the Division of Cognitive Labor." *Child Development* 73: 1073–1084.

Malt, B. C., and Johnson, E. C. 1992. "Do Artifact Concepts Have Cores?" *Journal of Memory and Language* 31: 195–217.

Medin, D. L., and Ortony, A. 1989. "Psychological Essentialism." In S. Vosniadou and A. Ortony (eds.), *Similarity and Analogical Reasoning*. Cambridge: Cambridge University Press, 179–195.

Putnam, H. 1975. "The Meaning of 'Meaning'." In his *Mind, Language, and Reality*. Cambridge: Cambridge University Press, 215–271.

Rozenblit, L. R., and Keil, F. C. 2002. "The Misunderstood Limits of Folk Science: An Illusion of Explanatory Depth." *Cognitive Science* 26: 521–556.

Russell, B. 1924. "Logical Atomism." In J. H. Muirhead (ed.), *Contemporary British Philosophy: Personal Statements, First Series*. London: G. Allen and Unwin, 359–383.

Ryle, G. 1938. "Categories." *Proceedings of the Aristotelian Society* 38: 189–206.

Schwartz, S. (ed.). 1977. *Naming, Necessity, and Natural Kinds*. Ithaca: Cornell University Press.

Schwartz, S. 1978. "Putnam on Artifacts." *Philosophical Review* 87: 566–574.

Sommers, F. T. 1959. "The Ordinary Language Tree." *Mind* 68: 160–185.

Sommers, F. T. 1963. "Types and Ontology." *Philosophical Review* 72: 327–363.

Sommers, F. T. 1964. "A Program for Coherence." *Philosophical Review* 73: 522–527.

Sommers, F. T. 1965. "Predicability." In M. Black (ed.), *Philosophy in America*. Ithaca: Cornell University Press, 262–281.

Sommers, F. T. 1971. "Structural Ontology." *Philosophia* 1: 21–42.

Sommers, F. T. 1973. "Existence and Predication." In M. Munitz (ed.), *Logic and Ontology*. New York: New York University Press.

Sperber, D., Premack, D., and Premack, A. J. 1995. *Causal Cognition: A Multidisciplinary Approach*. New York: Oxford University Press.

Wilson, R. A., and Keil, F. C. 1998. "The Shadows and Shallows of Explanation." *Minds and Machines* 8: 137–159.

5   General Terms, Anaphora, and Rigid Designation

Alan Berger

Introduction

Modern logicians in the twentieth century, in developing their formal logic systems, have rejected traditional Aristotelian semantic categories of general terms. Instead, they have replaced the semantic category of general terms with the semantic category of predicates. Whereas general terms were often taken to denote each of their instances, predicates do not play the same semantic role. For Frege, a predicate is a function that maps objects onto truth-values; for Russell, predicates denote propositional functions that map objects onto propositions. And in standard Tarskian semantics, predicates do not denote at all. Rather, they are assigned an extension, namely the class of objects that the predicate is true of. I want to argue in what follows that contemporary discussions in semantics often confuse the semantics of predicates with the semantics of terms, something less likely to occur if those who engaged in such discussions studied the semantics of term logic.

Fred Sommers, a long-time champion of term logic, has defended several terminist theses in his book, *The Logic of Natural Language*.[1] This book concentrates on formulating a special syntax that makes use only of the category of terms and shows how one can express and deduce at least as much within its system as can be done in modern predicate logic. Although there is some discussion of the semantics of various terms in LNL, this semantics is less known but further developed elsewhere and in conversation. This is unfortunate, since Sommers's semantics of various terms is every bit as astute and pioneering as his single-handed development of the formal logic of terms.

A moment's reflection on the vocabulary of various subjects with which philosophers are concerned, especially in science, reveals that this vocabulary is best represented by general terms rather than regimented as predicates. Chemists, for example, identify various substances with atomic and molecular structures. Gold is identified with Au_{79}, water with H_2O. In biology, the germ theory of diseases is prevalent. Each disease is to be identified with a particular germ. In physics, natural phenomena, such as lightning and colors, are identified with a stream of photons and specific wavelengths, respectively. Indeed, even future scientific projects make identifications a central goal. Molecular biology promises to identify various species with a specific genotype, for example. And in the days of logical positivist philosophy of science, the deductive-nomological (D-N) model was prevalent and scientific laws were formulated as universal conditional statements with predicates; in retrospect, the model seems a gross inadequacy in representing such laws, since these are also typically expressed as identifications. Newton's laws, for example, are standardly represented in physics by equations such as $F = ma$. And perhaps the most famous equation, due to Einstein, is $E = mc^2$. In all these cases, it should be apparent that the vocabulary of science is the vocabulary of terms.

A central project in *Naming and Necessity*[2] is Saul Kripke's analysis of certain terms and their semantics. Kripke has dramatically demonstrated the deep philosophical implications and applications of analyzing certain terms as rigid designators. A rigid designator is a term that designates its referent(s) in all possible worlds in which its referent(s) exists, and fails to designate otherwise.[3] The prevalent attitude within the philosophical community is to regiment natural language into the formal language of modern predicate logic. This often leads to confusion in endeavoring to make Kripke's views regarding rigid designation plausible or even coherent. Indeed, some of the most sympathetic and intelligent followers of Kripke have gone astray in this regard. Scott Soames, for example, argues that Kripke's criteria for a general term to be a rigid designator are inconsistent at worst, unclear at best. His confusion, in my opinion, stems from the confusion between the semantics of predicates and the semantics of terms. Although I am not suggesting that Kripke is required to be a term logician or that his views regarding rigid designation cannot be expressed in modern predicate logic, it is of special interest to investigate how

Sommers's semantics of terms applies to many of Kripke's theses regarding the rigid designation of certain terms.

1

What is a term? Although there is no general agreement in usage, typically a term is viewed as any linguistic expression that denotes (perhaps with respect to given context, time and place). By and large, such an expression is thought of as denoting an individual or individuals. We will not restrict a term in this way. We will permit a term to denote a substance, species, or other abstract entities, for example. A term that denotes a single individual is called a *singular term* and is contrasted with a *general term* that could denote any number of individuals. In the sentence 'Spot is a dog', 'Spot' functions as a singular term, 'dog' as a general term. Proper names and personal pronouns are paradigmatic singular terms in English. A definite description ⌈the *NP*⌉ is for the most part also taken to be a singular term, except, of course, following Bertrand Russell's analysis, as a first-order uniqueness-restricted quantifier equivalent to ⌈a unique *NP*⌉.[4] In contrast, common nouns and most adjectives are paradigmatic general terms in English.

Clearly, terms seem to be primary, at least in a primordial sense, to predicates. Terms, syntactically speaking, can be used to serve as a primitive category to which we can apply a function to form predicates. Thus, for example, Nathan Salmon introduces two such predicate-forming functions that apply to terms. First, there is a predicate-forming operator on adjectives (whether single words or adjectival phrases) and mass nouns. The copula in 'is blue', for example, is formally represented as '*is*{ }'. Second, there is a similar predicate-forming operator on count nouns. The expression 'is a' in 'is a tiger', for example, is represented as '*is-a*{ }'. Accordingly, the predicate 'is blue' is formalized as '*is*{blue}' and the predicate 'is an albino tiger' as '*is-a*{albino tiger}'.

2

One central thesis that Kripke holds in N&N is that certain general terms, such as natural kind terms (e.g., 'water' and 'tiger'), phenomenon terms ('heat', 'hot', and 'lightning'), and color terms (e.g., 'blue' and 'yellow'), are rigid designators solely as a matter of semantics, that is, independently of empirical, extralinguistic facts. Consequently, Kripke argues that identity statements involving these general terms are like identity statements involving proper names (e.g., 'Hesperus = Phosphorus') in that, solely as a matter of semantics, they express necessary truths if they are true at all. But whereas it is reasonably clear what it is for a (first-order) singular term to designate, Kripke does not explicitly say what it is for a *general* term to designate. In modern predicate logic, general terms are regimented into (usually monadic) predicates. But predicates have (semantic) extensions, which, if anything, are best seen as their designation. Alternatively, in the spirit of Frege, we may think of a predicate as a characteristic function of the class that is the extension of the predicate. But what is the extension of a general term, such as 'tiger'? It is the class of actual tigers (or its characteristic function), and clearly the term does not rigidly designate its extension, since the class of tigers in one possible world may differ from the class of tigers in another. What, then, is it for 'tiger' to be rigid?

Scott Soames addresses this question in his recent book, *Beyond Rigidity*,[5] and considers two interpretive hypotheses that he deems the most promising, strongly favoring one of the two.[6] On the preferred interpretation, a general term is *rigid*, by definition, if it expresses a property (e.g., being a tiger) that is essential to anything that has it at all, that is, a property of an object that the object could not fail to have (except perhaps by not existing). Soames characterizes this hypothesis as a "natural extension" to predicates of N&N's definition of singular-term rigidity, a characterization I do not understand. The whole point of Kripke's rejection of the Frege–Russell descriptivist view is to deny that proper names—a paradigm example of a rigid singular term—express any property. Be that as it may, I consider the proposal obviously false. One obvious problem with the proposal is that color terms are then considered nonrigid, contrary to Kripke's apparent labeling of them as rigid. For most things that have a certain color do not have that color essentially. This problem applies also to terms like 'heat' and 'pain', since hardly anything has them essentially.

A second problem with the definition is that it does not provide any obvious candidate to be the rigid designatum of a predicate like 'is a tiger'. If the predicate 'is a tiger' is to be regarded as designating the property of being a tiger, rather than as designating the class of actual tigers, then it would appear that any predicate should be seen as designating the property that it expresses. But in that case, every predicate, even 'is a bachelor', emerges as a rigid designator, since the attribute (property or relation) expressed by a predicate with respect to a possible world does not vary from world to world. Nothing special about natural-kind predicates, color predicates, and so on, has been identified to demarcate them from the rest. So we are back to the question of what it is for a general term to be a rigid designator.

As for the question of what the designatum is for a general term that is a rigid designator, Kripke tells us that such a term designates a kind (e.g., a species, substance, phenomenon, etc.). Accordingly, the term 'tiger' designates the species *Tiger* (*Felis tigris*). In general, a biological taxonomic general term should be seen as designating a biological taxonomic kind (a species, a genus, an order, etc.), a chemical-element general term ('gold') should be seen as designating an element (gold), a chemical-compound general term as designating a compound (water), a color general term as designating a color (red), a natural-phenomenon general term as designating a natural phenomenon (heat), and so on. But as Nathan Salmon has pointed out, "now the threat is faced anew that every general term will emerge as a rigid designator of some appropriately related universal or other. If 'bachelor' designates the gendered marital-status category, *Unmarried Man*, it does so rigidly. Even a common-noun *phrase*, like 'adult male human who is not married', emerges as a rigid designator."[7] Soames objects to this proposal for the same reason: "there is no point in defining a notion of rigidity for predicates according to which all predicates turn out, trivially, to be rigid."[8] Soames concludes that there is no notion of rigidity that is simultaneously analogous to singular-term rigidity, a natural extension of singular-term rigidity to general terms, and a notion according to which certain general terms (especially, natural-kind terms) are rigid but many other general terms are nonrigid.[9] And this, he maintains, paves the way for a "demotion of the status of rigidity in Kripke's overall semantic picture" of terms singular and general.[10]

The problem with Soames's discussion of the rigidity of general terms is that it fails to distinguish sharply between a general term like 'tiger' and its corresponding predicate, 'is a tiger'. Even if every common count noun (whether a single word or a phrase) emerges as a rigid designator on this counterproposal, it does not follow that every general term is rigid. This is most evident when a definite description is in predicative position. Definite descriptions are typically singular terms—or, alternatively (following Russell), quantificational expressions that merely appear to be singular terms. But definite descriptions can sometimes function as if they were adjectives or mass-noun phrases. Consider the renowned definite description 'the present king of France' in the sentence

(1)   Chirac is the present king of France.

Unlike the use of this definite description in the famous sentence

(2)   The present king of France is bald,

there is no intuition that (1) is in some sense incomplete or fails to express a definite proposition. Instead, we just consider (1) to be false. Moreover, if France were still to have a monarchy, then (1) might have been true. The term 'the present king of France' simply fails to designate. The difference between the occurrence of 'the present king of France' in (1) and its use in (2) is that in (2), as Strawson taught us, there is a presupposition that there is a present king of France. On my view and Sommers's, this presupposition is part of an anaphoric background.[11] But in (1), there is no anaphoric background. We are not presupposing that there is a present king of France in order to make sense of the sentence or understand the definite proposition expressed by (1). Indeed, such uses, as Sommers has always maintained, better fit the Russellian model of having the definite article contextually defined and thus having the definite description represented as a restricted quantifier expression rather than as a singular term. Using the predicate-forming operator 'is-a', the predicate in (1) can be represented as 'is-a{unique present king of France}'. If we are to think of 'unique present king of France' as a general term restricted to one individual, then this general term fails to designate in the actual world but could have were France still to have a monarchy. This would then be an example of a nonrigid general term, and thus not all general terms would be rigid designators.

Nevertheless, the copula 'is' in (1) might not be correctly analyzed as the 'is' of predication as opposed to the 'is' of identity. As such, the definite description functions as a singular term, and the question still remains, are there any general terms that are nonrigid? One candidate is the description 'the color of the sky', as it occurs in the sentence

(3)   My true love's eyes are the color of the sky.

Soames sees the definite description in the predicate of (3) as a singular term rather than a general term.[12] Yet the copula 'are' here cannot be the pluralization of the 'is' of identity, since the color blue is a single universal whereas the speaker's lover's eyes are two particulars, and hence not both identical to a single (universal) thing. Nor can the copula be the 'is' of constitution. So it appears that the description 'the color of the sky' is a general term that, when appearing after the copula 'are' in (3), forms a predicate. Making use of the predicate-forming operators, the term 'the color of the sky' may then be rendered formally as a second-order definite description:

$(\iota F)[is\text{-}a^2\{color\}(F)$ & $is\{F\}($the sky$)]$,

where 'F' is a variable ranging over appropriate universals. (The superscript '2' indicates that the resulting predicate is second-order.) As a second-order term, the description designates even while combining with the 'is' of predication. This is a central view dictated by Sommers's system of term logic. Indeed, so understood, we can make sense of the following valid argument:

(3)   My true love's eyes are the color of the sky.

(4)   Blue is the color of the sky.

Therefore,

(5)   My true love's eyes are blue.

This inference is best seen as a special instance of Leibniz's Law, or Substitution of Equality. According to (4), the color blue is identical with the color of the sky. Since the speaker's true love's eyes are the color of the sky, it follows by substitution that those same eyes are blue. To draw this inference, the copula in (4) must be the 'is' of identity, attached to general terms instead of singular terms, and forming a sentence that is true if and only if the terms flanking the 'is' are codesignative.

   Nathan Salmon, in formalizing this inference in modern predicate logic, says: "Formalization of the inference might help to make the point:

(P1′) $(x)[is\text{-}a\{$eye of my true love$\}(x) \rightarrow is\{(\iota F)[is\text{-}a^2\{color\}(F)$ & $is\{F\}($the sky$)]\}(x)]$

(P2′)   blue $=^2 (\iota F)[is\text{-}a^2\{color\}(F)$ & $is\{F\}($the sky$)]$

(C′) $(x)[is\text{-}a\{$eye of my true love$\}(x) \rightarrow is\{$blue$\}(x)]$

(Then again, it might not.)"[13]

Indeed, as Salmon notes, this simple valid inference is moderately complicated when expressed in modern predicate logic.

Not surprisingly, even famous linguists say confusing things about the logical form and analysis of such descriptions. Robert May, for example, has challenged the view that 'the color of the sky' is a general term. He has argued that insofar as 'the color of the sky' is to be classified either as a singular term or as a general term, it is a singular term even in (3).[14] He endorses this conclusion on the ground that definite descriptions are nominal phrases that can occur in positions occupied by singular terms—as, for example, in 'Max and the color of the sky are two of my favorite things'. In addition, May cites the particular sentences, 'Max is the man for the job' (due to James Higginbotham) and the sarcastically understated 'Max isn't the best cook in town', as further examples—allegedly like (3)—of the 'is' of predication combined with an English singular term rather than a general term to form an English monadic predicate.

It should be obvious that May is mistaken to think that the mere fact that an expression can grammatically occupy a singular-term position, that is, a subject position, suffices to show that the expression is a singular term. At best, this is, a necessary condition on singular terms, not a sufficient condition. Mass terms in English, for example, can occur in singular-term position ('Water is H_2O', 'Max and gin are two of my favorite things'), but they also occur in general-term position, combining with the 'is' of predication to form English monadic predicates ('The liquid in this cup is water'). Likewise, canonical color terms ('red') and number terms ('three') can occur in singular-term position, as in 'Nine is the number of planets', but they also combine with predicative 'be' to form a predicate, as in 'The planets are nine'.[15] Contrary to May, the latter is something singular terms cannot do, at least not while functioning as singular terms, or even as first-order restricted quantifiers in the manner of Russell and Montague. (The fact that mass terms and the like can occur grammatically in singular-term position in addition to general-term position might be taken as independent grounds for recognizing at least some general terms as *second-order singular terms*.)

Second, English also includes sentences like 'What I am is nauseated', in which the subject is a general term—or, at least, would appear to be one. Indeed, this sentence appears to be an identity statement and its subject a second-order definite description (or, alternatively, a second-order restricted quantifier). Insofar as English includes second-order definite descriptions, phrases like 'the color of the sky', 'Henry's favorite beverage', and 'the chemical compound composed of two parts hydrogen and one part oxygen' are as good candidates as any.[16] Although these descriptions can occur in singular-term position, they also combine with the 'is' of predication to form monadic predicates, wherein they cannot function as singular terms. In fact, at least some of these same definite descriptions appear to function as mass-noun phrases and/or as color-term noun phrases. (Consider (P2') and 'Water is the chemical compound composed of two parts hydrogen and one part oxygen'.) As such, these descriptions would be general terms rather than singular.

Most important, as Sommers has long advocated, whether a term is singular or general is a matter of logical form, and logical form, in turn, is dependent on semantics. That 'blue' and 'the color of the sky' are general terms is a fact about logical form. It is not a fact about syntactic form—about *grammar* in the syntactic sense of the term (which does not conform to current usage in theoretical linguistics). The following sentences, on their standard readings, have the same syntactic form.

(6) Henry's favorite shirt is the color of the sky.

(7) Henry's favorite color is the color of the sky.

Each is a copular sentence constructed from a definite description of the form ⌜Henry's favorite N⌝ as subject, the appropriate conjugation of the verb 'be' as copula, and the definite description 'the color of the sky' as predicate nominal. Nevertheless, they differ sharply in logical form. Sentence (6) is a monadic predication, whereas sentence (7) is (equivalent to) an identity/equation, on a par with (4) and with May's examples (e.g., 'Max is the man for the job'). Correspondingly, (7) is logically equivalent to its converse and supports Leibniz's Law substitution; (6) is not and does not.

It would be a mistake to infer that, since they differ in logical form, (6) and (7) also differ in syntactic/grammatical form. Compare the following two sentences, on their standard readings:

(8) Henry's favorite shirt is blue.

(9) Henry's favorite color is blue.

These sentences are semantically related exactly as (6)–(7). All four sentences, (6)–(9), share a common syntactic structure. Like the pair (6)–(7),

(8) and (9) differ in the replacement in their subjects of 'shirt' by 'color' (count nouns both), and are otherwise structurally identical. Here the lexical switch in the subject issues in a categorial (nonstructural) switch in the predicate. The word 'blue' occurs as an adjective in (8), as a noun in (9), reflecting the change in logical form. This grammatical switch in the predicate does not occur with (6)–(7). As already noted, abstracting from their meanings and their logic—which are indeed very different—(6) and (7) share the same syntactic analysis in terms of both constituent structure and lexical and phrasal categories. Yet the same change in logical form that occurs in (8)–(9) also occurs in (6)–(7), where it is concealed behind a veil of superficial syntactic similarity. Though 'the color of the sky' is a nominal phrase, it plays exactly the same logico-semantic role in (6) and (3) that the adjectival 'blue' plays in (8) and (5)—a role reflected in the grammar of the word but not in that of the description.

Here again, contrary to May, recognition that the copula in (3), on its standard reading, is the same 'is' of predication that occurs in (8) and (5) reveals that the predicate nominal in (3)—regardless of its syntax—is a general term, since a term that combines with the 'is' of predication (without an intervening article) to form a monadic predicate cannot function as a singular term in the predicate so formed.

3

Before turning to Sommers's term logic and semantics of terms, let us summarize what has been shown thus far. I have argued that there can be definite descriptions that are general terms. Such descriptive general terms include 'the color of the sky'. Though the general-term description 'the color of the sky' designates blue, the corresponding predicate 'is the color of the sky' semantically expresses the property of having the same color as the sky, as opposed to the more specific property of being blue (in color). The two properties in the actual world share the same extension—the class of all blue things—but they differ in extension in some counterfactual situations, and so differ in intension and in what they designate in all possible worlds. It is important to notice also that whereas 'the color of the sky' is a nonrigid general term, the gerund phrase 'being the color of the sky' evidently rigidly designates a particular property—that of having the same color as the sky.

The noun/adjective 'blue' designates the color blue, and the definite description 'the color of the sky' designates the color of the sky. Given these two facts and the empirical fact that the sky is blue, the general terms 'blue' and 'the color of the sky' are codesignative. But whereas the 'blue' is surely rigid, 'the color of the sky' clearly is not. The latter designates red with respect to some possible worlds, making (4) contingent. If the copula in (4) is indeed an 'is' of identity to be placed between general terms, then Kripke's claim is vindicated that identity statements in which only rigid general terms occur are, unlike (4) but like identity statements involving proper names, necessary if true at all. Examples are close at hand: 'Furze is gorse'; 'Gold is Au'; 'Water is H_2O'. As already noted, even some descriptive general terms, like 'adult male human who is not married', are rigid designators. Still, nonrigid general terms are everywhere. These include such definite descriptions as 'the species that serves as mascot for Princeton University', 'the liquid compound that covers most of the Earth', 'the most valuable of elemental metals', 'the color of the sky', and so on.[17]

It remains to show how to formalize in standard quantification theory what it is for a general term to be rigid, and then show how much simpler it is in Sommers's term logic. For the sake of simplicity, we shall consider the case where a term rigidly designates in every possible circumstance. We shall say that a general term τ designates a kind k if and only if the extension of τ with respect to any possible world w is the class of instances of k in w. Making use of the predicate-forming operators discussed above that apply to mass nouns and count nouns, respectively, and letting 'v' stand for any common noun or common noun phrase, we get '$is\{v\}$' and '$is\text{-}a\{v\}$'. Then if 'α' is any term denoting with respect to the actual world the kind designated by v, we can express what v designates by one of two well-formed formulas, respectively:

(8) $(\exists k)[k = \alpha \ \& \ \Box(x)(is\{v\}(x) \leftrightarrow x \in k)]$ (for mass nouns)

(9) $(\exists k)[k = \alpha \ \& \ \Box(x)(is\text{-}a\{v\}(x) \leftrightarrow x \in k)]$ (for count nouns).

These formulas say that there is a kind k such that $\alpha = k$, and necessarily anything is v iff it is an instance of k, and there is a kind k such that $\alpha = k$, and necessarily anything is a v iff it is an instance of k, respectively.

Notice that the above definitions distinguish between a general term that rigidly designates, such as 'blue', and a general term that does not, such as 'the color of the sky'. The former on the above analysis rigidly denotes a specific color, whereas although the latter denotes the same color in the actual world, it does not denote that color in all possible worlds. This should not be confused with the latter term's corresponding predicate 'is the color of the sky', which semantically expresses the property of having the same color as the sky as opposed to the more specific property of being blue (in color). The general term 'the color of the sky' should also not be confused with the gerund expression 'being the color of the sky'. Whereas the former is a nonrigid designator, the latter rigidly designates the particular property—that of having the same color as the sky.

We turn now to Sommers's semantics of terms. In his terminology, a term both *signifies* and *denotes*. A term denotes the extension of its associated predicate, and it signifies the property had by all members of its extension. It is to be the property that all members of any possible extension (or denotation in Sommers's terminology) have. Sommers identifies the signification of a term with whatever the associated gerund of the term rigidly designates. The denotation of the term 'the color of the sky' is certainly the class of all things that are the color of the sky. But on the basis of semantics alone, we are not told what color that is. When we are told that the term's denotation is the class of blue things, we are given which color all things in the denotation class have. Thus, to be semantically informative about what color all things in the class's extension have, we must mention the name of that color. And, in general, whatever that property is that all members of the extension of that term have, to be semantically informative that term must be a name of that property. We may think of these terms as something like logically proper names. Thus 'tiger', 'gold', 'water', and standard names of colors are such names. What I have in mind is what Kripke, in his Whitehead Lectures, has called a *buckstopper*. A *buckstopper* is a term denoting a person, place, thing, etc., such that when we are presented with such a term, we no longer ask, 'And what person, place, thing, etc., is that?'

My thesis expressed in the terminology of Sommers is that a given term is a rigid designator if what it signifies is necessarily coextensive with the designation of the buckstopper term for what the given term signifies. In such a case, the given term is thus a rigid designator whose denotation is the class of things with respect to a possible state of affairs denoted by the buckstopper term with respect to that possible state of affairs. Other terms are generally not rigid designators unless they are rigid de facto.

So, for example, the given terms 'H_2O' and 'water' are buckstopper terms. The former signifies the property (state) of being two hydrogen atoms combined with one oxygen atom. This property is necessarily coextensive with the property designated by the buckstopper terms, 'being H_2O' or 'being water'. Thus the term 'H_2O' rigidly designates the chemical compound water, or H_2O, whose denotation is the class with respect to a possible state of affairs that is denoted by the buckstopper terms 'being H_2O' or 'being water'. That is, all members of the class of H_2O with respect to a given possible state of affairs have the property of being two hydrogen atoms combined with one oxygen atom. In contrast, the term 'the color of the sky' is not a buckstopper. The term signifies the property of being the color of the sky. But given the semantics of the term alone, we can rightly ask, 'And what color property is that?' The name that is a buckstopper for this color property is 'blue'. Hence the property of being the color of the sky must necessarily be coextensive with the property blue if the general term 'the color of the sky' is to count as a rigid designator. This is clearly not the case. For, in some states of affairs, the color of the sky is red.

I end by formalizing the notion of a rigid general term and the above argument in Sommers's traditional formal logic (hereafter, TFL). Sommers has a very simple logical form for propositions in the algebraic language of TFL. The general form of a proposition in this algebraic language is the following:

$\pm(\pm(\pm\alpha) \pm (\pm\beta))$,

where 'α' and 'β' are two terms. This general form has the following interpretation:

yes/no some/every α/non-α is/isn't β/non-β,

where the plus sign in each case is to be interpreted by the corresponding affirmative expression, and the negative sign by the corresponding negative expression.

Sommers talks about a term being introduced by means of some anaphoric background. We see a strange animal and believe it to be of an unknown species (kind), $S^{\blacklozenge}$, where the superscript '$\blacklozenge$' signifies that 'S' is a term that is uniquely designative. So, using 'T' to stand for 'thing', we begin with 'some T is an $S^{\blacklozenge}$', in which '$S^{\blacklozenge}$' is *the species in question*. In the algebraic language of TFL, this becomes: $+T + S^{\blacklozenge}$.[18]

We decide to name the species '$\alpha^\blacklozenge$'. Then to say that '$\alpha^\blacklozenge$' rigidly designates this species (kind), we add that the following holds in all possible states of affairs:

$$-\alpha^\blacklozenge + S^\blacklozenge \ \& \ -S^\blacklozenge + \alpha^\blacklozenge.$$

In English this translates as 'All $\alpha^\blacklozenge$s are $S^\blacklozenge$s' and 'All $S^\blacklozenge$s are $\alpha^\blacklozenge$s'. Analogous remarks apply to mass terms.

We next consider the following valid argument that required much effort on Salmon's part to formalize in predicate logic:

(3)   My true love's eyes are the color of the sky.

(4)   Blue is the color of the sky.

Therefore,

(5)   My true love's eyes are blue.

Let 'A' be the term 'eye of my true love', '$B^\blacklozenge$' be the term 'blue', and '$C^\blacklozenge$' be the term 'the color of the sky'. Then (3) becomes:

(P3) $-A + C^\blacklozenge$,

which translates as 'Every (thing that is the) eye of my true love is the color of the sky'.

In TFL, an identity statement is a monadic predication both of whose terms are uniquely designative. Sommers's way of formalizing an identity statement is:

$$\pm X^\blacklozenge + Y^\blacklozenge,$$

an expression that may be read as 'X is identical to Y', where '$\pm$' represents "wild quantity".[19] Accordingly, premise (4) is formalized as:

(P4) $\pm B^\blacklozenge + C^\blacklozenge$.

This allows us to read (P4) as '$+B^\blacklozenge + C^\blacklozenge$' or 'some $B^\blacklozenge$ is $C^\blacklozenge$', and to derive its converse, '$+C^\blacklozenge + B^\blacklozenge$'. But since '$C^\blacklozenge$' is also uniquely designative, it too takes wild quantity. That is, '$+C^\blacklozenge + B^\blacklozenge$' entails the universal form '$-C^\blacklozenge + B^\blacklozenge$'. Adding '$-C^\blacklozenge + B^\blacklozenge$' to (P3) gives us the conclusion

(C5) $-A + B$,

which represents 'Every eye of my true love is blue'.

In TFL we now see the ease with which the above argument is formulated and deduced as a valid argument. This contrasts sharply with the effort to get straight what the premises are and how to formulate them in predicate logic. We have also seen the ease with which we may formalize whether a term is a rigid designator. Thus, the likelihood of confusion of these different terms decreases. Indeed, as Fred Sommers seems to have been saying all along: what could be simpler?

Acknowledgments

I wish to thank David Oderberg and Nathan Salmon for comments on an earlier version of this essay.

Notes

1. F. T. Sommers, *The Logic of Natural Language* (Oxford: Clarendon Press, 1982) (hereafter LNL).

2. S. Kripke, *Naming and Necessity* (Oxford: Blackwell, 1980) (hereafter, N&N).

3. N&N, pp. 117–144, *passim,* and especially at 134, 139–140. There are other notions of rigid designator, such as an obstinate and persistent rigid designator. For details, see Nathan Salmon, *Reference and Essence* (Oxford: Blackwell, 1982).

4. But I shall argue that a definite description can also function as a general term.

5. S. Soames, *Beyond Rigidity* (New York: Oxford University Press, 2002).

6. Ibid., pp. 249–263, 287–288, and *passim.*

7. See *Reference and Essence*, pp. 52–54, 69–75, and his forthcoming article, "Are General Terms Rigid?" In his article, as well as in the book, Salmon argues for the position that although general terms that are rigid include all common nouns (whether a single word or a phrase), the proposal meets the above challenge that not all general terms are rigid.

8. *Beyond Rigidity*, p. 251.

9. Ibid., p. 263.

10. Ibid., p. 264.

11. See LNL, pp. 207–226; and my *Terms and Truth: Reference Direct and Anaphoric* (Cambridge, Mass.: The MIT Press, 2002).

12. *Beyond Rigidity*, p. 261. More accurately, he sees the description as a quantifier phrase, which he "assimilates to the broader class of singular terms" (p. 316, n.17). In other words, Soames neither sees the description in (3) as a general term nor assimilates it to the class of such terms.

13. N. Salmon, "Naming, Necessity, and Beyond: Critical Notice of Scott Soames, *Beyond Rigidity*," *Mind* 112 (2003): 475–492, at p. 484.

14. "Comments on Nathan Salmon, 'Are General Terms Rigid?'," presented to the 2003 Princeton Workshop on Semantics. The following criticism of May's views comes in part from Salmon's unpublished reply to May.

15. The predicate formed by combining 'be' with a canonical number term might be regarded as *multiadic* (rather than as monadic, or dyadic, etc.). More accurately, such numerical predicates should be seen as applying collectively rather than individually (or equivalently, as applying to pluralities or multiplicities, i.e., to groups having a number that may be other than one).

16. The threat of Russell's Paradox applies pressure to see some definite descriptions as differing from others in logical form, despite sharing the same syntactic form. The kinds that come readily to mind are always of the following sort (*R*): *a kind K that is not itself something of kind K*. The species, *Tiger*, for example, is not itself a tiger. (Indeed, precious few kinds are not of this kind (*R*).) Consider now the very kind just specified: the kind (*R*) such that, necessarily, something is of (*R*) iff it is a kind *K* that is not itself something of kind *K*. The preceding definite description, despite its syntax, cannot be first-order on pain of contradiction (assuming that it designates a kind, and assuming obvious logical properties of definite descriptions).

17. Some definite descriptions are rigid, e.g., 'the only even prime number'. In *Naming and Necessity*, Kripke calls such descriptions *rigid de facto*, in contrast to proper names, which are termed *rigid de jure* (p. 21n.).

18. For simplicity here and in what follows, I have followed Sommers's custom of omitting extraneous signs, leaving only the plus signs for 'some' and 'is'.

19. See LNL, chapter 6, for details.

6 The Syntax and Semantics of English Prepositional Phrases

Patrick Suppes

For just over twenty years now, I have been an admirer of Fred Sommers's work in the logic of natural language, especially as summarized extensively in his 1982 book of this title. Before I knew many details about Fred's work, I wrote in the 1970s Suppes and Macken 1978, and Suppes 1979a,b, 1981. All four of these earlier articles of mine, the first one with Elizabeth Macken, concentrated on the elimination of variables entirely in semantics, and also on a semantics that was organized to reflect directly the structure of natural English, not the structure of first-order logic. My agreement with Fred on these matters could not be more complete.

In this early work of my own and in Fred's well-known book (1982), as well as his more recent textbook on logic (Sommers and Englebretsen 2000), there is really no systematic semantical treatment of prepositional phrases, yet prepositional phrases carry a considerable load in expressing our cognitive ideas about space and time and many other kinds of relations between ourselves and objects. In various places, Fred occasionally uses a verb phrase that contains a prepositional phrase modifying, in the ordinary grammatical sense, the main verb. But in his analysis of canonical sentences, he would simply treat this as a verb phrase and not analyze it into parts, for example, in the verb phrase, *lived among the heathen*—not that this is one of his examples. I can also equally well cite such unanalyzed complex predicates of my own in my logic text (Suppes 1957/1999).

There are some fundamental reasons for shying away from a detailed analysis of prepositional phrases. I pointed out a central difficulty in the final two paragraphs of Suppes 1979b. Here is the simple example I tried to analyze:

John is pouring water in the pitcher.

This is an ordinary sentence that certainly has a clear meaning. But when we analyze it in terms of the usual formal logic of relations and operations on relations, as exemplified in the 1979 article cited, and which certainly appears in work by many other people as well, the ordinary logic ends up with the inference that John is in the pitcher, which is clearly not meant to be a valid consequence of the sentence. The difficulty is that the prepositional phrase locates the action denoted by the main verb phrase and does not spatially locate the subject of the sentence, that is, where *John* is. So, if we try to analyze this sentence in terms of just the natural context-free semantics for noun phrases, verb phrases, and the obvious extension of a verb phrase to prepositional phrases, we cannot get out of this difficulty. It is clear that the models used must exceed in richness the arbitrary relational structures that are the workhorse of the model theory ordinarily associated with the semantics of context-free languages. This applies as well to the extended relation algebras I have introduced in several articles and that are characterized in Suppes 1979b.

A very general response to what I have written is that we could certainly provide adequate logical machinery by going beyond relation structures or the extended relation algebras just mentioned by introducing an unbounded set-theoretical hierarchy of the sort much used by Montague. But this is really not the focus I want to highlight here. What I said in the earlier article I still hold to. I am not sure Fred would agree with this point. I am especially skeptical of making any analytic–synthetic distinction in the use of prepositions. I regard, for example, prepositional phrases using the preposition *in* often to be making spatial claims, claims that are not logical at all but much richer in character, as in the sentence 'The broom is in the next room'. So the real difficulty I want to consider here is that of understanding the subtlety of the correct use of such prepositions in English. I will not, in the discussion to be given here, undertake at all to provide a formal treatment of their semantics, for example by giving a logic for such phrases.

There is also another aspect of analysis that I do not intend to entertain in any detail in this essay. This is the attempt to indicate, without a full formalism, the semantics of various spatial prepositions, especially 'in' and 'on'. In an earlier paper, Crangle and Suppes 1989, Colleen Crangle and I tried to spell out some of the intricate geometric and physical aspects of the usage of these prepositions. Some of the considerations we entered into there were of the following sort. Did the use of a given preposition or prepositional phrase imply a point of view, as when one says 'The house you are looking for is to the left of the yellow one'? In many accounts, the correct interpretation of the preposition 'to the left of' requires a point of view, for reasons that are obvious. Here is another kind of example. It is natural to think of many relations of 'on' as being purely geometric, as when I say 'The book is on the table'. But, on further reflection, it is obvious there is a physical concept of support implied that is not at all geometric in nature. It might, of course, be argued that we can eliminate the need for a separate concept of support by enriching Euclidean geometry with a restrictive notion of oriented verticality—so that, with Aristotle, we could meaningfully talk about *up* and *down*. But this is certainly not something we can accomplish in ordinary Euclidean geometry, for which no notion of *up*, *down*, or *on* is invariant.

There is another usage of 'on' in geometry that is appropriately invariant, and that is when we say that point *a* is *on* line *l*. The preposition 'on', especially, is a wonderful source of puzzles. We might be inclined, working through things in a purely mathematical way, to think that 'on' should be transitive. But in an ordinary sense it is not. So, we can say 'The table is on the floor' and we can also say 'The book is on the table', but it would be a mistake to say that the book is on the floor.

Still other kinds of example require the introduction of time as well as space. Here are some standard examples: 'When you are going to school, walk in the shade'; 'If you are smart, you will run under the bridge when the rain starts'; 'The pencil is rolling on the table, can you catch it?'. Crangle and I certainly offered no general solution for this wilderness of cases. We did, I hope, make some progress in classification and clarification.

In this essay, I want to do something else—to take note of how inadequate the ordinary, purely grammatical classification of nouns and noun phrases can be in terms of their being objects of prepositions. We need a much finer classification than the ordinary grammatical one to eliminate nonsense. For example, we say, in a quite appropriate way, 'The water is running in the bucket', but we can't say, 'The water is running in the minute'. In other words, 'in' has a kind of spatial quality that, of course, can be used in a temporal fashion, but only in a special way. So, for example, I can say 'I will be home in five minutes.' But it sounds weird to say 'I'll be home in the minute'. Similar restrictions, devious in nature when all examples are considered, are needed for 'on'. I can say 'The books are on the table', but it is nonsense to say, in a literal sense, 'Five minutes are on the table'.

A different kind of problem is raised by the implied motion that is so often associated with the use of the preposition 'into'. It is fine to say 'He walked into the room', but not 'The book is into the table', or even, perhaps, 'He is into the room', in contrast to 'He is in the room'. Here we need a sense of motion underway or just completed. However, for many kinds of motion, if we have the right kind of verb, we can use 'in', as in the following example: 'He is running in the water', or, even more interesting, 'He is turning the pages in the book'.

I give these many examples in the conviction that it is the responsibility of a full analysis of a language to exclude nonsensical examples from being accepted. I have been careful in formulating the last sentence not to say whether the strings that are not accepted—that I have been calling nonsense—are rejected for grammatical or semantical reasons. My general view of such matters is that this distinction is a mistake. We cannot really draw a sharp line between the grammatical and the semantical, just as we cannot between the analytic and the synthetic. Not everyone agrees with this view. My purpose here, however, is not to argue for its correctness, but rather to point out how hard it is to exclude the nonsense sentences, whether one assigns them to the grammatical or semantical side of the fence.

Three obvious context-free production or parsing rules for prepositional phrases (PP) are the following:

(1)   PP → Prep + NP   'Maria ran to the house'

where 'to the house' is the prepositional phrase, and 'the house' is the noun phrase (NP). The noun phrase is referred to as the complement of the preposition. The second rule permits an adjectival phrase (AdjP) to be a prepositional complement:

(2)   PP → Prep + AdjP   'She worked for little, but liked it'.

However, standardly, prepositional complements are noun phrases, and much more rarely adjectival phrases. More common, but still not standard, are clausal complements of prepositions, with and without 'that':

(3)   PP → Prep + (*that*) + Clause   'I left before he did'.

Here the clause 'he did' is the complement of the preposition 'before'. The use of 'that' is much more restricted, but here is an example: 'I left provided that she stayed'.

These three rules are only a small sample of the many required to chart the syntactic varieties of correct prepositional use. The new *Cambridge Grammar of the English Language* (2002) gives a wonderfully detailed survey, without actually writing down formal rules. It would seem to be a good thing for someone to attempt, a matter I return to later.

The issue I want to turn to now is the important one of imposing restrictions on the range of rules. Violations of rules (2) and (3) are obvious, since very few adjectival phrases can serve as prepositional complements and many clauses cannot. For example:

(4)   *He ran to unsettled.

(5)   *She walked in very heavy.

(6)   *She left in he said he would.

But such infelicities are easy to construct as well for prepositional complements that are noun phrases. Here are some examples using the familiar prepositions 'on', 'in', 'into', and 'at':

(7)   *She ran quietly on her ideas

in contrast to

(8)   She ran quietly on the empty street;

(9)   *He slept in his notebook

as opposed to

(10)   He wrote in his notebook;

(11)   *The pencil was into the box

as compared to

(12)   He put the pencil into the box;

(13)   *She stated her views at the room

in contrast to

(14)   She stated her views at the graveyard.

That the starred expressions are ungrammatical is uncontroversial and obvious even by a liberal standard of usage. That is not the problem. The problem is restricting the grammatical production or parsing rules to rule out such usage while permitting the usage that is acceptable.

Before making any concrete suggestions, I want to state my general view that the task of giving nearly all the rules governing prepositional usage in standard written English is a difficult if not impossible task, as yet not really attempted by anyone, although some of the efforts at writing large computer-based grammars of English may in the not too distant future produce significant approximation.

In mentioning "rules" I deliberately did not mention "grammatical" rules, for many would regard a number of the additional rules we need as embodying semantical rather than grammatical notions. I am, as already mentioned, skeptical of making this distinction precise and will not make an effort to do so in any detail in what follows.

It is commonly noted as important that probably a majority of the most frequently used prepositions, such as the four just discussed, have an essentially spatial or temporal character, often extended by spatial or temporal metaphors:

(15)   She searched in the oldest parts of the house

but as well

(16)   She searched in her oldest memories of him.

The subtlety of what constitutes acceptable usage is well exemplified by the starred (13) and the proper (14). The preposition 'at' most often has a spatial focus that marks the occurrence of some event at a given place. This spatial marking of place is implicit in (14) but not in (13). Why? Because the bare noun 'room' has a primary sense of being a container rather than a place to be, which is not the case for 'graveyard', although it is certainly acceptable to say:

(17)   Her mother was buried in the graveyard.

These last examples suggest how we might begin to generate new and better rules by restrictions on the old one. So we replace (1) with

(1.1)   Container PP → Container Prep + Container NP

and

(1.2)   Place PP → Place Prep + Place NP

(The rules seem awkward when written with such repeated modifier words, but because of their nonstandard character I will not abbreviate them.) As sentences (14) and (17) illustrate, nouns such as 'graveyard' have both a container and a place sense. Which sense is being used depends on the preposition being used, or, in some cases, on the sense of the preposition, which may be illustrated by again using 'in'. I take

(18)   The balls were in two different places

to be a case of 'in' being used in the sense of place, as expressed by rule (1.2), but in the following the sense is one of measure of a quality or property:

(19)   (i)   They differ in temperature.

(ii)   They differ in weight.

(iii) They differ in attitude about freedom.

In the three examples under (19), (i) and (ii) differ in type of measure. Using the traditional distinctions, temperature is an intensive property and weight an extensive one, but this distinction does not seem to matter much for the use of 'in'. Some might object that qualitative distinctions are needed for (19), but because I think it is important not to distinguish the kind of quality, extensive or intensive, referred to by the prepositional complement, I lump them together under measure. I do mean, however, to restrict measure to qualities that at least admit of a comparative judgment about them. Moreover, another terminology could be proposed, but I shall not examine the matter further here.

   The preposition 'in' can be used in all three senses introduced: container, place, and measure. What about 'on'? It does not easily have a sense of container, but certainly does of place, including not just spatial place but also temporal place, as in

(20)   They burst on boiling.

This example might also be interpreted as using 'on' in the sense of measure, as in the similar

(21)   The pipes burst on freezing.

But at least (20) and (21) seem to illustrate a singularity, or change of state, associated with the measurable property or quality.

These last two examples do move us toward another sense, that of movement, as in

(22)   She walked into the room.

Movement generally implies change in both space and time. Unlike the first three senses we have been discussing, 'in' does not have this sense except in a rather indirect way, as in

(23)   She danced in one room and then another.

Another sense of frequent usage is that concerning causes, expressed by prepositions such as 'because', 'because of', 'due to', and 'in spite of'. Note that 'in spite of' takes as a complement a negative cause. Intuitively, a negative cause is a cause that tends to prevent an event or action from happening, as in

(24)   Mary saw Henry in spite of the advice of her parents.

Of course, negative causes can also be successful in preventing an action:

(25)   Rosa did not go out because of the illness of her mother.

For a formal analysis of negative causes, see Suppes 1970, p. 43.

Also important is the sense of prepositions expressing goals, e.g., 'to' and 'straight to', as in:

(26)   I ran to the shelter.

(27)   I ran fast straight to the shelter.

Prepositions used to express higher or more general goals fall under this sense as well.

Without claiming that I have given a complete list of basic senses, I stop the enumeration. And, as should be obvious, I have stopped even sooner the elaboration of syntactic expressions for prepositions, which is, fortunately, explored thoroughly by Huddleston and Pullum (2002). They describe many complex prepositions, which syntactically means those using several words, such as 'in spite of', 'in front of', 'with reference to', 'for the sake of'—note the occurrences of familiar simple prepositions beginning and ending these complex prepositions.

Linguists tend to classify lexical categories as open or closed. Noun phrases are open because there is in English no obvious fixed, finite bound to their number. But prepositions, simple and complex, taken together, form a closed class. On the other hand, the total number of prepositions, even restricting the list to those that are uncontroversial, seems to be very large.

As far as I know, no one has as yet attempted anything like a complete enumeration of just those that appear intuitively to be widely acceptable.

Perhaps as essential would be an agreed, more or less complete list of what I have called senses, which in many cases correspond to what in traditional philosophy have been called categories. Certainly, it seems to me, such a list, which has only been begun here, can no longer be claimed to have the privileged epistemological or ontological status of the categories, as proposed by such philosophers as Aristotle or Kant and those who have been their followers on this matter. Taken more pragmatically, however, many of the distinctions introduced by Aristotle in *The Categories* can be useful for the kind of analysis begun here.

References

Crangle, C., and Suppes, P. 1989. "Geometrical Semantics for Spatial Prepositions." In P. A. French, T. E. Uehling, Jr., and H. K. Wettstein (eds.), *Midwest Studies in Philosophy XIV*. South Bend: University of Notre Dame Press, 399–422.

Huddleston, R. D., and Pullum, G. K. 2002. *The Cambridge Grammar of the English Language*. Cambridge: Cambridge University Press.

Sommers, F. T. 1982. *The Logic of Natural Language*. New York: Oxford University Press.

Sommers, F. T., and Englebretsen, G. 2000. *An Invitation to Formal Reasoning: The Logic of Terms*. Burlington: Ashgate.

Suppes, P. 1957/1999. *Introduction to Logic*. New York: Van Nostrand. (Spanish translation by G. A. Carrasco: *Introduccion a la logica simbolica* [Mexico: Compania Editorial Continental, SA., 1966]. Mandarin translation by Fu-Tseng Liu [Taiwan: Buffalo Book Co., 1968]. Reprinted 1999 [New York, Dover].)

Suppes, P. 1970. *A Probabilistic Theory of Causality*. Amsterdam: North-Holland.

Suppes, P. 1979a. "Variable-Free Semantics for Negations with Prosodic Variation." In E. Saarinen, R. Hilpinin, I. Niiniluoto, and M. P. Hintikka (eds.), *Essays in Honour of Jaakko Hintikka*. Dordrecht: Reidel, 49–59.

Suppes, P. 1979b. "Logical Inference in English: A Preliminary Analysis." *Studia Logica* 38: 375–391.

Suppes, P. 1981. "Direct Inference in English." *Teaching Philosophy* 4: 405–418.

Suppes, P., and Macken, E. 1978. "Steps Toward a Variable-Free Semantics of Attributive Adjectives, Possessives, and Intensifying Adverbs." In K. E. Nelson (ed.), *Children's Language*, vol. 1. New York: Gardner Press, 81–115.

7 Modeling Anaphora in TFL

William C. Purdy

1 Introduction

Term functor logic (TFL) represents pronouns by employing superscripts to co-index a pronoun with its antecedent. Terms carrying the same superscript are defined to have the same denotation. This approach suffices for most pronouns, but further refinement is possible. The present essay describes a refinement that takes cognizance of the work of Slater with the epsilon-calculus as well as work with ontological foundations of conceptual modeling to provide a richer and more extensive treatment of anaphora. First, an analysis of anaphora in English is undertaken to identify the requirements to be imposed on the refinement. This analysis concludes that generic descriptions as well as indefinite descriptions and definite descriptions among others must be considered. Further, it concludes that fundamentally different treatment of plural and singular anaphors is required. Next, as a basis for what follows, a formal syntax and semantics of (superscript-free) TFL is given. The refinement is then formally defined as an extension of TFL. An advantage of the refinement here described is that it makes reference and attribution independent. It can be shown that this independence permits construal of ascriptive pronouns and even fictions. A number of examples are presented. Finally, two issues—donkey sentences and coordinating conjunctions—are examined and related to the refinement here described.

2 Anaphor and Antecedent

To define anaphor and antecedent, first a few subordinate concepts must be introduced.

A *noun* names a person, place, thing, or concept. Nouns are subdivided into *proper nouns* ('John', 'Mary', 'Toledo', ...), *pronouns* ('he', 'she', 'it', ...), and *common nouns* ('man', 'dog', 'grass', ...).

A proper noun or a proper noun preceded by modifier(s) ('Bob', 'big bad John', 'my friend Flicka', ...) is called a *proper noun group*. A common noun or a common noun preceded by modifier(s) ('man', 'dog', 'big brown dog', 'tall blonde man', ...) and/or followed by a relative clause ('man who wears a red hat', ...) is called a *common noun group*.

A *noun phrase* is any of the following:

1. A proper noun group

2. A pronoun

3. A common noun group preceded by a determiner (typically 'a', 'the', 'some', 'all', ..., but demonstratives and possessives can also function as determiners)

4. A plural common noun group (called a *bare plural*).

A noun phrase that begins with the determiner 'a', 'some', or equivalent is called an *existential* description. A noun phrase that begins with the determiner 'all', 'every', or equivalent is called a *universal* description. More specifically, a noun phrase that begins with the determiner 'a' is called an *indefinite description*. A noun phrase that begins with the determiner 'the' is called a *definite description*. The indefinite and definite descriptions have a long and involved history in the logic of natural language (Neale 1990).

The indefinite description and definite description can be used generically as well as particularly. For example, 'A good student completes his homework' uses 'A good student' in the sense of a generic representative. When so used, these descriptions are called *generic descriptions*. In the subsequent development, the notion of a generic representative plays an important role in the explication of several types of anaphora. A bare plural, that is, a plural common noun group, also can be a generic description (examples: '*Rabid dogs* must be avoided', '*Beautiful women* often get special treatment'). Finally, a universal description can be a generic description (see section 3.2).

In view of these observations, descriptions are classified (and simultaneously defined for the purposes of this paper) as follows:

1. Proper description: '*John* is a teacher'

2. (Particular) indefinite description: '*A boy* rides a bike'

3. (Particular) definite description: '*The boy* has red hair'

4. Generic indefinite description: '*A child* needs discipline'

5. Generic definite description: '*The spotted owl* is endangered'

6. Bare plural: '*Men* are from Mars'

7. Universal description: '*Every man* needs a job'

8. Generic universal description: '*Every man* chooses a partner. He bows'.

An *antecedent* is a phrase whose denotation does not require reference to another phrase. By contrast, an *anaphor* acquires its denotation by reference to its antecedent. The anaphor acquires the same denotation as its antecedent. *Anaphora* refers to the relation between anaphor and the antecedent that supplies the anaphor's referent. (These definitions come from *The Concise Oxford Dictionary of Linguistics*.) Each of the above descriptions, except for (3), the (particular) definite description, acquires a denotation by virtue of its own structure. Each can therefore function as an antecedent. An anaphor is a third-person pronoun or a definite description. Note that although a definite description can be an anaphor, not all definite descriptions are anaphors. For example: 'John Adams was the president' uses the definite description as a predicate. Similarly, whereas an indefinite description can be an antecedent, not all indefinite descriptions are antecedents. Example: 'Felix is a cat' uses the indefinite description as a predicate.

The anaphoric reference is determined by the parse. It is indicated in the parse by a numerically identical superscript (on the antecedent) and subscript (on the anaphor). For example: 'A^1 boy shouted. Then he_1 ran away'. The superscript and subscript are appended to the determiner, if present, that "quantifies" the phrase. When a determiner is not present, as in the case of bare plurals, the superscript is appended to the last word in the phrase. For example: 'Beautiful $women^1$ often receive special treatment. $They_1$ expect such treatment'. Where necessary to avoid ambiguity, the phrase can be parenthesized: '(Beautiful women)^1 often receive special treatment. $They_1$ expect such treatment'. A similar device can be used for conjoined noun phrases. For example: '(A father and a son)^1 entered the petting zoo. $They_1$ chortled with delight'. Again: '(Mary and Sue)^1 came to the party. $They_1$ brought cookies'. Conjoined noun phrases present other, more serious difficulties (see section 7). The sentence 'Alice screamed at her mother that she is too fat' is ambiguous and admits two parses that assign different references to the anaphor 'she'. Again, consider the sentences 'A father and a son entered the petting zoo. He chortled with delight'. The second sentence is ambiguous with respect to the reference of the anaphor 'He'. Thus it is clear that the parse, determined by intent of the speaker and/or understanding of the listener, defines the reference. This is a linguistic rather than logical consideration.

In many instances, the gender of a pronoun is sufficient to disambiguate the reference. When it is not, a definite description with sufficient content for disambiguation is often used. For example: 'A^1 quick red fox jumped over a^2 lazy brown dog. The$_1$ fox was gone in an instant'.

A generic description is denoted by a *prototype* of the denotation of the immediate descriptive content (see section 3.1). A prototype is an element that possesses all and only those properties possessed by every member of the denotation of the immediate descriptive content. In this essay, all generic descriptions will be denoted by prototypes. Note, however, that some linguists believe that each generic has a different meaning: that the generic indefinite refers to the *definition* of its immediate descriptive content; that the generic definite refers to the *prototype* of its immediate descriptive content; and that the bare plural refers to the *norm* of its immediate descriptive content (see Lawler 1997).

The genericity of a description is determined by the parse. In general, a sentence containing a generic description is ambiguous, admitting also a nongeneric reading. A generic description will be indicated in the parse by prefixing g to the superscript attached to that description. Example: 'The ^{g1} spotted owl is endangered. It$_1$ is protected by law'.

3   Types of Anaphora

Anaphora to be considered involve pronouns of types B, E, and A, and definite descriptions. B (for bound) and A (for ascriptive) come from Sommers (1982), E (for Evans) comes from Evans (1980). These are nominal anaphora. They do not exhaust the possible types of anaphora. Examples of anaphora not considered are the following.

1. John said Bob might lose his job. That scared Bob.

2. John drives a truck. Bob drives one too.

3. Linguists earn less than computer scientists. That is unfair.

3.1 B-Type

Prior to Evans's important paper (1980), it was generally thought that all pronouns were analogous to the bound variables of quantification theory. Evans argued that this is true only of some pronouns, namely those that occur "in construction with" their antecedents, that is, those pronouns that are located in the same quantifier scope as their antecedents. But this characterization is not altogether satisfactory in that it presupposes a certain construal of pronouns.

The theory of grammar can provide a more satisfactory characterization. Parse trees will be represented in linear fashion as follows. A nonbranching node A dominating a subtree t is represented $[A[t]]$. A branching node A dominating two subtrees t_1 and t_2 is represented $[A[t_1, t_2]]$. The grammarian's notion "c-command" can be defined as follows. Let A and B be nodes of a parse tree. Then A *c-commands* B iff the first branching node that dominates A also dominates B, and A does not itself dominate B (Riemsdijk and Williams 1986). Now it can be stated that a pronoun is B-type (bound) iff it is c-commanded by its antecedent. An example of a B-type pronoun is provided by the sentence: 'A^1 boy walks his$_1$ dog'. The parse tree is

[S[[NP[[DET[a]],[N[boy]]]],[VP[[V[walk]],[NP[[PRON[his]], [N[dog]]]]]]]].

(S = sentence, NP = noun phrase, VP = verb phrase, DET = determiner, N = noun, V = verb, PRON = pronoun.) It is easily seen that the noun phrase 'a boy' c-commands the pronoun 'his'. An example of pronouns that are not bound is provided by the sentences: 'A^1 boy walks a^2 dog. He$_1$ feeds it$_2$'. When a pronoun occurs in a sentence different from the sentence in which its antecedent occurs, it cannot be c-commanded by its antecedent. Pronouns that are not c-commanded by their antecedents are E-type and A-type.

The c-command relation can also assist in defining the descriptive content of descriptions. The *immediate descriptive content* of a description is the common noun group or proper noun group of that description. The immediate descriptive content of a description corresponds to the quantifier restriction in modern predicate logic (MPL), and to the subject term of a dyad in TFL. The *total descriptive content* of a description is the immediate descriptive content of the description conjoined to the subtree c-commanded by that description. The total descriptive content corresponds to the conjunction of the quantifier restriction and the scope of the restricted quantifier in MPL, and to the conjunction of the subject and predicate terms of a dyad in TFL.

3.2   E-Type

On the traditional view, all pronouns were treated as bound variables. Evans (1977, 1980) argued that although such treatment is appropriate for pronouns that occur in construction with their antecedents, it is not appropriate when the anaphoric pronoun occurs in a different construction from its antecedent. Evans called the latter *E-type pronouns*. He analyzed the semantics of these pronouns at length.

An example is: 'John owns a^1 horse and Mary rides it$_1$'. Here the pronoun ('it') refers to a horse that John owns.

Evans also discussed a variation of the E-type pronoun. It is similar to E-type defined above, but the pronoun is plural. An example is 'John owns some^1 horses and Bill vaccinates them$_1$'. The pronoun 'them' refers to some horses that John owns. Although the reference is ambiguous, it is usually taken to be all of those horses that John owns rather than some of those horses that John owns.

There is another variation of the E-type pronoun. It has been claimed that a universally quantified common noun cannot function as antecedent to a singular anaphoric pronoun (see Groenendijk and Stokhof 1991). For example, the following is anomalous: 'All^1 soldiers march past. He$_1$ salutes'. But not all sentences of this form are anomalous. A counterexample (from Groenendijk and Stokhof 1991) is: 'Every^1 player chooses a^2 marker. He$_1$ puts it$_2$ on square one'. Now consider the following list of examples:

(1)   All^1 soldiers march past. He$_1$ salutes.

(2)   Every^1 soldier marches past. He$_1$ salutes.

(3)   Each^1 soldier marches past. He$_1$ salutes.

(4)   Each of the^1 soldiers marches past. He$_1$ salutes.

(1) is definitely anomalous. (2) may be questioned. But (3) and (4) are quite proper. The explanation is linguistic rather than logical. Nida (1975, p. 106) points out that the determiners 'all', 'every', 'each', 'each of the', 'each one of the' are logically equivalent in that they all possess the "meaning components" *definiteness* and *plurality*, but they are not linguistically equivalent because they differ in the meaning component *distribution*.

When the determiner is low in the distribution component, the phrase in its scope denotes an undifferentiated collection. It is referred to by a *plural* pronoun, as in 'All[1] soldiers march past. They$_1$ salute'. However, when the determiner is high in the distribution component, the phrase in its scope denotes a collection of individuals. The collection may be referred to by either a singular or plural pronoun. If the pronoun is plural, the reference is to the undifferentiated collection. However, if the referring pronoun is *singular*, as in 'Each[1] soldier marches past. He$_1$ salutes', the pronoun refers to a generic representative or prototype of that collection of individuals. With this reading, the description is a generic universal description, indicated as follows: 'Each^{g1} soldier marches past. He$_1$ salutes'.

Some variations of this example are the following:

Every^{g1} player chooses some[2] markers. He$_1$ puts them$_2$ on square one.

Every^{g1} player chooses some[2] markers. He$_1$ puts some of them$_2$ on square one.

These examples again illustrate the point that linguistic considerations contribute to defining the relationship between antecedent and anaphor, and therefore must be used in determining the logical representation.

3.3 A-Type

Sommers (1982) pointed out that a pronoun can be ascriptive and not descriptive, denoting something that is antecedently believed (mistakenly) to exist. These he calls *A-type pronouns*. For example (ibid.): 'There is a[1] man at the door. No, it$_1$ is not a man. It$_1$ is a woman'. Here the first sentence is retracted but the reference is preserved. That is, the second sentence denies the first but still uses it to provide the anaphoric reference. The third sentence uses the same anaphoric reference to make the correction.

It is not necessary that these pronouns involve mistaken belief. An A-type pronoun can also find its reference in a sentence denied at the outset. For example, 'It is not true that a[1] dog dumped your garbage. It$_1$ was a bear'. This example also demonstrates that negation does not necessarily prevent an antecedent from remaining active.

3.4 Definite Description

As noted previously, a definite description may be used in place of a pronoun when the pronoun reference is ambiguous. Otherwise it functions like a pronoun, and may be E-type or A-type.

4   Syntax and Semantics of TFL

To provide a basis for the extension of TFL, a formal definition of TFL (without superscripts) is given. Define $\omega := \{0, 1, 2, \ldots\}$, the nonnegative integers, $\omega^* :=$ the finite strings over ω, and let $\alpha \in \omega^*$. $|\alpha|$ denotes the length of the string α. $\{\alpha\}$ denotes the set of integers occurring in α. The phrase 'term X with indices β' in TFL corresponds to the phrase 'formula X with free variables $\{x_i : i \in \beta\}$' in MPL.

The syntax of TFL with lexicon L (L is the set of nonlogical symbols) is defined as follows. (For every L, $\mathsf{T} \in L$, where T is the universal unary predicate denoting the entire universe.)

1. If $R \in L$ is an m-ary predicate and $|\alpha| = m$, then R_α is an n-ary term with indices β, where $\beta = \{\alpha\}$ and $n = card(\beta)$.

2. If X is an n-ary term with indices β, then $-(X)$ is an n-ary term with indices β.

3. If X, Y are l, m-ary terms (respectively) with indices β, γ (respectively), then $\langle +X + Y \rangle$ and $\langle -X + Y \rangle$ are n-ary terms with indices δ, where $\delta = \beta \cup \gamma$ and $n = card(\delta)$.

4. If X is a unary term with index i, and Y is an $(n + 1)$-ary term with indices β, where $i \in \beta$, then $(+X + Y)$ and $(-X + Y)$ are n-ary terms with indices $\beta - \{i\}$. (Remark: $(+X + Y)$ and $(-X + Y)$ are called *dyads*, with X the *subject term* and Y the *predicate term*. i is the *cropped index*.)

5. If X, Y are unary terms with index i, then $[+X + Y]$ and $[-X + Y]$ are nullary terms (*statements*) with indices ϕ.

6. If p, q are statements, then $[+p + q]$, $[-p + q]$, $+p$, and $-p$ are statements.

The following abbreviations will be used on occasion.

1. $[+R + Q]$ for $[+R_i + Q_i]$
2. $[-R + Q]$ for $[-R_i + Q_i]$
3. $\langle - -X - -Y \rangle$ for $-\langle +(-X) + (-Y) \rangle$
4. $(*X + Y)$ for $\langle +(+X + Y) + (-X + Y) \rangle$
5. $\langle +X + Y + Z \rangle$ for $\langle +\langle +X + Y \rangle + Z \rangle$
6. $+X + (Y + Z)$ for $+X + (+Y + Z)$
7. $+[X + Y]$ for $+[+X + Y]$
8. $(+Y + X)$ for $(+X + Y)$
9. $(+Y - X)$ for $(-X + Y)$

Note that TFL (in *dyadic normal form*) is an SOV (subject-object-verb) language. To bring it closer to English (an SVO language) the last two abbreviations will frequently be used. The result will be called *modified dnf*.

The semantics of TFL can be defined directly as follows. An *interpretation* of TFL with lexicon L is a pair $I = (I, F)$, where I is a nonempty set and F is a mapping on L such that for each $R \in L : F(R) \subseteq I^{ar(R)}$ ($ar(R)$ is the arity of R) and $F(\mathsf{T}) = I$. Let $\boldsymbol{d} = (d_0, d_1, \dots) \in I^\omega$ and $\boldsymbol{d}_{d_i}^d = (d_0, d_1, \dots, d_{i-1}, d, d_{i+1}, \dots)$. Y is *satisfied by* $\boldsymbol{d}$ in I, written $I, \boldsymbol{d} \models Y$ (or $I \models Y$ if Y is a statement), iff one of the following holds.

1. $Y = R_\alpha$, where $R \in L$ has arity m, $\alpha = i_0 i_1 \dots i_{m-1}$, and $(d_{i_0}, d_{i_1}, \dots, d_{i_{m-1}}) \in F(R)$.

2. $Y = -(X)$ and $I, \boldsymbol{d} \not\models X$.

3. $Y = \langle +X + Z \rangle$ and $I, \boldsymbol{d} \models X$ and $I, \boldsymbol{d} \models Z$.

4. $Y = \langle -X + Z \rangle$ and $I, \boldsymbol{d} \models X$ implies $I, \boldsymbol{d} \models Z$.

5. $Y = (+X + Z)$, where X is a unary term with index i, Z is a $(n + 1)$-ary term with indices β, $i \in \beta$, and there exists $d \in I$ such that $I, \boldsymbol{d}_{d_i}^d \models X$ and $I, \boldsymbol{d}_{d_i}^d \models Z$.

6. $Y = (-X + Z)$, where X is a unary term with index i, Z is a $(n + 1)$-ary term with indices β, $i \in \beta$, and for every $d \in I$: $I, \boldsymbol{d}_{d_i}^d \models X$ implies $I, \boldsymbol{d}_{d_i}^d \models Z$.

7. $Y = [+p + q]$, where p, q are statements, and $I \models p$ and $I \models q$.

8. $Y = [-p + q]$, where p, q are statements, and $I \models p$ implies $I \models q$.

5   Epsilon Terms and Gamma Terms

The syntax of TFL with lexicon L is extended to include epsilon terms and gamma terms as follows. Items 1 through 6 are the same as in the definition of the syntax of TFL given in section 4. The extension adds the following items.

7. If X is an n-ary term with indices β, where $i \in \beta$, then $\varepsilon_i(X)$ is an n-ary term with indices β.

8. If X is an n-ary term with indices β, where $i \in \beta$, then $\gamma_i(X)$ is an n-ary term with indices β.

The semantics of this extension of TFL is defined as follows. An *interpretation* of extended TFL with lexicon L is a tuple $J = (J, \Phi, \Psi, F)$, where

1. $J = I \dot{\cup} G$ is a disjoint union of nonempty sets (I is the set of *individuals*, G is the set of *prototypes* or *generics*);

2. $\Phi : Pow(I) \rightarrow I$ is a function (the *choice function*) with the property that $\Phi(D) \in D$ if $D \neq \phi$ and $\Phi(D) \in I$ otherwise;

3. $\Psi : G \rightarrow (Pow(I) - \{\phi\})$ is a function (the *extension function*), with the property that $g_1 = g_2$ iff $\Psi(g_1) = \Psi(g_2)$ (i.e., Ψ is injective); and

4. F is a mapping on L such that for each $R \in L : F(R) \subseteq J^{ar(R)}$ and $F(T) = J$, subject to the restriction that if $\boldsymbol{a} := (d_0, \ldots, d_{ar(R)-1}) \in F(R)$ and $g \in G$, then $\boldsymbol{a}^g_{d_i} \in F(R)$ iff $\Psi(g) \subseteq \{d \in I : \boldsymbol{a}^d_{d_i} \in F(R)\}$.

As before, let $\boldsymbol{d} = (d_0, d_1, \ldots) \in J^\omega$ and $\boldsymbol{d}^d_{d_i} = (d_0, d_1, \ldots, d_{i-1}, d, d_{i+1}, \ldots)$. Y is *satisfied by d in J*, written $J, \boldsymbol{d} \models Y$, iff one of the following holds. Items 1 through 8 are the same as in the definition of the semantics of TFL given in section 4, but with J substituted for I. The extension adds the following items.

9. $Y = \varepsilon_i(X)$, where X has indices β and $i \in \beta$, and $d_i = \Phi(\{d \in I : J, \boldsymbol{d}^d_{d_i} \models X\})$.

10. $Y = \gamma_i(X)$, where X has indices β and $i \in \beta$, and $d_i \in G$, and $\Psi(d_i) = \{d \in I : J, \boldsymbol{d}^d_{d_i} \models X\}$.

I and G correspond to the particular and universal (respectively) "urelements" of some ontological systems (see, e.g., Guizzardi, Herre, and Wagner 2001). An inconsistently ascribed individual, for example, 'the man at the door who is not a man after all', can be the value of the choice function Φ given a nonexistent class. In contrast to individuals, prototypes are never inconsistent. Prototypes are viewed as abstract elements, rather like the abstract objects of mathematics. As such, they exist *in re* (ibid.), that is, by virtue of their concrete instances (particular elements). Therefore, if $g \in G$ then $\Psi(g) \neq \phi$.

It is important to observe that ε- and γ-terms are singular terms (also called *uniquely denoting terms* or *UDTs*). Singular terms have the important property that Sommers refers to as "wild quantity": $(+X + Z) \equiv (-X + Z)$, where X is singular and Z is arbitrary. ε-terms have the additional property (the fundamental axiom of the ε-calculus)

(ε) $(+X + Z) \equiv (*\varepsilon_i(\langle +X + Z \rangle) + \langle +X + Z \rangle)$;

γ-terms have the additional property

(γ) $(+\gamma_i(X) + Z) \equiv (-X + Z)$.

These properties are imposed by the semantics. To simplify the following explanation, assume that X is unary with index i. Item 9 requires that $\varepsilon_i(X)$ denotes an arbitrary element of the denotation of X if the denotation of X is not vacuous; otherwise $\varepsilon_i(X)$ denotes an arbitrary element of I. Item 10 requires that $\gamma_i(X)$ denotes a generic element $g \in G$ such that the extension of g is the denotation of X in I. The restriction on F entails that the denotation of X includes every element of the extension of $g \in G$ iff it includes g as well. This claim is proved by straightforward induction on the structure of X. The generalization of this explanation to n-ary X is obvious. It simply requires restriction throughout to index i. An ε-term is intended to be an (arbitrary) *exemplar* of the total descriptive content of the existential description that gives rise to that ε-term. A γ-term is intended to be a *prototype* of the immediate descriptive content of the generic description that gives rise to that γ-term. It will be convenient in subsequent discussions to refer to the ε-terms and γ-terms as exemplars and prototypes, respectively.

The semantics presented above is extensional with respect to ε-terms. That is, $\varepsilon_i(X)$ denotes an arbitrary choice from the denotation of X. If Z is a term whose denotation is the same as the denotation of X, then $\varepsilon_i(X)$ and $\varepsilon_i(Z)$ have the same denotation as well. In some models 'rational animal' and 'human' might have the same extension. But they do not have the same intension or sense. Thus, it might be argued, they should not have the same representative or exemplar.

An extensional semantics is not the only possibility. An intensional alternative is also possible. The extensional semantics is simpler, but offers no compelling advantage. Indeed, it may impose a limitation that constitutes a disadvantage.

The following is a sketch of an intensional semantics. Define I to be the set of all closed ε-terms, where $\varepsilon_i(X)$ is *closed* if it has i as its only index. For construction of an interpretation in the universe of closed terms, see Mendelson 1987, lemma 2.16. Consider the dyad $(+X + Z)$, where X is a unary term with index i and Z is a $(n + 1)$-ary term with indices β and $i \in \beta$. Let $\beta' = \beta - \{i\}$, and $j \in \beta'$. Define

1. $\varepsilon_i(\langle +X + Z \rangle)[d_j] := \varepsilon_i((d_j + \langle +X + Z \rangle))$

2. $\varepsilon_i(\langle +X + Z \rangle)[\{d_j : j \in \beta'\}] := \varepsilon_i((d_j + \langle +X + Z \rangle))[\{d_k : k \in (\beta' - \{j\})\}]$

Note that $\varepsilon_i((d_j + \langle +X + Z \rangle)) \equiv \varepsilon_i(\langle +X + (d_j + Z) \rangle)$, and these ε-terms have indices $\beta - \{j\}$.

Now item 9 of the extensional semantics can be rewritten as

9'. $J, \boldsymbol{d} \models \varepsilon_i(\langle +X + Z \rangle)$, where X is a unary term with index i and Z is a $(n + 1)$-ary term with indices β and $i \in \beta$, iff $d_i = \varepsilon_i(\langle +X + Z \rangle)[\{d_j : j \in (\beta - \{i\})\}]$ Thus the exemplar of $\langle +X + Z \rangle$ is a closed ε-term, distinct for distinct $\langle +X + Z \rangle$. The choice function Φ is no longer needed. This alternative semantics was inspired by a suggestion of Slater.

6   Construal of Anaphora

Since this paper is concerned with anaphora, it will not address the more general issue of translation from English into TFL. Rather, the implicit definition of translation from English into TFL given in Sommers and Englebretsen 2000 will be assumed. Briefly, this definition is as follows. First each English sentence is *regimented* into *canonical form*. Examples of canonical form are: no X is Y, every X is Y, some X Rs a Y. Canonical form so closely parallels TFL (in modified dnf) that direct transcription usually can be performed. In the sequel, this will be referred to as the *standard translation*.

However, as some of the examples illustrate, a direct transcription between the English sentence and TFL is not always possible. In TFL, the construct $(+X + Z)$ requires that X is unary with index i and Z has indices β where $i \in \beta$. When direct transcription would lead to the ungrammatical $(+X + Z)$, where X has indices α ($card(\alpha) > 1$) and Z has indices β ($card(\beta) > 1$) and $i \in (\alpha \cap \beta)$ is to be the cropped index, the transcription must be modified to yield the equivalent $(+T_i + \langle +X + Z \rangle)$. (If this leads to another ungrammatical dyad, this stratagem must be repeated.) Failure to observe this requirement led to a spurious criticism of Sommers's Dictum de Omni (DDO) in my book review of Sommers and Englebretson 2000 appearing in my 2002. In the special case where this modification yields $(+T_i + \langle +X + Z + W_i \rangle)$ (W a unary predicate), the equivalence $(+T_i + \langle +X + Z + W_i \rangle) \equiv (+W_i + \langle +X + Z \rangle)$ can be used to get a more direct construal. This construal is used in several of the examples presented in the sequel.

The antecedent-anaphor combinations to be considered are as follows.

type	antecedent	anaphor		
		sing.pron.	plur.pron.	def.desc.
B	PNS	B-PNS-PS		
	ID	B-ID-PS		

	ED	B-ED-PS	B-ED-PP	
	UD		B-UD-PP	
	GID	B-GID-PS		
	GDD	B-GDD-PS		
	BP		B-BP-PP	
	GUD	B-GUD-PS		
E	PNS	E-PNS-PS		
	ID	E-ID-PS		E-ID-DD
	ED	E-ED-PS	E-ED-PP	E-ED-DD
	UD		E-UD-PP	E-UD-DD
	GID	E-GID-PS		E-GID-DD
	GDD	E-GDD-PS		E-GDD-DD
	BP		E-BP-PP	E-BP-DD
	GUD	E-GUD-PS		
A	ID	A-ID-PS		A-ID-DD

(PNS = proper noun singular, ID = indefinite description, ED = existential description, DD = definite description, UD = universal description, GID = generic indefinite description, GDD = generic definite description, BP = bare plural, GUD = generic universal description, PS = pronoun singular, PP = pronoun plural.)

Examples of these antecedent-anaphor combinations follow.

B-PNS-PS: John^1 loves his$_1$ mother.

B-ID-PS: A^1 boy loves his$_1$ mother.

B-ED-PS: Some^1 boy eats a^2 candy that he$_1$ likes.

B-ED-PP: Some^1 boys eat a^2 candy that they$_1$ like.

B-UD-PP: All^1 children love their$_1$ mothers.

B-GID-PS: A^{g1} lioness protects her$_1$ cubs.

B-GDD-PS: The^{g1} wolf hunts with its$_1$ pack.

B-BP-PP: Pretty women^{g1} get their$_1$ way.

B-GUD-PS: Every^{g1} man loves his$_1$ mother.

E-PNS-PS: Caesar^1 came. He$_1$ conquered.

E-ID-PS: A^1 boy ran in. He$_1$ shouted.

E-ID-DD: A^1 boy waved to a^2 man. The$_1$ boy smiled.

E-ED-PS: Some^1 boy sees a^2 dog. He$_1$ smiles.

E-ED-PP: John owns some^1 horses and Bill vaccinates them$_1$.

E-ED-DD: John owns some^1 horses and Bill vaccinates the$_1$ horses.

E-UD-PP: All[1] bikes were shiny. They$_1$ were new.

E-UD-DD: All[1] soldiers saluted all[2] officers. The$_2$ officers saluted them$_1$ back.

E-GID-PS: A^{g1} Corvette is expensive. It$_1$ always draws attention.

E-GID-DD: A^{g1} dog always likes to chase a^{g2} cat. The$_2$ cat is not amused.

E-GDD-PS: The^{g1} border collie is full of energy. It$_1$ needs daily exercise.

E-GDD-DD: The^{g1} dog is a natural enemy of the^{g2} cat. The$_2$ cat runs away.

E-BP-PP: Cats^{g1} are difficult to train. They$_1$ do not try to please.

E-BP-DD: Women^{g1} are more sensitive than men^{g2}. The$_1$ woman is generally smarter too.

E-GUD-PS: Every^{g1} man grabbed a^2 hat. He$_1$ put it$_2$ on his$_1$ head.

A-ID-PS: A[1] boy is selling cookies. No, it$_1$ is a girl, not a boy.

A-ID-DD: A[1] boy is selling cookies. No, the$_1$ boy selling cookies is actually a girl.

6.1 B-Type

When the antecedent c-commands the anaphor (i.e., a B-type anaphor), the anaphor is translated *null* if the pronoun is nominative or reflexive, and is translated *poss$_{jk}$* (and conjoined to the object of the pronoun) if the pronoun is possessive. j is the index of the antecedent, and k is the index of the object of the pronoun. The following examples illustrate this. 'John[1] loves his$_1$ mother' translates to $*J_1 + (\langle +L_{12} + poss_{12}\rangle + M_2)$. In this and subsequent translations, a word is symbolized by the first letter of the word, or if that letter has been used, by the next consonant of the word. 'A[1] boy eats a candy that he$_1$ likes' translates to $+B_1 + (\langle +E_{12} + L_{12}\rangle + C_2)$. The latter translation of B-type pronouns is essentially the same as using superscripts to co-index the translations of the antecedent and anaphor, then applying IPE (internal pronoun elimination) to remove the redundant anaphor translation.

6.2 E-Type

Slater (1986, 1988a,b) supports Evans's claims and further argues that Hilbert's ε-logic is especially well suited for representation and explication of E-type pronouns. The treatment given here closely follows Evans and Slater.

Recall the example from section 3: 'John owns a[1] horse and Mary rides it$_1$'. It was observed that the pronoun 'it' refers to the indefinite description 'a horse that John owns'. This reference is precisely rendered by the ε-term $\varepsilon_1(\langle +H_1 + (+J_2 + O_{21})\rangle)$. Therefore a translation is $+[+J_2 + (+O_{21} + H_1)]$ $+ [+M_3 + (+R_{31} + E_1)]$, where E is $\varepsilon_1(\langle +H_1 + (+J_2 + O_{21})\rangle)$. By property (ε), one obtains $+[+J_2 + (+E_1 + O_{21})] + [+M_3 + (+E_1 + R_{31})]$, which is equivalent to $+E_1$ $+ (\langle +\langle +H_1 + (+J_2 + O_{21})\rangle + (+M_3 + R_{31})\rangle)$, that is, E is a horse that John owns and Mary rides.

This treatment is easily extended to sentences such as 'A[1] farmer owns a[2] horse and he[1] rides it[2]'. Here the pronoun 'he' refers to 'a farmer who owns a horse' and 'it' refers to 'a horse that is owned by that farmer'. Therefore the sentence is translated $+[+F_1 + (+O_{12} + H_2)] + [+E_1 + (+R_{12} + E_2')]$, where E is $\varepsilon_1(\langle +F_1 + (+O_{12} + H_2)\rangle)$ and E' is $\varepsilon_2(\langle +H_2 + (+E_1 + O_{12})\rangle)$. This is equivalent to $+E_1 + (\langle +F_1 + (+E_2' + \langle +H_2 + \langle +O_{12} + R_{12}\rangle\rangle)\rangle)$.

Where the antecedent is existential but not indefinite, the anaphor is plural. For example, 'John owns some[1] horses and Bill vaccinates them[1]' and 'John owns some[1] horses and Bill vaccinates the[1] horses'. Here the translation is $+[+J_1 + (O_{12} + H_2)] + [+B_3 + (+V_{34} - \langle +H_4 + (J_5 + O_{54})\rangle)]$.

Where the antecedent is universal, the anaphor may be either singular or plural. An example of the former is: 'Every[1] man chose a[1] hat. He[1] put it[2] on his[1] head'. This is translated: $+[-M_1 + (C_{12} + H_2)] + [*G_1 + (\langle +(P_{123} * E_2)$ $+ poss_{13}\rangle + D_3)]$, where $G = \gamma_1(M_1)$ and $E = \varepsilon_2(\langle +H_2 + (*G_1 + C_{12})\rangle)$.

An example of the latter is: 'All[1] bikes were shiny. They[1] were new'. This is translated: $+[-B_1 + S_1] + [-B_2 + N_2]$.

6.3 A-Type

Recall the example of an A-type anaphor from section 3: 'There is a[1] man at the door. No, it[1] is not a man. It[1] is a woman'. The unary expression $\langle +M + D\rangle$ denotes $\emptyset$ and so $\varepsilon(\langle +M + D\rangle)$ denotes an arbitrary choice from I. Use of ε-terms permits reference and attribution to be independent. This facilitates ascriptive anaphora as well as fictions (Slater 1987). This feature of the ε-operator is not shared by similar operators (e.g., the η-operator). For an extensive discussion of the value of this feature, see Slater 1988. The translation of this example is similar to an E-type translation: $+[*\varepsilon_1(\langle +M_1 + D_1\rangle) + (-M_1)] + [*\varepsilon_1(\langle +M_1 + D_1\rangle) + W_1]$.

6.4 Summary of Translation

This subsection gives in summary form a formal definition of the translation of antecedent-anaphor pairs to TFL. It is assumed that the English sentence(s) have been regimented into canonical form SP, where S is the subject and P is the predicate, also in canonical form. The anaphor may be located in the first sentence (if it is B-type) or may be located in a subsequent sentence (otherwise). If the parse is appropriate, the exemplar $\varepsilon_i(X)$ (or prototype $\gamma_i(X)$) is fully instantiated (closed), that is, all free indices (except i) are instantiated.

For brevity, let π represent the translation of the immediate descriptive content of the antecedent, and τ represent the translation of the total descriptive content of the antecedent.

1. The anaphor is c-commanded by its antecedent (the anaphor is located in the first sentence):

   (a) The antecedent is proper:

      i. The anaphor is singular:

         antecedent: translated standardly (i.e., $*\pi$)

         anaphor: translated *null* if nominative or reflexive; $poss_{ij}$ if possessive (i is the index of the antecedent, j is the index of the object of the pronoun)

   (b) The antecedent is existential:

      i. The anaphor is singular:

         antecedent: translated standardly

         anaphor: translated *null* if nominative or reflexive; $poss_{ij}$ if possessive (i is the index of the antecedent, j is the index of the object of the pronoun)

      ii. The anaphor is plural:

         antecedent: translated

         standardly anaphor: translated *null* if nominative or reflexive; $poss_{ij}$ if possessive (i is the index of the antecedent, j is the index of the object of the pronoun)

   (c) The antecedent is universal:

      i. The anaphor is plural:

         antecedent: translated standardly

         anaphor: translated *null* if nominative or reflexive; $poss_{ij}$ if possessive (i is the index of the antecedent, j is the index of the object of the pronoun)

(d) The antecedent is generic:

    i. The anaphor is singular:

       antecedent: translated $*\gamma_i(\pi)$

       anaphor: translated *null* if nominative or reflexive; $poss_{ij}$ if possessive (i is the index of the antecedent, j is the index of the object of the pronoun)

    ii. The anaphor is plural:

       antecedent: translated $-\pi$

       anaphor: translated *null* if nominative or reflexive; $poss_{ij}$ if possessive (i is the index of the antecedent, j is the index of the object of the pronoun)

2. The anaphor is not c-commanded by its antecedent:

  (a) The antecedent is proper:

    i. The anaphor is singular:

       antecedent: translated standardly (i.e., $*\pi$)

       anaphor: translated $*\pi$

  (b) The antecedent is existential:

    i. The anaphor is singular:

       antecedent: translated standardly

       anaphor: translated $*\varepsilon_i(\tau)$

    ii. The anaphor is plural:

       antecedent: translated standardly

       anaphor: translated $-\tau$

  (c) The antecedent is universal:

    i. The anaphor is plural:

       antecedent: translated standardly

       anaphor: translated $-\pi$

  (d) The antecedent is generic:

    i. The anaphor is singular:

       antecedent: translated $*\gamma_i(\pi)$

       anaphor: translated $*\gamma_i(\pi)$

    ii. The anaphor is plural:

       antecedent: translated $-\pi$

       anaphor: translated $-\pi$

Using this definition of the translation, the previous examples of antecedent-anaphor combinations are given below.

English: John[1] loves his[1] mother.

TFL: $*J_1 + (\langle +L_{12} + poss_{12} \rangle + M_2)$

English: A[1] boy loves his[1] mother.

TFL: $+B_1 + (\langle +L_{12} + poss_{12} \rangle + M_2)$

English: Some[1] boy eats a[2] candy that he[1] likes.

TFL: $+B_1 + (\langle +E_{12} + L_{12} \rangle + C_2)$

English: All[1] children love their[1] mothers.

TFL: $-C_1 + (\langle +L_{12} + poss_{12} \rangle + M_2)$

English: A[g1] lioness protects her[1] cubs.

TFL: $*\gamma_1(L_1) + (\langle -poss_{12} + P_{12} \rangle - C_2)$

English: The[g1] wolf hunts with its[1] pack.

TFL: $*\gamma_1(W_1) + (\langle +H_{12} + poss_{12} \rangle + P_2)$

English: Pretty women[g1] get their[1] way.

TFL: $*\gamma_1(\langle +P_1 + W_1 \rangle) + (\langle G_{12} + poss_{12} \rangle + Y_2)$

English: Every[g1] man loves his[1] mother.

TFL: $*\gamma_1(N_1) + (\langle +L_{12} + poss_{12} \rangle + M_2)$

English: Caesar[1] came. He[1] conquered.

TFL: $+[*C_1 + M_1] + [*C_1 + N_1]$

English: A[1] boy ran in. He[1] shouted.

TFL: $+[B_1 + R_1] + [*E_1 + S_1]$, where $E = \varepsilon_1(\langle +B_1 + R_1 \rangle)$.

English: A[1] boy waved to a[2] man. The[1] boy smiled.

TFL: $+[B_1 + (W_{12} + M_2)] + [*E_1 + S_1]$, where $E = \varepsilon_1(\langle +B_1 + (W_{12} + M_2) \rangle)$

English: Some[1] boy sees a[2] dog. He[1] smiles.

TFL: $+[B_1 + (S_{12} + D_2)] + [*E_1 + S_1]$, where $E = \varepsilon_1(\langle +B_1 + (S_{12} + D_2) \rangle)$

English: John owns some[1] horses and Bill vaccinates them[1].

TFL: $+[*J_1 + (O_{12} + H_2)] + [*B_3 + (V_{12} - (\langle +H_2 + (*J_1 + O_{12}) \rangle))]$

English: John owns some[1] horses and Bill vaccinates the[1] horses.

TFL: $+[*J_1 + (O_{12} + H_2)] + [*B_3 + (V_{12} - (\langle +H_2 + (*J_1 + O_{12}) \rangle))]$

English: All[1] bikes were shiny. They[1] were new.

TFL: $+[-B_1 + S_1] + [-B_1 + N_1]$

English: All[1] soldiers saluted all[2] officers. The$_2$ officers saluted them$_1$ back.

TFL: $+[-S_1 + (L_{12} - O_2)] + [-O_2 + (B_{23} - S_3)]$

English: A[g1] Corvette is expensive. It$_1$ always draws attention.

TFL: $+[*\gamma_1(C_1) + E_1] + [*\gamma_1(C_1) + D_1]$

English: A[g1] dog always likes to chase a[g2] cat. The$_2$ cat is not amused.

TFL: $+[*G_1 + (L_{12} * G_2')] + [*G_2' + (-A_2)]$, where $G = \gamma_1(D_1)$ and $G' = \gamma_2(C_2)$

English: The[g1] border collie is full of energy. It$_1$ needs daily exercise.

TFL: $+[*\gamma_1(B_1) + F_1] + [*\gamma_1(B_1) + N_1]$

English: The[g1] dog is a natural enemy of the[g2] cat. The$_2$ cat runs away.

TFL: $+[*\gamma_1(D_1) + (E_{12} * \gamma_2(C_2))] + [*\gamma_2(C_2) + R_2]$

English: Cats[g1] are difficult to train. They$_1$ do not try to please.

TFL: $+[-C_1 + D_1] + [-C_1 + (-P_1)]$

English: Women[g1] are more sensitive than men[g2]. The$_1$ woman is generally smarter too.

TFL: $+[*\gamma_1(W_1) + (R_{12} + *\gamma_2(M_2))] + [*\gamma_1(W_1) + (S_{12} * \gamma_2(M_2))]$

English: Every[g1] man grabbed a[2] hat. He$_1$ put it$_2$ on his$_1$ head.

TFL: $+[*G_1 + (R_{12} + H_2)] + [*G_1 + (\langle + (P_{123} * E_2) + poss_{13}\rangle + D_3)]$, where $G = \gamma_1(M_1)$ and $E = \varepsilon_2(\langle +H_2 + (*G_1 + R_{12})\rangle)$.

English: A[1] boy is selling cookies. No, it$_1$ is a girl, not a boy.

TFL: $+[*E_1 + G_1] + [*E_1 + (-B_1)]$, where $E = \varepsilon_1(\langle +B_1 + S_1\rangle)$

English: A[1] boy is selling cookies. No, the$_1$ boy selling cookies is actually a girl.

TFL: $+[*E_1 + G_1]$, where $E = \varepsilon_1(\langle +B_1 + S_1\rangle)$

7 Discussion

The treatment of anaphora presented here is successful in handling a variety of anaphora in a manner that is both accurate and in the spirit of Sommers's term logic. It enjoys another notable success and suffers a notable failure. These are described in this section.

7.1 Donkey Sentences

The so-called donkey sentence (Geach 1962) presents a puzzle that has inspired a number of theoretical developments. Consider 'If a[1] farmer owns

a^2 donkey, he_1 beats it_2'. Although this sentence appears to contain only indefinite descriptions, it imparts universal force to both subject and object, to entail: for every farmer and for every donkey, if the former is in the *own* relation to the latter, then the former is in the *beat* relation to the latter as well. However, this sentence contains not particular indefinite descriptions, but generic indefinite descriptions. Thus a more accurate parse is: 'If a^{g1} farmer owns a^{g2} donkey, he_1 beats it_2'. That is, such a sentence should be read as an assertion about generic representatives. It is therefore translated: $-[*\gamma_1(F_1) + (*\gamma_2(D_2) + O_{12})] + [*\gamma_1(F_1) + (*\gamma_2(D_2) + B_{12})]$. Because γ-terms are singular and have property (γ), this translation is equivalent to: $-F_1 + (-D_2 + \langle -O_{12} + B_{12}\rangle)$. That is, for every farmer and for every donkey, if the farmer owns the donkey, then he beats it.

Sentences having similar structure are the following. They are translated similarly.

If a^{g1} hotel has a^{g2} thirteenth floor, it_2 is assigned number fourteen.

If a^{g1} man has a^{g2} beard, he_1 trims it_2.

A more challenging example is (see Groenendijk and Stokhof 1991):

If a man has a quarter, he puts it in the parking meter.

This sentence has two possible parses:

If a^{g1} man has a^2 quarter, he_1 puts it_2 in the parking meter.

If a^{g1} man has a^{g2} quarter, he_1 puts it_2 in the parking meter.

Common knowledge dictates that the first is the appropriate one. The second parse entails that every man puts every quarter that he has in the parking meter. Given the first parse, the translation is:

$$-[*\gamma_1(M_1) + (+H_{12} + Q_2)] + [*\gamma_1(M_1) + (+P_{12} * \varepsilon_2(\langle +Q_2 + (*\gamma_1(M_1) + H_{12})\rangle))]$$

This translation entails $-M_1 + (+E_2 + \langle -\langle +Q_2 + (*\gamma_1(M_1) + H_{12})\rangle + P_{12}\rangle)$, where $E = \varepsilon_2(\langle +Q_2 + (*\gamma_1(M_1) + H_{12})\rangle)$.

It might be mentioned in passing that one can hold the view that conditional sentences are by their nature ambiguous relative to universal versus existential (or probabilistic) reading. For a presentation of this position, see Slater 1988b.

7.2 Coordinating Conjunctions

The theory of the logic of English as represented in TFL is characterized by Englebretsen as "Aristotelian" (Englebretsen 1989). In Aristotelian theories a statement consists of a subject term and a predicate term combined by a "formative" or functor such as 'some . . . is/are. . . .' Coordinating conjunctions pose a problem for any theory of the logic of English, but are particularly troublesome for Aristotelian theories (Böttner 1994; Purdy 1991). When anaphora are a part of the theory, coordinating conjunctions become extremely problematic.

Consider the sentence 'John likes Mary and Sue'. Employing the translation assumed thus far, one translates $*J_1 + (+\langle *M_2 * S_2\rangle + L_{12})$. But $\langle *M_2 * S_2\rangle$ has an empty denotation unless Mary is Sue. One might be tempted to infer that 'and' is used to form a union 'and' so take and as synonymous with 'or' to get the translation $*J_1 + (+\langle - -M_2 - -S_2\rangle + L_{12})$. But this statement is consistent with $+[*J_1 + (*M_2 + L_{12})] + [*J_1 + (-(*S_2 + L_{12}))]$, which is certainly not intended. Note too that 'and' and 'or' have essential uses as in 'John or Mary will attend, but John and Mary will not attend (because one must babysit)'.

A more promising view (Harris 1982) is that occurrences of coordinating conjunctions derive from coordinating conjunctions between sentences and that their occurrences elsewhere are simply "locutions of laziness." Thus 'John likes Mary and Sue' is a lazy rendition of 'John likes Mary and John likes Sue'.

But coordinating conjunctions cannot always be raised to sentence level. Consider 'Some boys like Mary and Sue'. Raising 'and' to sentence level results in 'Some boys like Mary and some boys like Sue'. This is consistent with 'No boy likes Mary and likes Sue', which is unintended. In this case, 'and' must be raised only to the verb phrase level: 'Some boys like Mary and like Sue'.

Now introduce anaphora. B-type anaphora require more complex treatment but are tractable. For example, 'John and Bill love their mother'. A translation is: $+[+J_1 + (L_{13} + \langle +\langle +M_3 + (+J_1 + poss_{13})\rangle + (+B_2 + poss_{23}))\rangle)] + [+B_2 + (L_{23} + \langle +\langle +M_3 + (+J_1 + poss_{13})\rangle + (+B_2 + poss_{23}))\rangle)]$. This translation preserves the meaning that both John and Bill have the same mother.

E-type anaphora are less tractable: 'A man and a boy entered. They smiled'. When expanded these sentences become: 'A man entered and a boy entered. The man smiled and the boy smiled'. The plural pronoun is replaced by two (singular) definite descriptions. A similar example is: 'A boy and a girl visited. They brought cookies'.

It appears that the regimentation necessary constitutes a *transformational phase* of the translation.

An alternative approach was proposed by Montague (Dowty, Wall, and Peters 1981). In the Montagovian approach, a noun phrase denotes a set of properties (i.e., a set of sets) called a *sublimation*. These sets can be operated on by intersection (denoting 'and') and union (denoting 'or'). This approach is not as intuitive and is not in the spirit of the terminist approach of Sommers.

Acknowledgment

I am indebted to Michael Böttner and B. Hartley Slater, who read earlier versions of this paper and offered valuable suggestions for improvement.

References

Böttner, Michael. 1994. "Open Problems in Relational Grammar." In Paul Humphreys (ed.), *Patrick Suppes: Scientific Philosopher*, vol. 3, 19–39. Dordrecht: Kluwer.

Dowty, David R., Robert E. Wall, and Stanley Peters. 1981. *Introduction to Montague Semantics*. Dordrecht: D. Reidel.

Englebretsen, George. 1989. "Formatives." *Notre Dame Journal of Formal Logic* 30 (1989): 382–389.

Evans, Gareth. 1977. "Pronouns, Quantifiers, and Relative Clauses (I)." *Canadian Journal of Philosophy* 7: 467–536.

Evans, Gareth. 1980. "Pronouns." *Linguistic Inquiry* 11: 337–362.

Geach, P. 1962. *Reference and Generality*. Ithaca: Cornell University Press.

Groenendijk, J., and M. Stokhof. 1991. "Dynamic Predicate Logic." *Linguistics and Philosophy* 14: 39–100.

Guizzardi, Giancarlo, Heinrich Herre, and Gerd Wagner. 2001. "On the General Ontological Foundations of Conceptual Modeling." *21st International Conference on Conceptual Modeling: Lecture Notes in Computer Science*. Berlin: Springer-Verlag.

Harris, Zellig. 1982. *A Grammar of English on Mathematical Principles*. New York John Wiley and Sons.

Lawler, John. 1997. "Ask a Linguist for May 1997–June 1997." At URL: http://www.linguistlist.org/~ask-ling/archive-1997.5/msg00000.html.

Matthews, P. H. 1997. *The Concise Oxford Dictionary of Linguistics*. Oxford: Oxford University Press.

Mendelson, Elliot. 1987. *Introduction to Mathematical Logic.* Monterey: Wadsworth and Brooks.

Nida, Eugene A. 1975. *Compositional Analysis of Meaning.* The Hague: Mouton.

Neale, Stephen. 1990. *Descriptions.* Cambridge, Mass.: The MIT Press.

Purdy,W. C. 1991. "Coordinating Conjunctions in Aristotelian Theories of English." *School of Computer and Information Science Technical Report,* Syracuse University, Syracuse.

Purdy, W. C. 2002. Book Review: Fred Sommers and George Englebretsen, *An Invitation to Formal Reasoning: The Logic of Terms,* Ashgate, Aldershot, 2000. In: *Bulletin of Symbolic Logic* 8: 97–100.

Riemsdijk, Henk van, and Edwin Williams. 1986. *Introduction to the Theory of Grammar.* Cambridge, Mass.: The MIT Press.

Slater, B. H. 1986. "E-type Pronouns and ε-terms." *Canadian Journal of Philosophy* 16: 27–38.

Slater, B. H. 1987. "Fictions." *British Journal of Aesthetics* 27: 145–153.

Slater, B. H. 1988a. *Prolegomena to Formal Logic.* Aldershot: Avebury.

Slater, B. H. 1988b. "Subjunctives." *Critica* 20: 97–106.

Sommers, Fred. 1982. *The Logic of Natural Language.* Oxford: Clarenden Press.

Sommers, Fred, and George Englebretsen. 2000. *An Invitation to Formal Reasoning.* Aldershot: Ashgate.

8 An Elementary Term Logic for Physically Realizable Models of Information

Steven Lindell

Conceptual Introduction

Traditional logic has nearly faded into obscurity in the twentieth century, eclipsed by tremendous developments in modern logic. The purpose of this volume is to recognize the pioneering work of Fred Sommers, who has championed its revival on philosophical grounds by articulating its familiar correspondence with natural language and emphasizing a deductive system that is cognitively more similar to human thought than that of modern predicate logic. Indeed, a beautifully succinct summary of this view is that Sommers believes in "the classical idea of having a psychologically realistic theory of reasoning based on ordinary grammatical analysis."[1]

Inspired by his approach, one of the primary aims of this essay is to show that traditional logic may provide important insights when describing properties of symbolic information represented in physical form. The goal of showing that classical subject-predicate term logic may have application to fundamental principles in the philosophical foundations of computation can be seen as a stepping stone toward a "physiologically realistic theory of computing based on ordinary informational analysis." (Here, the term 'physiological' is being used in its more obscure but original meaning of 'pertaining to the material universe or to natural science'.)

Although originally inspired by the close connection between traditional logic and natural methods of representing information, I hope to show how an enhanced symbolic version might also provide a more perspicuous tool for the analysis of first-order definability over physically scalable models of information—identified as highly uniform classes of finite structures. In bridging an immaterial view of data with its material realization in memory, I hope to shed light on the ultimate limits of a physically constrained mathematical theory. After all, human thought is also presumably physically based (though probably not indefinitely scalable).

Computer Science

Computer science is unique among the sciences in that it encompasses both *software*, abstract ideas whose underlying theory is mathematical, and *hardware*, material objects governed by physical law. The fundamental mathematical theory behind software can be broken down further into *data structures*, which model the information stored in a computer, and *algorithms*, the computational processes that transform that information. Algorithms are always developed so that in theory they could operate on any amount of data, given sufficient time and space to do so, and efficiency ratings (computational complexity) are based on their asymptotic consumption of these resources. Computers are complex machines carefully engineered to execute algorithms, storing and processing information according to precisely specified rules of behavior. When provided with a program that defines those rules (the algorithm) and the input on which to operate (the data), these theoretical aspects can materialize in a hardware implementation, requiring *matter* for information and *energy* for computation. The focus in this essay will be on the informational aspects; computations will be the subject of a subsequent paper.

When information is stored as data in memory, it takes on properties of *size* and *shape*. The amount of data that can fit is limited by the memory's capacity, and how that data is arranged limits the memory's access speed. Aside from reliability, capacity and speed are the two most important aspects of memory performance. To acquire a deeper understanding of this, we will embark on a theoretical analysis of how information makes its way from logical structure to physical representation. What possible connection could there be between the mathematics of information and the technology of data storage? The answer can be found when the quantity of data exceeds any predetermined bound.

Section Summary

The essay begins in section 1 by arguing that the material requirement of storing arbitrarily large amounts of information at bounded density necessitates an asymptotic view of how data is shaped in space. In section 2, I illustrate the various ways that information in the form of relational facts can be represented mathematically. In section 3, I explain the various methods of memory organization that are used to store data physically. Section 4 describes the uniform symbolic structures I am using as models of information, upon which the specially designed logic will work. This logic, consisting of functionally defined terms that are numerically quantified into statements, is detailed in section 5. Immediately following is the main result in section 6, which demonstrates equivalence with first-order definability. The essay is summarized in section 7. Other than a basic understanding of first-order logic, no additional background in mathematics or physics is required to understand this essay.

1 Philosophical Foundations

Plenty of Room at the Bottom

In 1959, Richard Feynman gave his now famous lecture on the hitherto enormous untapped potential of nanotechnology to store information at incredibly high density, challenging engineers and physicists to reproduce the entire contents of the *Encyclopedia Britannica* on the head of a pin. He showed that there was more than enough room to accomplish what seemed at the time like an incredible task. Indeed, this much information storage is already available in a consumer device about the size of a quarter, and the ability to write atomically has already been demonstrated in the laboratory. All of this has been made possible by the exponential growth in computer technology, currently doubling storage density in under a year. What this means is that the size and cost of storing a *bit*, the smallest unit or datum of information, has been periodically halving as a result of improvements that have made it possible to read and write data at progressively smaller scales of distance using ever smaller amounts of material.

But Not an Unlimited Amount

This rapid growth in information density might lead one to believe that there are no practical limits to the amount of data that can be stored in various types of storage devices. For example, in under a decade it will be possible to store the entire contents of the Library of Congress in a device the size of a postage stamp. But despite these startling accomplishments, such increases in density cannot go on forever. In just a few decades we will reach scales at which the very structure of matter itself prohibits further progress. No amount of cleverness will be able to exceed these limits without breaking the known laws of physics. At these minuscule scales, when we have reached the density limit of matter, the ideas put forward here begin to have application.

No Room to Go But Out

There is an obvious impact of the above issues on the field of computers due to a fundamental philosophical difference between mathematics and physics: the quantum nature of our universe implies that there is a smallest scale (say, the Planck length); but the infinitude of natural numbers implies that there is no largest number. No arbitrary limit can be placed on the amount of data that a mathematical model of information must deal with: it is clearly boundless. But the amount of matter that can be confined to a given amount of space is not. When storing arbitrarily large amounts of information, there is nowhere to go but out.

Large Numbers

We are used to dealing with numbers in ordinary life up to a certain size, and assuming by extrapolation from those experiences that operations such as counting could, at least in principle, go on forever. From these simple observations we can deduce at an early age that there is no largest integer, even if the notion of infinity does not yet sit entirely comfortably with us. But this essay requires something more—a fact about numbers that is not often appreciated even by adults. Just as there is no largest number, there are no large numbers. It is only by context that we can assign relative notions of largeness to numbers. In an absolute sense, compared with the unbounded infinitude of all numbers, no number can be deemed mathematically large.

The Importance of Scale

Though simple to state, this principle can be hard to accept. Perhaps it is because most scientific endeavors study phenomena at some scale or other, even though that scale may be extremely small (say, particle physics) or large (say, astronomy). On the other hand, mathematics does not even concern itself with scale, being as comfortable with one real number as any other. Mathematics also deals with ideas concerning arbitrary, even infinite, size. But the difference here is more substantial—in most situations there is no "implementation" envisaged. Even in areas of mathematics where computational techniques are available, "experiments" are necessarily finite approximations of more general cases that involve arbitrarily large discrete instances or continuous precision.

Why should the existence of physical limits place any restriction on mathematical ideas? The answer is it does not, until one wants to implement those ideas. Basically, this is what computer science is all about: taking abstract objects and making them real. This is different than engineering, where one wants a bridge of a certain length, a rocket of a certain size, or a train that can go at a certain speed. There is never the intention that the techniques should or could scale to an arbitrary degree. But this is exactly what happens in computer science. This requirement to operate at *any scale* illustrates the fundamental distinction between computer science and the rest of the sciences.

The Role of the Computer

Computers are unique in that they implement abstract mathematical concepts in the concrete physical world. It is not sufficient to have an idea of how to solve a problem; its efficacy must be demonstrated in the material world even if only on small examples. In part, this explains the importance of the "demo," which replaces the role of the experiment in the natural sciences (Hartmanis 1995). One can then argue by extrapolation how the implementation could be extended, at least in principle, to work on problems of any size. This will be an important guiding principle for what follows. For to really understand information and computation, we must also be concerned with the physical constraints nature places on their realization. Theoretical models should include their instantiation in the computer—in effect building in the tools required to carry them out.

Limits to Asymptotic Shape

The existences of limits imposed by nature are all that concern us here, not their actual values. All we really need is to acknowledge that matter cannot be compressed to arbitrarily high density. That is to say, there must be a fixed finite bound on the amount of information that can be stored in a given amount of space. This simple observation has profound implications for how data can be structured. Huge collections of bits cannot be arranged in completely arbitrary ways. Their imposition in space yields a more limited variety of possible models, which will be studied in this essay. In other words, since no amount of information is large in any absolute sense, the physics of storing arbitrarily large amounts of information determines the mathematical form of that information. In short, size ultimately influences shape. In the next sections we proceed from the abstract mathematical structure of information to its concrete material realization in physical space.

2   The Mathematical Representation of Information

Information can be seen as a collection of facts that impart knowledge by their context. Hence an individual piece of information can be viewed as a *fact* over a given domain of discourse. Each fact relates to one or more individuals of its domain. An example is:

Fact: John is married to Jane.

An information structure consisting of facts like these is represented mathematically by a *relational model*. In all such models, facts about a domain of discourse are represented as *tuples* between those elements, and similar types of facts are collected together to form relations. For example, the binary relation 'is married to' between husband and wife determines a set of ordered pairs *Couple* = {(m, f): male m is married to female f} so that the individual fact above is stated *Couple* (*John, Jane*). In general, a relation can be formed from any set of tuples of a common length, which determines its *arity*.

The Role of Logic

Logic is a formal language for expressing properties and explaining conclusions about the information being modeled. When a property is defined by a question it is called a *query*. For example, we might wish to check whether *Couple* represents a matching:

Query: Is each (male) person married to exactly one other (female) person?

In this essay we are concerned only with queries about static situations of information structures. First-order logic is well suited to this job, expressing many (but not all) properties of interest. A subsequent essay will focus on a fixed-point logic extension to cover dynamic properties in order to capture computations. Basic background on relational models from the computer science perspective can be found in any standard book on databases such as Ullman 1982. Basic foundations of mathematical logic are covered in any introductory textbook such as Enderton 2001.

Representing Relations

Relational models can be represented in various ways. In a *structure* they are abstract sets of tuples, in a *database* they are tables, and in a *graph* they are collections of nodes.

Abstract method: Finite structures   Since we are studying stored information, we assume relations with an arbitrarily large but finite number of facts, giving us a finite domain. Given a fixed collection of relations $R_1, \ldots, R_m$, where a_i is the arity of R_i, a *finite structure* $\mathbf{A} = \langle A, R_1, \ldots, R_m \rangle$ that combines them is said to have signature $a_1, \ldots, a_m$ (its total arity a is just the maximum arity of its relations). It will be sufficient for our purposes to assume that the domain $A = |A|$ is implicitly defined to be just the set of elements that participate in any of the relations, and that the number of (distinct) such elements $n = |A|$ is defined to be the *size* of $\mathbf{A}$.

Of course, we need a polynomially larger number of tuples in order to take into account the actual amount of physical storage required to represent $\mathbf{A}$. Most often, what we are really interested in is not the precise amount of space, but rather its asymptotic growth rate with respect to $|A|$, up to a constant of proportionality. So in actuality $\mathbf{A}$ would require SPACE$[n^a]$ to store. A graph (one binary relation) on n vertices could contain up to n^2 edges and hence require a quadratic amount of space. For example, in a group of $n = 6$ people (vertices), there are up to $n(n-1)/2 = 15$ ways (edges) for them to shake hands, as illustrated in figure 8.1.

First-order logic   To derive information from a structure, there needs to be a way to bring facts together. The standard language for describing properties of finite structures is first-order logic, or FOL, allowing simultaneous discourse about a variety of facts. For example, suppose the *Couple* relation above is represented symbolically by C, so that

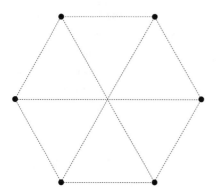

Figure 8.1
How n objects can be related by a quadratic amount of information.

(John, Jane) ∈ C or equivalently C(John, Jane)

Recalling that our marriage example is gender-sensitive (male followed by female) and consequently asymmetrical, a formula that expresses unique correspondence is:

¬ ∃z [∃x $C(x, z)$ ∧ ∃y $C(z, y)$] ∧ ¬ ∃xyz [$y \neq z$ ∧ $C(x, y)$ ∧ $C(x, z)$ ∨ $C(y, x)$ ∧ $C(z, x)$]

The first part says that no person appears on both sides of the relation, and the second part says that no person is related to two distinct people on the opposite side of the relation. In other words, nobody is both a husband and a wife, and no one is married to two different people. This boils down simply to saying that everyone currently participating in marriage does so exactly once.

Tabular method: Relational databases The information in a finite structure is contained in its relations, specifically, in the tuples of domain elements it relates. In practical applications, it is convenient to arrange this data in the form of tables, one for each relation. In a given table, there is one named column for each place in the corresponding relation. Hence, both the number of tables and their widths are fixed by the signature. Within tables, each row represents a fact—a tuple in the relation. Each entry in a row is simply a label for an element of the domain (the labeling scheme is irrelevant as long as distinct labels are assigned to distinct elements). This mechanism for storing information is known as a relational

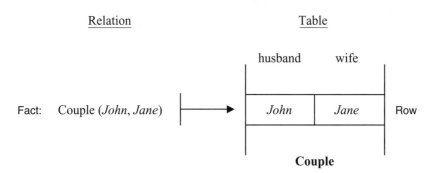

Figure 8.2
A tuple in a relation becomes a row in a table.

database (there are additional details but they are irrelevant). It becomes easy to see that the size of the database (measured by total number of entries) is proportional to the number of facts being stored.

Structured query language   One area of application in computer science where logic and information have combined in a particularly successful manner is the field of relational databases. It has become standard to obtain information from a database by writing a query in *structured query language*, or SQL. Although it is not necessary for us to deal with SQL code in this essay, it is important to realize that queries formulated for database programming are based on relational algebra, which is itself equivalent to FOL and known as the relational calculus (Ullman 1982). Hence first-order logic provides a foundation for the study of query theory—the fundamental underpinnings of how to access information stored in a database.

Graphical method: Data structures   To illustrate more clearly how a database might be stored in the memory of a computer, we can transform a (collection of) table(s) into a graph. Rows, representing tuples, become nodes that are labeled by the table they are part of, with labeled links to the atomic elements they are relating. Note that whereas atoms (always) point nowhere (see figure 8.3), many (other) nodes may point to the same atom.

It is easy to see how facts are determined by immediate adjacency between elements. For example, in the figure, the fact *Couple (John, Jane)* is determined from the existence of a *C*-node whose *h* and *w* links point

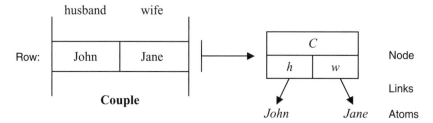

Figure 8.3
Rows from tables become nodes in a data structure.

to the atoms *John* and *Jane*, respectively. The idea that knowledge of facts can be based only on the proximity of elements being related is how we are going to connect each datum with its physical embodiment.

Language: Singular logic   The advantage of this graphical method is that it accurately shows how to convert an arbitrarily large amount of relational information into a structure whose elements each contain a bounded amount of data. Nodes have a single relation symbol, together with links to the atoms being related (the number of such links is fixed by the arity). Atoms contain only their identity. If we wanted to make all data elements uniform, we could enlarge each one of them to the maximum size (determined by the largest arity relation). This necessitates leaving some (or in the case of atoms, all) fields empty, so we introduce a special null atomic element called *nil* (an atom that points to itself) to fill the empty link fields. For example, atoms might now look as shown in figure 8.4. Atomic elements do not contain a relation symbol, indicating that they are not tuples in a relation. This yields a data structure whose size (number of data elements) is precisely equal to the amount of information being stored (the number of atoms being related, with nil, plus the number of tuples relating them), all without losing any information.

But there is yet more. It is possible to model these data structures in a particularly simple way: a signature with only unary relations and unary functions. The terminology *singulary logic* has been used to describe such a vocabulary (Church 1956). So now we have something whose size is at least roughly proportional to the amount of physical memory it might occupy. It is not difficult to show that every first-order query on the orig-

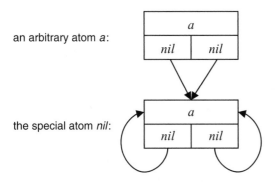

an arbitrary atom a:

the special atom nil:

Figure 8.4
How to fill empty fields in atoms.

inal database can be translated into a (typed) first-order formula (with equality) on the new data structure.

Referring to figure 8.4, this is accomplished by making the following substitution:

$$C(x, y) \mapsto (\exists z) [C(z) \wedge h(z) = x \wedge w(z) = y]$$

Note that many variables can occur together in the same formula even though the elementary symbols are themselves singulary. Later on, we will obtain what is essentially equivalent to a monovariable logic. This occurs only in special situations that are consequences of requirements that enforce physical scalability (basically where the in-degree of each atom is bounded). To understand how that can happen, we must turn to an analysis of how information is actually stored in a computer.

3 The Physical Storage of Data

It is generally accepted that in mathematics, any consistent requirement on the existence of an object can be witnessed by a (potentially infinite) set. This is fine for an abstract area like mathematics. But to be faithful to reality, information must have a material representation determined by the physical properties of the media in which it resides. So although it might be more elegant to study the concept of information independent of its representation, information must ultimately have a physical form. This section is concerned with the mechanics of how data is actually stored in memory and the theoretical consequences of those mechanics.

Information Theory

A beautiful probabilistic theory of information was developed by Shannon over fifty years ago to understand the amount of data required to reliably store or transmit redundant information in the presence of noise (see Hamming 1986 for an elementary treatment). This quantitative theory does not concern itself with how data is structured, usually assuming it takes the form of a binary string (a linear ordering of bits) because of the sequential nature of time in communications. However, this configuration could really be any rigid arrangement of symbols from a fixed finite alphabet that is previously agreed on by sender and receiver (such as the rectangular grid of color RGB pixels in a television screen). The only provision would be that the specified arrangement must be asymptotically scalable to support any (finite) amount of symbols. A linear sequence intuitively satisfies this constraint.

Arbitrary Amounts of Data

Our goal is to determine which classes of relational models admit practical implementation asymptotically. To accurately reflect the material requirements of storing *any amount* of information, we demand there be a uniform manner of storing an unbounded quantity of bounded size objects using matter in space, thereby taking into consideration the practical necessities of utilizing data at arbitrarily large scales.

We have already seen how, in a fixed vocabulary, relational information of arbitrary size and complexity can be represented by data structures—finite objects containing uniform collections of nodes that hold symbolic data and links to other nodes. To actually store this information requires a memory in which arbitrary arrangements of pointers can be embedded. This implementation is made possible by a powerful memory architecture in which every place in memory is immediately accessible from any other place by an access mechanism known as *addressing*. Although this is an appealing suggestion, we will see that there are difficulties in implementing this idea at arbitrarily large scales.

The Memory Hierarchy

Alan Turing introduced the first formal model of mechanical computing in 1936, originally to study the mathematical limits of computation. This model had to have the potential to manipulate arbitrarily large amounts

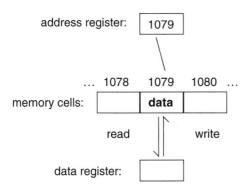

Figure 8.5
The logical layout of data in a pointer-based memory, showing that an address can reference any numbered location in memory. N.B.: locations are arranged linearly for purposes of illustration only; but they are really located in a hyperdimensional space, since cells are numbered and accessed by binary addresses.

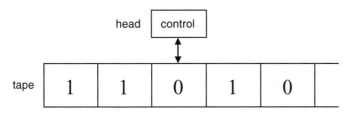

Figure 8.6
A Turing machine.

of information. Designed to be as simple as possible, it used a linear "tape" with a sequence of cells, infinite in one direction, each of which could hold one of finitely many symbols. A finite control reads from or writes to cells of the tape based on its state, modifying that state and moving left or right.

Turing soon observed that it would be unbearably slow to access the data of a computer whose memory was based on a linear sequential structure of cells (Turing 1992, p. 7). So he subsequently proposed an addressing scheme using a system of switches (akin to how a telephone network routes calls), which is conceptually equivalent to the way modern digital computers access an exponential amount of data compared to the address length. However, Turing carefully noted that this method runs into

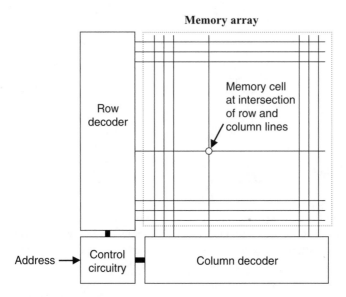

Figure 8.7
Physical layout of data in random access memory.

problems when addresses can no longer fit into a single location, a topic to which we will return shortly.

Main memory The current state of technology allows computers to use this addressable structure for their *main memory*, where it is called *random-access memory*, or RAM. It got this name because the speed at which data is accessed does not depend on its location. In actuality, as can be seen clearly in figure 8.7, the physical arrangement of a modern memory chip is two dimensional, with rows and columns that access the individual electronic cells. Given sufficiently high density, it is possible to make time differentials between distant locations small enough to be insignificant. However, it should be clear that in any finite-dimensional space, speed of light limitations prevent the construction of a memory that is always random-access, regardless of size. For this reason, computers need alternative methods of mass storage that rely on the inherent spatial arrangement of data.

Secondary storage Information that cannot fit in RAM is delegated to *secondary storage*, designed primarily for capacity, not speed. Secondary

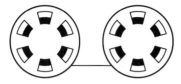

Figure 8.8
Linear tape (on reels).

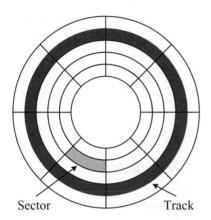

Sector   Track

Figure 8.9
Disk storage in tracks and sectors.

storage is usually much slower than RAM, as a result of its sequential nature of accessing data. An ordinary magnetic *tape* cassette used for audio or video is a perfect example of information that can only be accessed sequentially. Locations are linearly ordered in one dimension, so accessing one location from another requires scanning all intermediate locations (fast-forward and rewind). Indeed, early computers used tape storage extensively until more convenient methods utilizing a two-dimensional method became less expensive.

In the most familiar form of mass storage device in use today, an optical *disc*, radius and rotation are varied to access data stored in tracks and sectors respectively. Because they offer much faster access times than tape, audio (CD) and video (DVD) discs are often erroneously referred to as being random-access. In reality, their asymptotic speed can only approach the square root of their capacity, which is still significantly better than a purely linear arrangement.

Future developments promise techniques that utilize three-dimensional structures such as crystals or holograms, further improving both speed and capacity. But the asymptotic performance of a true RAM (essentially logarithmic access time) cannot be achieved in a finite-dimensional space.

Performance issues Special techniques involving caching have been developed to smooth the transition between different levels of the memory hierarchy so as to accommodate storage technologies that trade off speed for capacity. Since we are so very far away from the maximum storage density of data, one might think that such distinctions are a temporary artifact, and that RAM could eventually be scaled to any size, making it possible to store all information in high-speed memory. However, as we have seen through a closer investigation, there is sufficient cause to cast doubt on this assumption.

Scalability

Perhaps the first person to recognize that RAM cannot be scaled to any size was Alan Turing, in the very same breath as the discussion cited above (Turing 1992, p. 8). Even in proposing the now ubiquitous idea called RAM, Turing himself recognized the theoretical unfeasibility of such an approach. Eventually, he argued, no matter how cleverly one engineered the memory of such a "practical computing machine," a memory of arbitrarily large size must eventually degenerate into using sequential access to reach its data elements. In other words, the notion of immediate access to arbitrarily large amounts of information via an addressing scheme does not scale without breaking some law of physics. Actually, because of the exponential growth rate in technology, we are quickly (in a matter of decades) reaching those physical limits. (A relatively recent scientific investigation of the hurdles that current magnetic storage technology needs to overcome is presented in Toigo 2000.) Therefore, it will become necessary to take into account physical limits in our mathematical models of storage.

4   Models of Information

We have seen that representations of arbitrarily large finite mathematical structures can be stored in random-access memory. If it were possible to build (at least in theory) arbitrarily large instances of RAM, then there would be nothing further to say. However, we have seen that this is not the case. The storage hierarchy is imposed not by technological limitations, but by the physics of data storage—using matter that occupies space. Since the mass required must be asymptotically proportional to the amount of information being stored, and the density to which that mass can occupy space is ultimately limited, larger and larger amounts of information must take up more and more space (this should have been obvious to an engineer from the start).

Therefore, two mathematical principles follow naturally from an understanding of the restrictions that physical limits put on the arrangement and distribution of data with respect to locations in memory:

- A *bounded* amount of information per location: follows from bounded density
- A *bounded* number of neighbors per location: follows from finite dimensionality

The fact that matter cannot be compressed to an arbitrarily high density leads to the conclusion that at most one symbol of information can be stored in each location of memory. The bounded-degree requirement follows from the finite dimensionality of space, in that there is a fixed maximum number of adjacent locations that can be squeezed into a given radius. These local restrictions form what we will call *scalable* models of information and correspond to memories of fixed word size and degree.

Homogeneity

We now turn our attention to a special uniform case in which all the models of the class are embedded in a single homogeneous background structure—one that looks the same everywhere. Although this may seem overly restrictive, this assumption does not detract from the import of our main result—it remains true with minor modifications, which are discussed at the end of the essay.

Our key objective is to define what it means for a class of finite models to be *uniform*. Essentially, this will be a class in which each finite model lives in a physically symmetric universe. This homogeneous *universe* **U** consists of an infinite domain U of discrete *locations*, spatially related to one another by a finite number of *direction* functions $\Delta = \{\delta_1, \ldots, \delta_d\}$, and arranged so that all locations "look alike." Each location should be thought of as being equidistant from the d *neighbors* around it (to prevent over-crowding), and each direction is invertible, so that $\Delta^{-1} = \{\delta^{-1} : \delta \text{ in } \Delta\} = \Delta$. Any finite sequence of directions $\delta_{i_1}, \ldots, \delta_{i_m}$ can be composed, with the meaning 'go in direction δ_{i_1} first', then $\ldots$, finally 'go in direction δ_{i_m} last'. Note that adjacent inverses annihilate each other, and if directions were actual vectors in Euclidean space they would also commute, but we do not enforce this general requirement.

Indeed, arbitrary finite sequences from Δ, denoted Δ^*, form a group of bijections with respect to composition, acting on the elements of U in a way that makes them completely indistinguishable from one another. This means that if a certain sequence in Δ^* makes a cycle at some location, it will make a cycle at every location.

Definition: A *universe* is an infinite countable domain U of discrete locations related to each other by a uniform structure of direction functions δ_h. Specifically,

$$\mathbf{U} = \langle U, \delta_1, \ldots, \delta_d \rangle$$

where each $\delta_h: U \to U$ is a bijection over the domain $|U|$ of locations, also satisfying *homogeneity*: for each sequence $\delta \in \Delta^*$, $(\exists x \in U)\delta(x) = x \Leftrightarrow (\forall x \in U)\delta(x) = x$.

In particular, the set of cycles $C_U = \{\delta \in \Delta^* : \delta(x) = x\}$ is well defined and characterizes U up to isomorphism (provided it is connected). A direct consequence is that each position has exactly the same number d of immediately adjacent positions, called its *neighbors* (provided of course that each δ_h is nontrivial). Typical examples of these constant-degree structures are conveniently visualized geometrically, as shown in figure 8.10.

Typically, when studying embedded finite models such as constraint databases, the universe is a continuous structure such as the real numbers with ordinary arithmetic operations (Revesz 2002), but our structures are discrete in order to maintain consistency with the "tape" used in theoretical models of computation. Nevertheless, it is useful to imagine our discrete universe of locations as living in a more physical, continuous finite-dimensional metric space that is infinite in each dimension (so that the underlying algebraic structure becomes a torsion-free Abelian group). The most convincing examples are ones in which the elements are equidistant in Euclidean space from their nearest neighbors, as illustrated in figure 8.10.

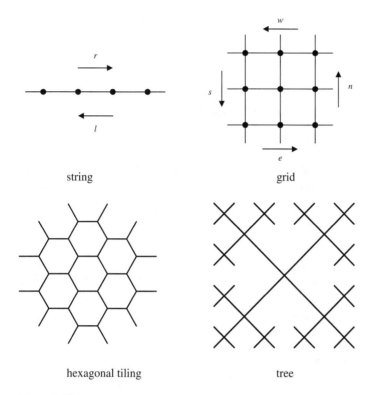

string   grid

hexagonal tiling   tree

Figure 8.10
Drawings of a string, grid, hexagonal tiling, and tree—the last requires an infinite dimensional space in order to maintain fixed distances between elements.

Embedding Models

These locations are thought of as potential places for storing information, like putting a finite amount of data in cells on an infinite tape. Hence, we insist that only a finite number of positions can hold symbols. For each symbol σ drawn from the tape alphabet Σ, we indicate its presence or absence at a given location by introducing a unary predicate (of the same name) to represent it, and adjoining all of these (nonoverlapping) predicates to the universe U.

Definition: An *embedded finite model* is an expansion $M = (U, \sigma_1^M \ldots \sigma_s^M)$ of U where the σ_i^M are pairwise disjoint finite subsets of U (we usually drop the superscripts), i.e. $\sigma_i \cap \sigma_j = \emptyset$ for $i \neq j$.

Although technically infinite, the model M contains only a finite amount of information, all within its *active domain* $A = \sigma_1 \cup \ldots \cup \sigma_s$. These occupied positions are the only locations of which it makes sense to ask what are the contents. Since unoccupied cells cannot contain any symbol (by definition) they are referred to as *empty*, and we will use a special *blank* symbol, '#', later on to represent their locations. The adjacency relationship between cells of the active domain is inherited from the "spatial" relationship determined by the directions of the universe U.

Data Structures

Restricting an embedded finite model to the contents of its active domain determines a finite relational data structure formed in the following natural way. The occupied cells become *nodes*, the symbols within them the *data*, with *edges* between them determined by directional adjacency. The relations $\{\sigma_i : 1 \le i \le s\}$ partition the active domain A, classifying each element according to its contents. Similarly, the functions $\{\delta_h : 1 \le h \le d\}$ assign a different type of (directed) edge to those pairs in A that are immediately adjacent in U. Note that no two edges of the same kind can both point to or from any vertex. Instead, like edges are incident only from head to tail. More precisely:

Definition: To each embedded finite model $M = (U, \sigma_1 \ldots \sigma_s)$ associate the finite relational substructure (essentially a labeled graph)

$$D_m = (A, \sigma_1, \ldots, \sigma_s, E_1, \ldots, E_d) \qquad \text{where } E_h = \{\langle x, \delta_h(x)\rangle : x, \delta_h(x) \in A\}.$$

In a certain precise sense, D_M (together with C_U) contains all the finite information needed to reconstruct M up to isomorphism.

Uniformity

These embedded relational structures represent structured data that conforms to an underlying homogeneous universe. It is now quite simple to define what it means for a class of such data structures to be uniform: when all of them "fit" into the same fixed universal background structure. This is similar in spirit to the notion of ultrahomogeneity in Hodges 1997, but with only unary functions and relations.

Definition: A class K of finite models is called *uniform* if each one has the same background structure and alphabet. I.e., for a fixed U and s, each model M in K is of the form $M = (U, \sigma_1 \ldots \sigma_s)$.

We now turn to the task of describing first-order properties of these uniform classes in logic.

5   Elementary Term Logic

This section develops in detail a specially designed elementary term logic (ETL) for describing properties of uniformly embedded finite models. Its key feature is that it has no variables in the conventional sense—rather, the formulas refer directly to the very symbols themselves, as classes appearing on the tape *en masse*. It is important to note that ETL utilizes the subject-predicate form of classical logic to effectively guard its quantifiers over the finite active domain. Yet despite this apparently strict limitation, it retains the full expressive power of first-order logic (FOL) with unrestricted quantification over the entire infinite domain. This active domain collapse was already observed by Libkin (2003) for structures of bounded-degree in the context of modern logic. My contribution is to demonstrate that it can be accomplished within the confines of a traditional logic applied to uniform classes of finite models.

Overview

It is important to recognize that the logical syntax will be bimodal: *terms* representing classes of cells and *statements* indicating truth-values (possible configurations of the entire tape). Do not be dissuaded by its deceptive simplicity. It retains the full expressive power of modern first-order logic, provided attention is restricted to the spatially motivated uniform classes of finite models.

The idea is to be able to say things like 'there are k elements, each of which resides in a certain kind of neighborhood'. In order to talk about neighborhood types and their quantity, we must extend classical Aristotelian logic while retaining its monadic appearance. Two essential features are added: unary functions and numerical quantification. Both additions maintain the essential character of a traditional approach to formal logic and permit the sacrifice of polyadic relationships, including equality.

Although it is common to examine the deductive power of logic (what we can *prove*), we are concerned here with definability (what we can *express*). The main result is that our term logic is equivalent in expressive power to closed formulas of first-order logic. This is analogous to the inferential parity that term-functor logic enjoys with its modern counterpart (McIntosh 1982). For the reader who might want to explore the possibility of developing a deductive logic, a section on simplification rules is provided.

Terms

A *term* is a property of a cell that depends on its symbolic contents and that of its neighbors. Terms represent a set of places on the tape. They are built up from symbols in Σ and adjacencies in Δ by functional composition, together with Boolean operators, in a completely ordinary fashion. Symbols are undefined concepts as in formal language theory.

Symbols as atomic terms The vocabulary of our logical language begins with the finite *alphabet* Σ of input symbols, which can appear on the tape (often written as digits). The principle is to let the atomic term σ represent the class of places where the very symbol σ appears (that way both the term and the symbol have the same intension and extension). They roughly play the role of variables in modern logic (but not really).

Definition: Let each tape symbol σ in Σ be an *atomic term*, denoting all the places σ appears. Technically, $\sigma^M = \{u \in U$: the cell at position u contains symbol $\sigma\}$.

Since by assumption only finitely many cells can be occupied by input symbols, atomic terms always denote finite classes. Also, since no two input symbols can be coincident and thereby occupy the same location, distinct atomic terms are disjoint. Note that the "blank" is not considered a symbol. Rather, empty cells are discerned by the absence of every other symbol.

In a fundamental sense, symbols represent the actual information in the model. They correspond with associating to each σ in Σ the property 'contains σ' of cells.

Example: the atomic term 0 represents the places containing the symbol zero. This is indicated by the underlined positions in the following string:

... ###<u>0</u>0<u>1</u>0<u>1</u>10<u>1</u>1###...

Directions for simple terms Augment the vocabulary by the fixed set of *directions* Δ that sets the adjacency relationships between cells on the tape. Functions are not entities unto themselves, only term modifiers. The principle is to use these functions to refer to the contents of nearby locations. Any bijection from Δ^* can be used to modify atomic terms via functional application.

Definition: For each δ in Δ^* and σ in Σ, let the *simple term* $\sigma\delta$ denote the class:

$$\delta[\sigma] = \{\delta(x): x \text{ in } \sigma\}$$

i.e., the places that can "see" a σ by looking back in the direction δ^{-1}. (Note that atomic terms are simple by choosing δ to be the identity.)

Example: Letting l stand for 'left of', the term $1l$ represents all cells that are to the left of a one. This is indicated by the underlined positions in the string:

$$\dots \#\#\#00\underline{1}0\underline{11}0\underline{11}\#\#\# \dots$$

Note: Using postfix notation avoids the confusing transposition caused by function composition in ordinary prefix notation: $fgS = (f \circ g)S = g(f(S))$. In contrast, even without parentheses, it is unambiguous to write $Sfg = S(f \circ g) = (Sf)g$.

Complementation   Given any property P it is often convenient to allow the complementary form non-P. These terms are written $\sim P$ and denote the places that do *not* satisfy the property P (and which may be infinite).

Definition: For any term P, let $\sim P$ denote the *complement* of P, i.e., $U \backslash P$.

Example: The term ~ 0 represents the locations that do not contain a zero. This is indicated by the underlined positions in the string:

$$\dots \#\#\#00\underline{1}0\underline{11}0\underline{11}\#\#\# \dots$$

Note: Parentheses are unnecessary for complements of simple terms because bijections pass right through: $(\sim\sigma)\delta = \sim(\sigma\delta)$.

Joining terms   Terms can be joined with the connective operations of union and intersection.

Definition: Given terms S and T, both their *union* $S \cup T$ and *intersection* $S \cap T$ are terms.

It is easy to verify that bijections pass cleanly through them, so for any sequence of directions δ:

$$(S \circ T)\delta = (S\delta) \circ (T\delta), \text{ where } \circ \text{ is either } \cap \text{ or } \cup$$

Normalization of terms   Without loss of generality we can express arbitrary combinations of $\{\cap, \cup, \sim\}$ and bijections very simply:

Fact: Any term can be written as a combination of monotone operators $\{\cap, \cup\}$ applied to simple terms or their complements.

Proof: Push complements to the bottom with De Morgan's laws, and distribute the bijections.

Referring to blank locations requires complementation. Consider the input alphabet $\{0, 1\}$.

Example: The term $\sim(0 \cup 1) = \sim0 \cap \sim1$ represents all empty cells, as indicated in the underlined positions of:

$\ldots$ ###001011011### $\ldots$

To summarize, here is a table that inductively defines the syntax and semantics of terms.

Terminology	Notation	Meaning	Conditions
Atomic term	σ	the class σ	σ is a symbol in Σ
Simple term	$\sigma\delta$	$\delta[\sigma]$	δ is in Δ^*
Complementation	$\sim P$	$U \backslash P$	P is any term
Compound terms	$S \cup T / S \cap T$	union / intersection	S and T are terms

There is a difference between how we will interpret the semantics of terms, depending on whether they are used as subjects or predicates, though this distinction is not essential. A *subject term*, representing members of the active domain A, is interpreted as a *class* or set of positions, so that, for example, $\sigma \subseteq A$ refers to the set of all cells that contain the symbol σ. Since by assumption A is finite, these classes are finite also. A *predicate term*, on the other hand, is a Boolean-valued characteristic function on the universe U, mapping all locations (including empty ones) to $\{true, false\}$, so that, for example, $\langle\#\rangle(u) = true$ if and only if $u \notin A$.

Statements

Unlike terms, which signify properties of individual things (i.e., cells in memory), statements signify facts about the state of the entire model (i.e., the contents of memory). The classical subject-predicate form provides a convenient way to include numerical quantity while still maintaining a finitely guarded domain of quantification.

Numerically quantified subject-predicate statements The two-term syntax for statements in traditional logic provides no way to count. To remedy this limitation, we introduce a natural extension in which quantifiers have numerical parameters in order to provide some sort of bounded counting capability, similar in spirit to Murphree 1991. Here is the syntax diagram for the general subject-predicate form of our statements:

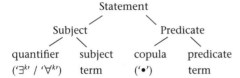

Compare the differences with modern logic, which relies on predicates applied to (functions of) variables. In particular, there are no atomic propositions in term logic following Sommers 1982, p. 5. Instead, every statement asserts a categorical proposition about how the subject term, according to its quantifier, satisfies the predicate term (the copula '•' reads as 'is' or 'are'). For each parameter $k \geq 0$, they come in two forms, duals of each other.

Existential form: $\exists^k S \bullet P$, meaning 'there are (at least) k S that are P'

Universal form: $\forall^k S \bullet P$, meaning 'all but (at most) k-1 S satisfy P'

For $k = 1$ (which we often omit) these are the usual '*some S* is *P*' and '*every S* is *P*', respectively. The sentential negation '*no S* is *P*' is given the usual treatment by converting it to term negation '*every S* is *non-P*' (universals do not have existential import). For $k = 0$ these forms trivialize to the Boolean constants *true* and *false* respectively, even for a vacuous subject (which we do not prohibit).

Basic statements Statements involving an atomic subject are intuitively elegant because they express categorical propositions about just one concept, even though the predicate term might be arbitrarily complex. This is the idea behind a basic statement.

Definition: If σ is an atomic term, and Q is either $\exists$ or $\forall$, then $Q^k\sigma \bullet P$ is called a *basic statement*.

Example: In a string, $\exists^1 0 \bullet \#r$ means the left endpoint is a zero (r stands for 'to the right of').

Figure: ... ###<u>0</u>1 ... 0### ...   (the witness is underlined)

Figure 8.11

Moreover, we shall see later that requiring an atomic subject is not a significant restriction, in that arbitrarily complex statements can be reduced to combinations of just basic statements.

Sentential negation   Despite numerical parameters, sentential denial still reduces to affirming the contrary with a reversal of quantity (the semantics were carefully chosen to make this happen):

For $k \geq 0$ $\neg \exists^k S \bullet P \Leftrightarrow \forall^k S \bullet {\sim}P$ & $\neg \forall^k S \bullet P \Leftrightarrow \exists^k S \bullet {\sim}P$

as illustrated respectively in figure 8.11.

So, without loss of generality, negation can be eliminated so that all Boolean combinations of statements can be expressed by using just the positive sentential connectives of conjunction and disjunction.

Combining statements   Statements can be combined using ordinary propositional connectives.

Definition: If s and t are statements, then so are their *conjunction* $s \wedge t$ and *disjunction* $s \vee t$.

As was just observed, it is unnecessary to include negation as it can be "pushed through" conjunction and disjunction.

To summarize, here is a table that inductively defines the syntax and semantics for statements:

Type of statement	Notation	Meaning	Conditions
Basic existential	$\exists^k S \bullet P$	$\|S \cap P\| \geq k$	S is atomic, P is any term
Basic universal	$\forall^k S \bullet P$	$\|S \setminus P\| < k$	S is atomic, P is any term
Denial	$\neg p$	negation	p is any statement
Compound	$s \wedge t / s \vee t$	conjunct / disjunct	s and t are arbitrary statements

Call the set of all such statements **ETL**, for elementary term logic.

Example: In a monosymbolic vocabulary, $\forall^2 O \bullet Or \wedge \forall^2 O \bullet Ol$ means there are no "gaps."

Figure: ... ###00 ... 0### ...   (internal ellipsis represents all zeroes)

Explanation: Since any finite string has two "external" endpoints, it generates one exception for each clause. The formula says that there are not two exceptions, precluding any "internal" endpoints.

Simplification Rules

This section is provided for the benefit of the reader who might be interested in seeing illustrations of syntactic transformations in ETL. Although it can be safely skipped, the reader should note the proposal on how to deal with the "head of an animal" problem. Note well that unnecessary parentheses have been removed, so close attention should be paid to the distinction between terms and statements.

Distributing over compound predicates   Just as in the nonnumeric case, existential quantification distributes over union and universal quantification distributes over intersection, but it is more complicated because we have to split the quantity by numerical partitioning, I shall illustrate just the existential case, but must first separate the predicate into a *disjoint* union:

$$P \cup Q = (\sim P \cap Q) \cup (P \cap Q) \cup (P \cap \sim Q)$$

Now we can distribute over any two disjoint terms U and V:

$$\exists^k S \bullet U \cup V \Leftrightarrow \bigvee_{0 \le i \le k} \exists^i S \bullet U \wedge \exists^{k-i} S \bullet V$$

The universal case is similar.

Breaking up compound subjects   In this section we show how a statement $Q^k S \bullet P$ containing a compound subject S (without complementation) can be broken down into a combination of basic statements. Reducing everything to atomic quantification gives further credence to the idea that subjects are tangible, in the sense that they refer to physically existing data in a bounded region of space. Although this can be deduced from the corollary to our main result by a semantic argument, our syntactic treatment here will help illustrate an important way to deal with unique correspondences (among other things).

Intersections in the subject are easily dealt with by moving one of them into the predicate:

$$\exists^k(S \cap T) \bullet P \Leftrightarrow \exists^k S \bullet T \cap P$$

$$\forall^k(S \cap T) \bullet P \Leftrightarrow \forall^k S \bullet {\sim}T \cup P$$

Unions can be broken up by quantifying over the pieces:

$$\exists^k(S \cup T) \bullet P \Leftrightarrow \bigvee_{1 \leq i,j \leq k} \exists^i S \bullet P \wedge \exists^j T \bullet P \wedge \forall^{i+j-k+1}(S \cap T) \bullet {\sim}P$$

$$\forall^k(S \cup T) \bullet P \Leftrightarrow \bigvee_{1 \leq i,j \leq k} \forall^i S \bullet P \wedge \forall^j T \bullet P \wedge \exists^{i+j-k-1}(S \cap T) \bullet {\sim}P$$

Verifying these identities is straightforward via the identity $|Q \cup R| = |Q| + |R| - |Q \cap R|$, where in the existential case, Q is a set of i witnesses in S for P, and R is a set of j witnesses in T for P (in the universal case they are sets of fewer than i or j violations respectively).

To remove functions from the subject, observe that bijections preserve cardinality via the one–one correspondence between terms $S \approx Sf$.

For $Q \in \{\exists, \forall\}$ $Q^k Sf \bullet P \Leftrightarrow Q^k S \bullet Pf^{-1}$ where $k \geq 0$.

This can be illustrated as follows, where s and p are representative elements of S and P, respectively:

$$s \xrightarrow{\,f\,} p \quad \Leftrightarrow \quad s \xleftarrow{\,f^{-1}\,} p$$

That is, a P can be reached from an S iff an S can be reached from a P by going in reverse.

This observation allows us to formulate and solve the famous "head of an animal" problem very simply, provided we assume a one–one correspondence between animals and their heads. In subject-predicate form, letting h stand for 'head of':

Premise: Every Horse is an Animal: $\forall H \bullet A$

Conclusion: All heads of Horses are heads of Animals: $\forall Hh \bullet Ah$

The conclusion is actually equivalent to the premise via the aforementioned transformation:

$$\forall Hh \bullet Ah \Leftrightarrow \forall H \bullet Ahh^{-1} \Leftrightarrow \forall H \bullet A$$

Put another way, the logical equivalence between $H \subseteq A$ and $Hh \subseteq Ah$ depends crucially on h being a unique correspondence.

It should be noted that eliminating the complement in the subject requires a more complex argument using finiteness. For the sake of completeness, I sketch how this could be done. Without loss of generality, assume it is applied directly to an atomic subject term by pushing all complements to the bottom and using the transformations above. Take $Q^k\text{-}\sigma \bullet P$ and change it by breaking $\text{-}\sigma$ into a disjoint union of all the other symbols in the alphabet together with the "blank" # (which has infinite extension). Applying the transformation for subjects joined by union repeatedly will result in a combination of statements in which the only nonbasic statements will be of the form $Q^k\# \bullet P$ for some compound predicate P. Use duality so that we consider only the existential form $\exists^k\# \bullet P$. Distribute the quantifier over union so that P consists entirely of intersections between simple terms of the form $\sigma\delta$ and blank terms of the form $\#\delta$ (converting complements as before). If P contains any nonblank term $\sigma\delta$, rewrite the whole formula with respect to the subject σ. Otherwise, if P consists entirely of blank terms, see that $\exists^k\# \bullet P$ is equivalent to just *true* since there are infinitely many blank neighborhoods consistent with P.

6   Results

In this section I show that elementary term logic is as powerful as first-order logic with equality in expressing properties of our embedded finite models. As a consequence of the proof, we will also obtain an atomic subject normal form for ETL.

ETL = FOL

Recall that in a model of information M, finitely many tape symbols reside in a fixed infinite background structure U, naturally forming a finite model D_M within it. Furthermore, being uniform, there is a well-defined set of cycles $C_U = \{\delta \in \Delta^* : \delta(x) = x\}$. Both of these ideas will be used in the proof of the following result.

Theorem: Fix a universe U. For each sentence ϕ expressible in FOL(=), first-order logic with equality, there is an equivalent ϕ' in ETL, elementary term logic, and vice versa, so that ϕ and ϕ' agree on all models M embedded in U:

$$M \models \phi \Leftrightarrow M \models \phi'$$

Proof: (ETL $\subseteq$ FOL) This is the easy direction because it is straightforward to design a syntactic translation.

Simple terms in ETL correspond to atomic propositions in FOL with one free variable in an obvious way:

ETL term	FOL formula
$\sigma\delta$	$\mapsto \quad \sigma(\delta^{-1}(x))$

Translation of simple terms for symbol $\sigma \in \Sigma$ and function $\delta \in \Delta^*$.

Although compound terms are trivially dealt with as Boolean combinations of these, it is important to use a common free variable.

The only really interesting construction arises from numerical quantification, which relies on equality in a critical way. For the sake of a nice corollary, we translate existential statements in ETL having both arbitrary subject and predicate terms into FOL sentences:

ETL term	FOL formula
$\exists^k S \bullet T$	$\mapsto \quad \exists x_1 \ldots x_k\ \sigma(x_1) \wedge \ldots \wedge \sigma(x_k) : \{x_i \neq x_j : 1 \leq i < j \leq k\} \wedge \tau(x_1) \wedge \ldots \wedge \tau(x_k)$

Translation of statements, where arbitrary S and T translate into $\sigma(x)$ and $\tau(x)$ respectively.

Just take Boolean combinations of these (including negation to get $\forall^k$) in order to translate compound statements.

(FOL $\subseteq$ ETL): This is the hard direction because it requires a semantic analysis and construction. Perhaps the first to realize that first-order formulas can speak about only local properties of a model was Gaifman (1982). But the easiest such normal form for our purposes comes from Hanf's Lemma, which for bounded-degree structures is most conveniently available from the treatment in Immerman 1999. Local properties are formalized using the concept of a *neighborhood*: a finite, connected group of locations. In particular, we can restrict our attention to regular neighborhoods, those whose boundary is equidistant from a central location. Imagine a ball of radius r around a central location n. This is a neighborhood consisting of all locations within distance r from the center n. We say that two such balls are isomorphic if they are identical except for the position of their centers. That is, their respective locations can be put into a one–one correspondence in a way that matches symbols and respects directions. Isomorphic balls look alike, and are said to have the same r-type. Below is an example of a 1-type in a grid:

Because our structures are uniform representations of models with bounded-density matter embedded in a finite-dimensional space, they have constant degree and a fixed amount of information per node. This means that for each r, there are only finitely many different kinds of r-types. On such structures, Hanf's lemma says that a first-order sentence of quantifier depth q can assert the occurrence (or omission) of r-types only where the radius $r \leq 2^q$. Moreover, it can distinguish the number of occurrences of a given r-type only up to a specified threshold t, which also depends only on q.

So basically, a first-order sentence is equivalent to a Boolean combination of sentences, each of which specifies a particular radius r neighborhood N along with the number of occurrences of N up to a certain threshold t. Although Hanf's lemma applies to purely relational structures, it is easy to make the appropriate modifications by interdefining functions and relations. We will construct terms to describe these neighborhoods, and statements to specify how many times they occur. For example, the neighborhood pictured above is described by $0 \cap 0w \cap 1n \cap 1s \cap \#e$ (where n, s, e, w, are compass directions in this context).

A neighborhood N is characterized by an isomorphism type that specifies the exact shape of its positions (its structure) together with the contents of each position (its data), all with respect to a central location. By definition, its local structure is constrained by the embedding into our fixed global universe U, so we can restrict attention to those isomorphism types whose shape is consistent with C_U, for otherwise any nontrivial such existential assertion is automatically false. So it remains to completely specify the contents of each cell in N. Such a term becomes a property of the center by describing the arrangement of symbols around it using an intersection term $T_N = T_1 \cap \ldots \cap T_n$, where each T_i is a simple term $\sigma\delta$ or $\#\delta$, using a variety of δ of length at most r. The quantity of neighborhood types N appearing in the model M can be described by a combination of statements using numerical quantifiers with parameters k of magnitude at most t applied to T_N.

So all that remains to be shown is that $\Pi \equiv \exists^k T_N$ is reducible to a canonical (basic) statement with an atomic subject term. There are two cases. If some $T_i = \sigma\delta$, i.e., $T = \sigma\delta \cap T'$, then manipulate Π to be $\exists^k \sigma\delta \bullet T' = \exists^k \sigma \bullet T'\delta^{-1}$, which is of the correct form. Otherwise, every T_i is of the form $\sim\sigma\delta$, which entails $\#\delta$ (recall that $\# = \sim\Sigma = \cap \{\sim\sigma : \sigma \in \Sigma\}$ stands for the blank, and that by definition completely empty neighborhoods can exist only outside the active domain). Therefore T_N is consistent with a sufficiently large empty neighborhood. Since there are infinitely many of these in M, Π is equivalent to just plain *true* and we are done. $\square$

As a consequence of the last paragraph in the proof we obtain the following additional result:

Corollary: An arbitrarily complex statement of ETL can be reduced to a combination of basic statements. That is, subjects can be made atomic without loss of generality. In particular, this means that all quantification can be guarded over the finite active domain.

Remark: As promised, we indicate what would need to be changed to accommodate the nonhomogeneous case, where we assume only that each node has bounded size and degree. Essentially, the main result remains true except that we would have to describe local paths, adding special terms that predicate about whether or not a given sequence of directions forms a cycle. A term of the form 'δ' would mean all those positions for which traveling along the sequence labeled by δ returns one to the original position (in the homogeneous case, this would be trivially true or false, independent of the origin). In the interest of elegance and simplicity, I have chosen to present the homogeneous case only, because it eliminates the need for such paths. Otherwise, various simplifications that push functions across term constructors no longer hold. But with enough work, it is easy to see that the main result remains true.

7 Summary

In this chapter, we have analyzed scalability requirements for models of information by examining simple physical restrictions on storing arbitrarily large amounts of data in memory. The resultant classes of models are those whose structure takes into consideration the density of matter in space. The unlimited size of those structures forced us to acknowledge a bounded locality requirement for each piece of information stored.

From this natural perspective, we studied a simple but natural term logic based directly on the symbolic representation of information. This logic, motivated and inspired by the work of Fred Sommers, incorporates the classical subject-predicate form with no use of variables or indexing. Our main result was that despite its appearance, it is just as expressive as ordinary first-order logic over these feasible models.

The ultimate goal of this research is an examination of the role that physical resources place on the potential limits of computability. Therefore, a second paper will study the role of energy and time in models of computation.

Acknowledgments

First and foremost, I would like to thank my wife Suzanne for her many intellectual contributions to the exposition and ideas expressed here. Though she is sometimes an unwilling participant, her tireless encouragement and efforts on my behalf made this paper possible. I am also grateful to my dear colleague Scott Weinstein for innumerable conversations over the years that led me to this work, and for his careful reading of a draft of this paper. Also appreciated were the many stimulating conversations with Sheila Greibach, Yiannis Moschovakis, Wilfried Sieg, Yuri Gurevich, and Leonid Levin. A special thanks goes out to my departmental colleague David Wonnacott for his penetrating insights into the nature of computer science and its relationship to both mathematics and physics. In addition, I would like to thank my son Natan for expertly drawing some of the figures.

Note

1. From Johan van Benthem's review of Sommers, *Philosophical Books* 24 (1983): 99–102.

References

Church, Alonzo. 1956. *Introduction to Mathematical Logic.* Princeton: Princeton University Press.

Enderton, Herbert. 2001. *A Mathematical Introduction to Logic.* San Diego: Harcourt/Academic Press.

Feynman, Richard. 1960. "There's Plenty of Room at the Bottom." Lecture of December 29, 1959, at the annual meeting of the American Physical Society, California

Institute of Technology. Transcript: February 1960 issue of Caltech's *Engineering and Science*, available at http://www.zyvex.com/nanotech/feynman.html.

Gaifman, Haim. 1982. "On local and non-local properties." In J. Stern (ed.), *Logic Colloquium '81*. Amsterdam: North-Holland.

Hamming, Richard. 1986. *Coding and Information theory*, second edition. Englewood Cliffs: Prentice-Hall.

Hartmanis, Juris. 1995. "On Computational Complexity and the Nature of Computer Science." Turing Award Lecture. *ACM Computing Surveys* 27: 7–16.

Hodges, Wilfred. 1997. *A Shorter Model Theory*. Cambridge: Cambridge University Press.

Immerman, Neil. 1999. *Descriptive Complexity*. New York: Springer.

Libkin, Leonid. 2003. "A Collapse Result for Constraint Queries over Structures of Small Degree." *Information Processing Letters* 86: 277–281.

McIntosh, Clifton. 1982. Appendix F of Sommers 1982.

Murphree, Wallace. 1991. *Numerically Exceptive Logic: A Reduction of the Classical Syllogism*. New York: Peter Lang.

Revesz, Peter. 2002. *Introduction to Constraint Databases*. New York: Springer.

Sommers, Fred. 1982. *The Logic of Natural Language*. Oxford: Clarendon Press.

Toigo, Jon William. 2000. "Avoiding a Data Crunch." *Scientific American* (May): 58–74.

Turing, Alan. 1992. "Intelligent Machinery." In D. C. Ince (ed.), *Collected Works of A. M. Turing: Mechanical Intelligence*. Amsterdam: North-Holland.

Ullman, Jeffrey. 1982. *Principles of Database Systems*, second edition. Rockville, Maryland: Computer Science Press.

9 Sommers's Cancellation Technique and the Method of Resolution

Aris Noah

Introduction

The general direction of my work on Fred Sommers's logic has been to reduce its apparent dissidence from conventional approaches by trying to understand its detailed relationship to more standard approaches and techniques. Without detracting from the originality of Sommers's work in logic, this allows for a more clear-headed and realistic assessment of his contributions.

The two bodies of work I have found most apt for a fruitful detailed comparison with Sommers's algebraic term functor logic have been Quine's predicate functor logic and Robinson's method of resolution (both developed in the 1960s and early 1970s, in parallel with Sommers's logic). As its title indicates, the present essay will concentrate on the method of resolution and the light it can throw on Sommers's work.

1

There are four defining elements in Sommers's programme that, in my opinion, have stood the test of time and criticism.

(1) *The coherence, depth, and promise of a term functor approach to logical inference.* Here Sommers's neo-Aristotelian research program in the logic of natural language merges fruitfully with Quine's very differently motivated work in predicate functor logic. The result is a reading of both singular and general predications as consisting of two terms joined by a copula/functor, in Quine's notation 'i' for particular and 'a' for universal predications (and indifferently 'i' and/or 'a' for singular predications, Sommers's 'wild quantity').[1]

The term functor reading of the copulas of predication, besides being logically fruitful, has considerable philosophical significance, perhaps best stated in negative terms: it debunks various pieces of philosophy that have made a living off the syntactical peculiarities of Fregean quantification—and there are quite a few.[2] This reading of the copulas has been castigated as deeply incoherent by Peter Geach and other followers of the syntactic and semantic doctrines of Gottlob Frege. Geach, aptly calling this reading "the two-term theory of predication," characterized it as "Aristotle's Fall," comparing it darkly with Adam and Eve's more well-known Fall.[3] It is somewhat ironic that Quine, a major proponent of quantification theory, has actually been a key figure in demonstrating the coherence of the term functor approach.

(2) *The reduction of the relation of identity to the copulas of predication.* Sommers has gone further than Quine in not only assimilating singular predications to predications indifferently particular and/or universal (of 'wild quantity'), but also in reinterpreting statements of identity as predications with both terms singular or uniquely denoting. The distinctive functions of the relation of identity are effectively discharged by the copulas of predication, a striking economy that Quine did not pick up on.[4]

(3) *The insight that all logical inference can be seen as proceeding through mutual cancellation of oppositely (positively or negatively) charged elements (whether terms or sentences).* This aspect of Sommers's work has been widely criticized, and I will shortly add my own voice to the criticism of his +/− notation. But I will also argue that his basic insight is supported by the success of the closely analogous method of resolution in offering an effective, sound, and complete account of logical inference.

(4) *The detailed development of a useful subsystem of term functor logic that includes not only classical syllogistic involving categoricals with monadic terms but also what we can call "relational syllogistic" or "nonclassical" syllogistic involving relations.*[5]   The inference rules of this system proceed in an essentially algebraic style, through simple, blocklike, term-for-term substitutions rather than relying on the standard methods of instantiation/generalization of the bound variables of quantification.

This paper will not touch on elements (1) and (2) above but will concentrate on (3) and (4), the themes of cancellation and syllogistic.

2

Let me begin with sentential logic, which does not involve any of the complexities associated with instantiation and is thus an ideal candidate for term functor, algebraic-style treatment. And yet, ironically, this has been the least fruitful application of Sommers's cancellation technique and the +/− notation that aims to implement it. I believe that the element lacking here is a systematic deployment of normal form. If such deployment is coupled with the technique of cancellation, we get a very efficient, comprehensive treatment of sentential inference.

Sommers's notation assigns +/− signs to both unary functors (here just sentence negation and its opposite, affirmation [explicitly marked by +]) and binary functors such as sentential conjunction, disjunction, and the conditional. In the case of binary functors, ordered pairs of +/− signs are assigned: $+p + q$ to $p \,\&\, q$, $-p + q$ to $p \rightarrow q$, and the confusing $--p\, --q$ to $p \vee q$. I will not repeat the frequently voiced criticisms, with which I am in substantial agreement, that the limited heuristic value of these assignments is more than offset by the numerous restrictions to the standard ways these algebraic signs interact in their usual arithmetical contexts—restrictions due to the semantical ambiguities of the +/− signs.[6] I will limit myself to the observation that the syllogistic provenance of these assignments, which raises conjunction and the conditional into prominence (because of their correspondence with the copulas 'i' and 'a' of particular and universal categoricals, respectively), helps plunge disjunction into relative obscurity. The result is a cumbersome and ambiguous representation for disjunction. However, it is disjunction with its commutativity and associativity, rather than the conditional, that plays the role of the major partner of conjunction in the two most influential treatments of normal form, the disjunctive (alternational) and conjunctive normal forms (from now on, DNF and CNF, respectively). Not surprisingly, the awkward representation of disjunction in Sommers's +/− notation has resulted in a cramped style of doing sentential logic.

Sommers's algebra, by itself, has difficulty handling inferences like the following:

(1) $(p \rightarrow q) \rightarrow r$

$\underline{-p}$

r

In Sommers's algebra, we get:

$-(-p + q) + r$

$\underline{-p}$

$-q + r$ (through cancellation of $-p$ and $--p$, after driving the
                 negation into the parentheses)

This conclusion, in Sommers's notation the equivalent of '$q \rightarrow r$', does indeed follow validly from the premises, but how are we to generate the conclusion 'r' by means of cancellation? (As we shall see, the method of resolution yields the conjunction 'r & $(q \rightarrow r)$', which implies both the above partial conclusions.)

Even worse is:

(2) p & q

      $(p \lor r) \rightarrow s$

      s

Sommers's algebra yields:

$+p + q$

$\underline{-(--p\ --r) + s}$

$+q - r + s$

As it stands, this algebraic representation of the conclusion can be interpreted in different ways in the absence of clear rules for handling parentheses. An available interpretation would be '$(q$ & $-r)$ & s', an invalid conclusion; another yields the valid but partial conclusion 'q & $(r \rightarrow s)$'. The problem here is twofold: first, the conclusion is not unambiguously determined, and second, there seems to be no way of getting a valid inference to 's'. (The method of resolution yields 'q & s & $(-r \lor s)$', which implies both 's' and 'q & $(r \rightarrow s)$'.)

Sommers's algebra is certainly not devoid of heuristic value, but it cannot by itself, without further guidance, reliably generate determinate conclusions. Prior doctoring of the premises into some more tractable form, something approaching a normal form, is clearly needed. It is no accident that Sommers has come to rely increasingly on the formulation of normal inference patterns for both sentential and syllogistic logic. His basic syllogistic rule has been an ingenious generalization of the Aristotelian/Scholastic "Dictum de Omni" (in Sommers's words, "what is true of every M is true of any M [M being the middle term of the syllogism]," Sommers 1990, p.

118). The sentential version of the generalized syllogistic rule can be formulated as follows, using Sommers's terminology for the two premises:

Rule S: $-p + q$ (the "donor" premise)

$$\frac{\overset{+}{\Phi}(p)}{\overset{+}{\Phi}(q/p)} \quad \text{(the "host" or "matrix" premise)}$$

$\Phi(q/p)$ (conclusion)

'$-p + q$' is Sommers's rendition of '$p \rightarrow q$'. $\overset{+}{\Phi}(p)$ represents a context in which sentence 'p' *occurs positively*, and $\Phi(q/p)$ represents the same context, but with 'q' having replaced the positive occurrence of 'p' in question.

To understand how Rule S works, notice that in the first premise 'p' has a negative occurrence, whereas in the second premise 'p' has a positive occurrence. The conclusion results through cancellation of these two oppositely charged occurrences, and it exactly mirrors the host or matrix premise except that the positive occurrence of 'p' in that premise has been replaced by 'q' (contributed by the donor premise). Here is the power of the rule: no matter how complicated the host or matrix premise may be, if 'p' occurs positively in it, then we can "jump to the conclusion" by simply plugging 'q' in place of 'p' and leaving everything else, that is, the entire structure of the matrix, undisturbed. (The reason I am placing the + sign *above* the letter p is that it represents the "overall charge" of p, not necessarily a + sign that may immediately precede it; hence it is not part of the actual sentential notation.)

It should be clear that the formulation of Sommers's Rule S cannot get off the ground without the key notion of a *positive*, as opposed to a *negative*, occurrence of a component sentence within a given sentence. The notion can be defined as follows. First, the scope of a negation sign '$-$' is given by the following rules: (i) If a '$-$' sign is immediately followed by a '(', then its scope is all of the material between that '(' and the corresponding ')'. (ii) Otherwise, the scope of a '$-$' is the atomic sentence that immediately follows it. An occurrence of a component sentence p (atomic or compound) within a sentence $\Phi(p)$ is then defined as *positive* if and only if it lies in the scope of zero or an even number of '$-$' signs. Such a case can be represented by $\Phi(\overset{+}{p})$. If p lies within the scope of an odd number of '$-$' signs in $\Phi(p)$, then the occurrence is defined as *negative*, and can be represented as $\Phi(\overset{-}{p})$.[7] For example, the occurrence of 'p' in '$(p \rightarrow r) \rightarrow s$' is positive, because in its algebraic representation $'-(-p + r) + s'$, $'p'$ is in the scope of two '−' signs.

Sommers may have begun with the central idea of cancellation in "The Calculus of Terms," but he was increasingly driven to substitution within a matrix in order reliably to guide the generation of the conclusion. Substitution, however, is closely connected to normal form. For example, since the premises in inferences (1) and (2) above are nowhere near the normal pattern required by Rule S as they stand, Rule S cannot get a grip, even though the opposed charges of p in the two premises hold a promise of eventual cancellation—but though only with prior doctoring.

3

Sommers's impressively powerful Rule S seems inextricably bound up with his +/− notation. Contrary to first impressions, however, it is not.[8] His innovative use of the notion of the overall positive/negative charge of a sentence (or term) can be shown to be completely independent of his otherwise problematic notation. I believe it to be the valuable nugget within it.

To see this, let us undo the +/− representation of all binary functors (sentential connectives), sticking to the standard notation of &, $\vee$, $\rightarrow$. Let us retain only the sign of sentence negation (unary functor), dropping the explicit + sign of sentence affirmation, as is customary. Since we will be working with CNF, let us use normal form notation, transcribing $'p \rightarrow q'$ as $'-p \vee q'$. We are now down to a notation consisting of $\vee$, &, and −, just like the notation of CNF and DNF.

We can now use the definition of positive or negative occurrence of a sentence p within a sentence Φ of which p is a component: the occurrence is positive if and only if it lies within the scope of zero or an even number of negation signs '−'; otherwise it is negative. In fact, the overall +/− charges of each sentence in this notation are identical with those of the same sentences transcribed in Sommers's notation. It is easy to see why: the translation of $'p \rightarrow q'$ as $'-p \vee q'$ parallels Sommers's $'-p + q'$ in terms of positive/negative charges, whereas his renditions of $'p$ & q' as $'+p + q'$ and $'p \vee q'$ as $'--p --q'$ leave the overall +/− charges unaffected. Thus, Sommers's +/− charges reflect something more fundamental than a peculiarity of his particular notation.

Sommers's Rule S can now be reformulated in more standard notation as follows:

RS: $-p \vee q$ donor premise (translation of '$p \rightarrow q$')

$$\overset{+}{\Phi(p)} \quad \text{matrix premise}$$

$$\overset{+}{\Phi(q/p)} \quad \text{conclusion}$$

To show the power of the rule, the following two examples will suffice:

(a) $-p \vee q$ {or $p \rightarrow q$}   donor premise   (b) $-p \vee q$

$$\overset{+}{(-r \vee s) \rightarrow (t \vee p)} \quad \text{matrix premise} \quad \overset{+}{(p \rightarrow r) \rightarrow s}$$

$$(-r \vee s) \rightarrow (t \vee q) \quad \text{conclusion} \quad (q \rightarrow r) \rightarrow s$$

4

The reformulation of Rule S in customary notation makes it easier to notice that RS includes as a special case *the resolution principle*, a powerful sentential inference rule that anchors a comprehensive (in fact, sound and complete) method of generating and testing inferences widely used in computer science and AI, namely, the method of resolution.[9]

The resolution principle operates on a pair of disjunctive clauses to yield a third disjunctive clause, their *resolvent*:

$-p \vee q$

$r \vee p$

$r \vee q$ (where p, q, r can be any sentences, atomic or compound)

The method of resolution, in its purely sentential application, works by reducing each sentence (premise) to CNF, that is, an n-place conjunction of disjunctive clauses of literals, that is, atomic sentences or their negations. Then the resolution principle is repeatedly called on to "resolve" pairs of distinct disjunctive clauses containing opposed (affirmative/negative) literals (like 'p' and '$-p$'). The effect is to "cancel" such pairs of opposed literals, so the method of resolution could be called, perhaps more aptly, *the method of cancellation*.

In the example above, the premise '$-p \vee q$' plays the role of the donor premise, '$r \vee p$' plays the role of the matrix premise, and the conclusion '$r \vee q$' is the same as the matrix, except that 'q' has been substituted for 'p', just as in Rule S. The inferential mechanism of the resolution principle can be seen to operate through a mutual *cancellation* of the pair of affirmative-versus-negative occurrences of the recurrent component p (the *middle term* of classical syllogistic) and the *substitution* of q (the partner of the negative occurrence of p) in the place of the positive occurrence of p. Thus we are back again to Sommers's themes of cancellation and substitution.

The claim I previously made that Sommers's idea of cancellation coupled with the notion of a normal form would result in a powerful and elegant treatment of inference is now firmly established, since the resolution principle is a special case of Sommers's Rule S. In the same way that Quine's predicate functor logic provides a theoretical underpinning for the feasibility of Sommers's programme of a term functor approach to logical syntax, the method of resolution provides an underpinning for his ideas of cancellation and substitution.

I conclude this section by showing how the method of resolution handles the Sommers-resistant examples of inferences (1) and (2) above:

(1) The premise $(p \rightarrow q) \rightarrow r$ is reduced to CNF: $-(-p \vee q) \vee r$, equivalent to $(p \& -q) \vee r$, equivalent to $(p \vee r) \& (-q \vee r)$. The CNF of the conjunction of the premises is $-p \& (p \vee r) \& (-q \vee r)$, which resolves to $r \& (-q \vee r)$. By simplification we can get both $-q \vee r$ and r as conclusions.

(2) The premise $(p \vee r) \rightarrow s$ is reduced to CNF through the following equivalence transformations: first to $-(p \vee r) \vee s$, then to $(-p \& -r) \vee s$, and finally to $(-p \vee s) \& (-r \vee s)$. Resolving the CNF of the conjunction of the premises, $p \& q \& (-p \vee s) \& (-r \vee s)$, yields $q \& s \& (-r \vee s)$.

5

Where does this leave us? Have I come to praise Sommers's account of inference by burying it safely in the method of resolution? Not really. Sommers's Rule S does much more than just include the resolution principle as a special case. The rule's distinctive power, based on Sommers's key notion of the positive/negative occurrence of a component sentence, is to generate a conclusion by simple substitution without going through the actual steps of reduction to CNF and cancellation. In a sense, it represents the triumph of substitution over cancellation, by "jumping to the conclusion" and shortcutting reduction to normal form.

How is this possible? And how is it related to Sommers's use of positive/negative charges? The answer, in a nutshell, is that as each premise (already couched in CNF notation, that is, expressed solely in terms of &, ∨, and –) is reduced to CNF, each sentence's overall charge remains invariant through all relevant equivalence transformations; hence, oppositely charged occurrences of a recurrent component p in the premises will be inherited (possibly multiplied) by CNF, and thus will be reliable predictors of forthcoming resolution/cancellation at the CNF stage. At that stage, resolution acts to substitute q for p, and the original matrix Φ in which p was positively embedded can then be reassembled sentence-for-sentence and functor-for-functor except that q now occupies the place of p in Φ.[10]

The economy afforded by Rule S is impressive, but how about examples like inferences (1) and (2) above that fall through the cracks? Is there anything more economical than full-dress reduction to CNF? Possibly in particular cases, but not in general. However, it is easy to show that virtually every premise of the form $\Phi(\overset{-}{p})$ can be reduced to the pattern '$(p \rightarrow \theta)$ & X', so that Rule S could then be applied to a matrix premise or premises of the form $\Phi(\overset{+}{p})$. To see this, $\Phi(\overset{-}{p})$ is reduced to CNF, with $-p$ appearing in one or more disjunctive clauses, whose conjunction, by the distributive law, is equivalent to a '$-p \lor \theta$' pattern, equivalent, in turn to '$p \rightarrow \theta$'. The entire CNF, then, has the form '$(p \rightarrow \theta)$ & X'. Inference (2) above can be handled this way.

The only exceptions to this general reduction are cases where X is absent, which does not affect the applicability of Rule S, or cases where θ is absent, or both. Inference (1) above is a case where both X and θ are absent, and Rule S does not strictly apply. However, by stipulating that '$-p$' is to be replaced in such cases by its equivalent '$p \rightarrow F$', the rule goes through, and we can get the desired result by simplifying '$F \lor r$' to 'r'.

Therefore, any case where the resolution principle applies to two premises of the form $\Phi(\overset{-}{p})$ and $\psi(\overset{+}{p})$ to generate an inference that cancels p is also a case that can be handled by Rule S. But since the above method of extracting a premise of the form '$p \rightarrow \theta$' is tantamount to full reduction to CNF, this result is of only theoretical, not practical import.

6

We are now in a position to move on to syllogistic logic—not just classical syllogistic inferences but also relational or nonclassical ones of the type that Sommers has pioneered in analyzing. The analysis will be along the same lines as that of sentential logic.

Here, too, Sommers has moved in the direction of subjugating algebraic cancellation to substitution within a matrix. His fundamental rule, a generalization of the Aristotelian–Scholastic Dictum de Omni (DDO), is the analogue in term logic of the sentential Rule S that I have already discussed. Expressed in Sommers's +/– notation, it can be formulated as follows:

DDO: $-M + P$ categorical or donor premise

$$\frac{\overset{+}{\Phi(M)}}{\underset{+}{\Phi(P/M)}}$$ matrix or host premise

$\Phi(P/M)$ conclusion

where P and M are now monadic terms instead of sentences and Φ represents a sentential context in which the "middle term" M *occurs positively*. '$-M + P$' is Sommers's representation of universal categoricals. The plus sign above the term letter M indicates, as before, the *overall* charge of the term M and is not a part of the actual notation. For example, the occurrence of M in 'Some S is R to everything that is F to every M' is positive overall (as its transcription in Sommers's notation shows: $+S + R - (F - M)$), yet it is immediately preceded by a '$-$' sign. The key notions of a *positive versus negative* occurrence of a term M (atomic or compound) within a sentence $\Phi(M)$ are defined exactly as before.

It should not come as a surprise that Sommers's essential innovation, the overall $+$ or $-$ charge of each term, proves to be not a peculiarity of his notation but rather eminently graftable onto the standard notation of quantification theory. Nor should it come as a surprise that this innovation, by helping us to syllogistically "jump to the conclusion" by substitution in a matrix, is as useful in nonsentential logic as it proved to be for sentential logic.

Adopting a standard notation for first-order quantification theory consisting of the quantifiers '$\exists$' and '$\forall$', variables 'x', 'y', 'z', etc., and atomic or compound open sentences, 'Px', 'Mx', 'Rxy', 'My & Rxy', etc., we can assign a positive or negative occurrence to every *closed sentence*, atomic or compound, and every *open sentence*, atomic or compound. In particular, we can assign a + or – overall charge to every open sentence with one free variable (which is the widest possible generalization of a traditional *monadic term*, and it is monadic terms that play the central role in syllogistic reasoning).[11] Again, it is only the even or odd number of the familiar unary negation signs that determines the overall charge; the quantifiers, like the binary sentential connectives, do not receive +/– representations.

We are still operating with a normal form (CNF) notation for sentential connectives, translating, for example, '$Fx \rightarrow Ryx$' to '$-Fx \lor Ryx$'. With this proviso, all assignments of overall +/– value again coincide with Sommers's. Thus assignments of overall +/– value are clearly not dependent or Sommers's particular notation but can be grafted onto any adequate notation, whether that of quantification theory or that of a form of term functor logic. The choice of notation for relational syllogistic is, therefore, wide open.

The DDO analogue in the notation of first-order quantification theory can now be formulated as follows:

Categorical (donor) premise: $(\forall x)\,(Mx \rightarrow Px)$ (or $(\forall x)\,(-Mx \lor Px)$)

Matrix (host) premise: $\overset{+}{\Phi(My)}$

Conclusion $\overset{+}{\Phi(Py/My)}$

where 'Mx', 'Px' are open sentences with one free variable x, and 'My', 'Py' are open sentences with one free variable y, not necessarily distinct from x.

This rule can be established as a derived rule in a standard system of natural deduction that uses the method of resolution for sentential inferences. The proof begins with chains of universal and existential instantiation to get down to sentential logic. It then proceeds to shortcut reduction to CNF and resolution by using substitution according to the sentential syllogistic Rule S, and finally ends up restoring quantifiers by universal and existential generalization corresponding to the initial uses of UI and EI.[12]

Viewing the operations of this syllogistic rule against the background of the full method of resolution, which includes instantiation, reduction to CNF, resolution, and generalization, we see DDO as "jumping to its conclusion" in full algebraic style through simple term-for-term substitution, successfully shortcutting the foregoing complex processes of inference. Therein lies its power and efficiency. And, of course, the intuitive simplicity and compactness of this "jumping to the conclusion" as compared to the complex bookkeeping of instantiation is the very basis of Sommers's claim that the DDO forms the backbone of our actual inferential cognitive processes. Note, however, that acceptance of this claim about the DDO need not commit us to Sommers's further claim that his +/– algebra models inferential cognitive processes. Sommers's algebra is one possible representation of the workings of the DDO, but it is neither the only one nor necessarily the most efficient. The cognitive status of the DDO can and should be assessed independently of Sommers's claims about his algebra.

I would like to conclude by proposing a general characterization of syllogistic inference strongly suggested by the foregoing analysis. It goes like this: in tractable, that is, syllogistic, cases, we can instantiate, disassemble in reducing to CNF, resolve, or "cancel," then reassemble and generalize to a conclusion whose structure matches that of the matrix premise up to a simple algebraic substitution. But there are less tractable cases where the conclusion, though still generated through resolution/cancellation, cannot be reassembled into a structure that can be effectively generated from the matrix premise by substitution or some other transformation rule of comparable simplicity. This, it seems to me, gets at the very essence of what syllogistic patterns are and where their boundaries lie, whether they occur in sentential logic or in the logic of terms or predicates. The *process* of inference can always be analyzed as one of cancellation, but the *result* is not always syllogistically predictable (that is, recoverable from the matrix).

Notes

This paper was presented at a conference on the work of Fred Sommers at the University of Ottawa in 1995.

1. For Sommers's treatment, see Sommers 1990 and, for more details, 1982. For Quine's late formulation, see "Predicates, Terms, and Classes," in Quine 1981. Note especially his adoption of a binary predication functor or copula on p. 168. Earlier formulations are to be found in "The Variable" (1972), "Algebraic Logic and Predicate Functors" (1970), both reprinted in Quine 1976, and "Variables Explained Away" (1960), reprinted in Quine 1966.

2. See Sommers 1982 and Noah 1987, 1973.

3. Geach 1980, 1.5, p. 47.

4. See Sommers 1990, section 6; Sommers 1982, ch. 6; Sommers 1969.

5. See Sommers 1990 and Sommers 1982, chs. 7 and 9.

6. See Charles Sayward, "Some problems with TFL," essay 12 in Englebretsen 1987.

7. The preceding definitions of the scope of a negation sign and the positive/negative occurrence of a component are indebted to Clifton McIntosh, appendix F to Sommers 1982, pp. 395–396.

8. Noah 1993.

9. The method of resolution was developed by J. A. Robinson (1965, 1968). A useful account of it can be found in Davis and Weyuker 1983, part 3, chs. 11 and 12.

10. For details and proofs, see Noah 1993, sections 6 and 7.

11. See Noah 1993, section 5.

12. See Noah 1993, section 8.

References

Davis, M., and Weyuker, E. 1983. *Computability Complexity, and Languages: Fundamentals of Theoretical Computer Science.* New York: Academic Press.

Englebretsen, G. (ed.). 1987. *The New Syllogistic.* New York: Peter Lang.

Geach, P. T. 1980. *Logic Matters.* Berkeley: University of California Press.

Noah, A. 1973. *Singular Terms and Predication.* Ph.D. thesis, Brandeis University.

Noah, A. 1987. "The Two Term Theory of Predication." In Englebretsen 1987: 223–243.

Noah, A. 1993. "Non-Classical Syllogistic Inference and the Method of Resolution." *Notre Dame Journal of Formal Logic* 34: 209–222.

Quine, W. V. O. 1966. *Selected Logic Papers.* New York: Random House.

Quine, W. V. O. 1976. *The Ways of Paradox and Other Essays.* Cambridge, Mass.: Harvard University Press.

Quine, W. V. O. 1981. *Theories and Things.* Cambridge, Mass.: Harvard University Press.

Robinson, J. 1965. "A Machine-Oriented Logic Based on the Resolution Principle." *Journal of the Association for Computing Machinery* 12: 23–41.

Robinson, J. 1968. "The Generalized Resolution Principle." In D. Michie (ed.), *Machine Intelligence* 3 (New York: Elsevier, 1968): 77–93.

Sommers, F. 1969. "Do We Need Identity?" *Journal of Philosophy* 66: 499–504.

Sommers, F. 1970. "The Calculus of Terms." *Mind* 79: 1–39. Reprinted in Englebretsen 1987: 11–56.

Sommers, F. 1982. *The Logic of Natural Language.* Oxford: Clarendon Press.

Sommers, F. 1990. "Predication in the Logic of Terms." *Notre Dame Journal of Formal Logic* 31: 107–126.

10 Predicate Logic and Bare Particulars

David S. Oderberg

1 Introduction

What is the relationship between logic and metaphysics? It goes without saying that we want our metaphysics to be logical; but do we want our logic to be metaphysical? To put it another way, do we want logic to do any metaphysical work? Logic is essentially a tool for getting at truth; it is *the* tool, for without it no reasoning is possible in any field of human enquiry whatsoever. But it cannot get to truth without already having truth on which to work: as G. K. Chesterton once remarked, "you can only find truth with logic if you have already found truth without it."[1] Armed with truth, we use logic to get more truth, even if what we get is "only" the actual combination or division of ideas that were already potentially combined or divided in the truth with which we started.

Since logic is a tool for truth, and since truth is about being, logic must in this sense be metaphysical. But since logic can be applied to fairies and phantoms as much as to bed knobs and broomsticks, we cannot say that logic must be about what is. I imagine Quine would agree with this last sentence. All propositions, for him, have the form of either assertions or denials of existence. In reasoning about the world, proponents of rival theories (his preferred term) advance competing existential claims (and denials). A claim is true only if the predicates it contains are true of the values of the variables. When we do not reason about the world, we do logic by evaluating existence claims that we entertain without necessarily asserting, and hence which quantify over objects to which we are not necessarily committed.

If that is all there is to the metaphysics of modern predicate logic (MPL), a traditionalist logician—by which I mean anyone adhering to the

Aristotelian/Scholastic syllogistic as a system of logic,[2] in particular to the contemporary traditional formal/term functor logic (TFL) devised by Fred Sommers—can happily agree with his Fregean counterpart. Maybe, for many Fregeans, that is as far as the relationship between logic and metaphysics goes. In Quine, however, something more seems to be at work, something at once mysterious and difficult to extract from his copious writings in defense of MPL. Whether it has ramifications for the philosophy of MPL as such is not easy to say. Certainly it indicates that, for one of its three most vocal defenders in the twentieth century (the other two being Michael Dummett and Peter Geach), MPL is far more ontologically laden than might appear to those who use it without philosophizing about it. We already know that for Frege MPL was metaphysical in the sense of requiring an ontology of concepts/functions that seemed to go proxy for old-fashioned universals and were to be contrasted with objects, as well as of making existence a second-level property of concepts.[3] These were not mere requirements of a semantic interpretation of sentences in MPL, but features suggested by the notation itself, part of the very syntax of quantification.

In Quine, scattered remarks and suggestions indicate an even more far-reaching metaphysical cast to predicate logic. For it appears that Quine's account of MPL commits it to the doctrine of *bare particulars*, the idea that there exist essentially featureless objects that ground numerical identity and difference between the objects of ordinary experience, these being no more than complexes consisting of bundles of features borne by the bare particulars. If so, it does not mean that MPL per se is indubitably committed to bare particulars. At most it suggests that the possibility should be taken very seriously. And since bare particulars should be rejected, we have some grounds for thinking that there is at least a metaphysical question mark hanging over MPL that its ideological defenders need to address.[4]

2 Syntactic Pointers

Beginning, as any logician should, with basic linguistic observations, Sommers has often pointed out the marked lack of resemblance between a sentence like

(1) All bakers rise early

and its proto-MPL translation

(1P) Everything is such that if it is a baker it rises early

which then goes into canonical MPL as

(1M) $(x)(Bx \rightarrow Rx)$.

For a start, (1P)/(1M) is in conditional form. Second, it contains two copulae and two predications: 'Everything *is* . . .' (copula), '. . . *is* a baker', (copula/predication), '. . . rises' (predication). Simple sentences of form (1P)/(1M) will contain a mix of copulation and predication depending on the kind of predicates used; but the copulation of 'Everything is . . .' will always be present. Of course, defenders of MPL, in particular Peter Geach, make much of the fact that no copulae actually appear in (1M), and hence that MPL gives "no special content" to the copula.[5] He is content to treat the copula as just "part of [the] predicable," with no "definite content."[6] Geach admits that this "does not settle the problem of the copula,"[7] but he does not then go on explicitly to settle it. Nevertheless, his idea is clear enough. Frege's distinction between saturated and unsaturated expressions obviates the need for any concern about the logical function of the copula: the Fregean logician just bundles the 'is' into the predicate and we thereby have a revival of the Platonic and early Aristotelian *onoma/rhema* (name/verb) theory of the proposition.

Traditional logic, on the other hand, according to Geach, warped the minds of pupils by "drilling" them in "twisting propositions into a form where they had a predicable beginning 'is' or 'are', and preferably one consisting of that prefixed to a noun (-phrase); this was a pernicious training, which might well disable the pupils for [*sic*] recognizing predicables that had not this special form."[8] Immediately we get a sense of the motivation behind what seems to be one of Quine's more outlandish doctrines. For suppose with the friends of MPL that the true form of the singular proposition is essentially the binary name-verb form (the atomicity thesis holding that all propositions are compounded from these building blocks by the sentential and quantificational rules of MPL). Since the copula is an irrelevant distraction with no "special content," we should not think it a mutation to move from 'Grass is green'—the copula being present in all its glory—to 'Gg', the copula having been swallowed by the predicate. But then how to read 'Gg' without insisting on the presence of the copula? Think of it as something like 'Grass greens', or 'Grass greenizes'. But then if speaking of something's *greenizing* is not to be taken as a weird distortion of logical syntax, neither should the same procedure as applied to names themselves: hence the 'Socratizing' and 'Pegasizing' so beloved of Quine in his elimination of names in canonical notation, to which we shall return.

Third, (1P) contains two pronouns and (1M) contains three variables, whereas (1) contains nothing that even looks like any of these devices. The connection between variable and pronoun is of course not accidental: Quine, as with Geach, holds that the bound variables of MPL just are the canonical representation of natural language pronouns; as Quine puts it, "The variable, properly considered . . . is simply the heir to the relative pronoun."[9] And again, he says: "[Y]ou may say that the objects of a theory are what the general terms are true of; or, again, what the pronouns can refer to. These versions do amount pretty much to saying that the objects are the values of the quantified variables. . . ."[10] Quine's emphasis on the relative pronoun is due to his belief that it is the syntactic key to objective reference.[11] More specifically, although natural language (for which English will stand as the representative, as it usually—and perhaps dangerously—does) contains both relative pronouns (e.g., 'who', 'which', 'that') and nonrelative pronouns (e.g., 'he', 'it', 'they', demonstratives, interrogatives), according to Quine, any sentence, however complex, containing a name can be transformed into a complex predication consisting of the name as subject and the remaining context, rendered into relative clause form, as predicate. So, for example:

(2) John went to the shop and bought some milk

becomes

(2R) {who went to the shop and (who) bought some milk} John.

(2R) has no natural English reading, and indeed the relative pronoun does not, as far as natural language syntax goes, seem well suited to this sort of manipulation since it is not always even part of a syntactically coherent whole, as Geach points out with sentences such as:

(3) A boy who was fooling her kissed a girl who loved him.[12]

Nevertheless, for both Quine and Geach this does not present a problem for the MPL rendering of any predication whether it contains an explicit relative clause or not. Quine points to the "variant of the relative clause, favoured by mathematicians for the simplicity of its syntax,"[13] namely, the 'such that' construction. (2) can be rendered as

(2R') John is such that he went to the shop and (he) bought some milk

or indeed as

(2R") John is a thing such that it went to the shop and (it) bought some milk

but in singular predication, as Quine says, the relative pronoun functions as a pronoun of laziness (Geach's term), that is, as a replacement for the antecedent singular term and replaceable by it without loss of sense.[14] Pronouns come into their own referentially or objectually, however, when used ineliminably in categorical propositions consisting, says Quine, of the "substantivized relative clause 'things which . . .' . . . preceded by 'every' or some'."[15] Here, he adds, there is no predication available for equating with the original sentence from which the relative construction is derived. We cannot render (1) as a relative predication, applying '. . . is a thing such that it rises early' to the subject 'all bakers', because, as the founders of MPL taught us, expressions like 'all bakers' are not syntactic or semantic subjects. Hence the rendering by (1P)/(1M). Bound variables that function only as pronouns of laziness are substitutional; but as ineliminable pronouns they are purely referential, taking objects as their values. So, according to Quine, the relative pronoun, construed in the broad way he does to encompass 'such that' constructions and repetitions of what linguists take to be personal and other nonrelative pronouns, is at the heart of objective reference.

3   Syntax and Reference

But we may now ask: *what* is referred to by the variable? One might think the answer is "Any kind of object you like," but this would be too quick. Let us return to common or garden proto-MPL formulas such as (1P) and its MPL translation (1M):

(1P) Everything is such that if it is a baker it rises early

(1M) $(x)(Bx \rightarrow Rx)$.

Another look at (1P) shows that it simply does not make sense because of the undivided word 'everything'. The natural linguistic urge is to look back for the reference of 'it', which, as we are told from the moment we begin studying MPL, is a misplaced urge because 'it' does not refer back to anything, least of all to everything since 'everything' does not itself refer. But surely 'it', being a noun, refers to something? The simple MPL answer is that it refers plurally ("ranges over" being the term of art) to its values. But we cannot bypass (1P): we still have to give an account of the quantificational idiom there if we are to have any understanding of how to construe 'refers plurally to its values' as applied to (1M). We can dispose quickly of Quine's famous warning that we do not find objecthood wherever we find a noun, his example being 'sake'; for 'sake' is quite clearly a kind of thing; it refers to the benefit, regard, or consideration with a view to which something is done, and the fact of its being a nonce-word (as the *OED* puts it), that is, a word used only in a very specific if unique context (as 'for the sake of'), is irrelevant.

Maybe, since (1P) makes no sense, we should split 'everything' into 'every' and 'thing'? After all, that will give us the sense-making

(1P') Every thing is such that if it is a baker it rises early.

Quine comes close to considering this when he seeks to differentiate between logical and nonlogical expressions.[16] He says that even if we split 'everything' into two morphemes it does not affect his proposed mark of distinction between the grammatical particles and the lexical elements (which he wants to use as a criterion marking the logical from the nonlogical) because the criterion is quantitative: "a morpheme is a particle or a lexical element according as there are fewer or many expressions in its grammatical category."[17] 'Every', like 'some', will qualify as a logical particle, and so will 'thing', since none of them accept many substitutes without incoherence. True enough for his example, 'There was something new on the Rialto', or indeed for just about any context one can think of; but one might as well say that 'grandfather', consisting of the morphemes 'grand' and 'father', is made up of two logical particles owing to the lack of grammatical substitutability. The same goes for treating 'something' as a single morpheme: in some contexts, such as the 'Rialto' one, the word admits of few coherent substitutions, which on Quine's criterion means it is logical; but in others, such as 'There was something on the ground', plenty of substitutions are available—so is 'something' logical or lexical?

We should drop the quantitative criterion, but the dual-morpheme proposal is suggestive. We have linguistic evidence for it inasmuch as, until about the nineteenth century, occurrences of the split 'some thing', 'any thing', and so on, were about as common as the undivided word. Why not go all the way and make the division? After all, it makes the sensical (1P′) out of the nonsensical (1P). Further, parallel logical form is not shown by 'Every baker is self-identical' and 'Everything is self-identical', but it is when the latter becomes 'Every thing is self-identical'. Moreover, splitting the word suggests, as it should, that 'thing' is a nonlogical expression: for why should it be considered logical when 'baker' or 'triangle' is not in the same sentential context? Quine is right that we should at least take our cue for logicality from the linguistic categories on which we have to work, and these are such that, quite clearly, 'thing' and its cognates 'object' and 'entity' are lexical and not grammatical. Yet he takes the variable to be a logical particle. It refers both back to its binding quantifier[18] and plurally to its values since it is *the* vehicle of objective reference. It is starting to look like a strange beast indeed.

Nor, from the viewpoint of basic syntax and intelligibility, does restricted quantification fare any better. For suppose the friend of MPL renders (1) as

(1PR) Everything that is a baker is such that it rises early

(1MR) $(x, \text{baker})(x \text{ rises early})$.

What has been gained? Restricted quantification does indeed approximate more closely to the categorical sentences of Aristotelian syllogistic—for one thing, universal and existential generalizations are not parsed as conditionals and conjunctions, respectively—but it is still not clear how the restricted sentences such as (1PR)/(1MR) are to be read. The reason is that they do not do away with variables; they are not mere notational variants of (1), for instance. They seem to be undesirable halfway houses between the syllogistic forms and the forms of unrestricted quantification. Like its unrestricted cousin, 'Everything that is a baker is such that it rises early' makes no sense without a mental splitting of the quantifier: 'Every thing that is a baker is such that it rises early'. To reinforce the idea that a mental splitting is necessary, ask yourself, upon reading (1P) and (1PR): 'But how could everything be a baker?' The predicate logician would, of course, respond to anyone who asked such a—silly—question that they had obviously not done Logic 101. But that is the point. One of the first things Logic 101 teaches us, if not explicitly then at least by implication, is that one must make a mental split of the quantifier corresponding to the syntactic split in '($\forall x$)' and '($\exists x$)'. (Whether '$\forall$' is present or absent is irrelevant—the same reading is taught for '(x)'.)

To see why (1PR)/(1MR) are not notational variants of the syllogistic forms and have more in common with the unrestricted formulas of MPL than with the former, consider first the reading of (1). We know that it is *not* to be read as

(1') Every man is such that if he is a baker then he rises early

precisely because the variable is unrestricted and so ranges over everything. The unrestricted rendering of (1') into proto-MPL is

(1P') Everything is such that if it is a man, then if it is a baker it rises early

whence

(1M') $(x)(Mx \rightarrow (Bx \rightarrow Rx))$.

So why can we not say that it is the restricted rendering that should follow (1')? Because (1'), when restricted quantification is used, becomes

(1PR') Everything that is a man is such that if it is a baker then it rises early

(1MR') $(x, man)(x$ is a baker $\rightarrow x$ rises early)

or, better

(1PR'') Everything that is a man and a baker is such that it rises early

(1MR'') $(x, man, baker)(x$ rises early).

In other words, the variable in restricted MPL is as necessary as in unrestricted MPL. So when the friend of restricted quantification charges unrestricted quantification with the counterintuitive feature of translating a universal generalization such as 'All bakers rise early' into a sentence that is not about bakers but about everything including boxers, boxes, and blocks—more precisely, about everything including things that happen to be boxers, boxes, or blocks—the ready response by the friend of unrestricted quantification ought to be a *tu quoque*: his rival might not translate 'All bakers rise early' into a sentence about things that happen to be boxers, boxes, or blocks, but he does turn it into a sentence about things that also happen to be bakers. And from the point of view of the friend of traditional logic, for whom 'All bakers rise early' is about *bakers*, not boxers, or things that happen to be boxers, or even things that happen to be bakers, it is a case of 'A plague on both your houses'.[19]

4   Names, Pronouns, and Bare Particulars

As noted earlier, for Geach—upholding as he does the Fregean position adhered to at least implicitly by all predicate logicians—there is no special content to the copula. The fact that there is no single verb for 'to be green' is a mere accident of language. Latin and Greek often do without the copula, as does Hebrew. We could just as comprehensibly say 'Green, the grass' or 'The grass, green'; or, to avoid ambiguity, we could neologize: 'The grass greenizes'. This way of thinking prepares us for the Quinean move to eliminate names from canonical notation through the process of socratization (otherwise known as quining the name and russelling the description). From

(4) Socrates is wise

we get

(4P) There is a thing that uniquely socratizes and is wise

(4M) $(\exists x)(Sx \;\&\; (y)(Sy \leftrightarrow y = x) \;\&\; Wx)$.

This is no mere matter of taste for Quine, but absolutely necessary so as to avoid wrinkles like singular negative existential statements. A sentence such as

(5) Hercules does not exist

cannot be translated into proto-MPL as

(5P!) Not: exists (Hercules)

because we could then existentially generalize to

(5PE) There exists a thing x such that x does not exist.

For the same reason the socratizing predicate 'herculizes' must not be thought of as a syntactically complex expression '... = Hercules' because the rogue existential generalization could still be carried out. Hence socratizing predicates are to be regarded as *indissoluble general terms*.[20] Where a socratizing predicate is not easily available one may keep the '$\ldots = \mathbf{a}$' locution (for some individual constant $\mathbf{a}$) as long as we remember that the '$=$' is simply the MPL rendering of the copula 'is', "which, as in 'is mortal' and 'is a man', serves merely to give a general term the form of a verb and so suit it to predicative position."[21] Hence for (5) we get the MPL-correct

(5P) There is no thing that uniquely Herculizes

(5M) ~$(\exists x)(Hx \ \& \ (y)(Hy \leftrightarrow y = x))$.

There are other ways around the problem, as is known. One is to resort to free logic, whereby empty names are allowed and existential generalization is only valid if the name is nonempty.[22] Another, which parallels TFL, is to deny that the existential quantifier expresses existence.[23] Another— the standard response—is to disallow empty names, and indeed empty domains altogether. But although the socratizing of names is usually only taught in Logic 101 as a curiosity, it is arguably more faithful to the spirit and intent of Fregean logic in its approach to predication and the copula. And even if it is not, and we take '$\ldots = \mathbf{a}$' to be syntactically complex, the russelling away of the description most certainly is central to the MPL approach, and we are still left with variables and predication.

Since it is the variable that is "simply the heir to the relative pronoun," what is it about the pronoun that licenses, for Quine, its canonization as the vehicle for objective reference? In French, as he points out, it is common to use pronominal reference even in monoclausal predication, as when one says, 'Le garçon, il ne fait jamais son travail'. Here, all characterization information, including identificatory, pivots around the pronoun; even the gender of the pronoun does not necessarily characterize. And although the same pivoting construction does not occur commonly in English, it is not ruled out by grammar either. Indeed, no natural language can do without pronouns. So what we have is the following situation in MPL, at least on the Quinean interpretation: (1) all characterization is given by predication; (2) the elimination of singular terms means all identification is given by predication; (3) in Quine's own words, this means that "designation goes by the board; there is only the variable";[24] (4) the variable says nothing about its values—this is all said by the open sentence;[25] (5) "the pronoun [variable] stands for pure and simple reference";[26] and (6) the way in which MPL characterizes the values of the variables entails that those values cannot be objects falling under certain kinds, but only objects *simpliciter*, as we saw in the discussion of restricted and unrestricted quantification. The objects cannot be essentially nameable because the names are eliminated in canonical notation. They cannot be objects essentially specifiable by general terms because the general terms are just part of the predication, even if the predication is simply a restriction on which values are taken to verify the formula. All instantiation is by means of the existential quantifier, and all generalization is from existential propositions. But existence, which is what the existential quantifier expresses in MPL, is univocal because the existential quantifier is itself a univocal second-level property of concepts or of propositional functions.

So if the values of the variables are pure objects characterized wholly by their predicates, and if they all exist in one sense—the sense in which the existential quantifier expresses existence—then these values can only be bare particulars. As Quine himself says: "The pronoun is the tenable linguistic counterpart of the untenable old metaphysical notion of a bare particular."[27] And again: "The variable is the legitimate latter-day embodiment of the incoherent old idea of a bare particular."[28] To which George Englebretsen has replied: "Quine does not make it clear just what is 'untenable' or 'incoherent' in the idea of a bare particular—perhaps just that it is an old idea, for he appears to like it well enough in its 'latter-day embodiment'."[29] Quine also tells us:

A notion scarcely separable from the identificatory use of terms is that of aboutness: what thing or things is some sentence about? Under the regimentation this lapses likewise, and good riddance. Sentences quantify over everything, and they fall into one or another special field depending on what general terms occur essentially in them; but the idea of their being about certain things and not others seems dispensable.[30]

We should not be misled by the last sentence into thinking that Quine allows "clothed particulars," as it were, by means of essentially occurring general terms; any necessity will only be *de dicto*, if even that, the truth being that the "essentially" occurring general terms are just those terms that happen to be most deeply entrenched in a given scientific theory. The bearers of the predicates expressed by the terms, or rather the members of the classes denoted by them, are just the objects pure and simple—the things over which a theory quantifies. But *every* theory, true or false, is about bare particulars, that is, the objects pure and simple. Not even a false theory can be about things that do not exist, as though we could truly say of a theory positing unicorns that the things it posits do not exist. All *we* can say—we who know there are no unicorns—is that there are no things that bear the features such a theory contains in its vocabulary of predicates terms: there are no such thing-predicate combinations as those posited by a theory asserting the existence of unicorns. We do not thereby deny there are things pure and simple—indeed if we do not include the empty domain, we presuppose that there *are*—rather, all we deny are the thing-predicate combinations asserted by the false theory. All we theorists, however, agree on *what* there is—everything, in Quine's words,[31] but more precisely, *every thing*. This leaves room for plenty of disagreement over *how* what there is, is—over what the bare particulars bear.

5   Categories, Terms, and Bare Particulars

According to Quine, there is only one sense of 'exists',[32] the sense expressed by the existential quantifier. This represents the standard view of MPL, since existence is a property of concepts or open sentences, namely, the property of their being instantiated or sometimes true. What sense could it make to say that there is more than one way for a concept to be instantiated or a sentence to be sometimes true? As Sommers points out, however, this seems to commit Quine to a denial of differences of ontological type altogether because he thinks 'exists' would be equivocal if true of things of different types.[33] The presupposition must be, then, that all predication of things of different types must be equivocal, given that there is no reason in principle why we should distinguish between multiple senses for 'exists' as applied to numbers and dogs, and multiple senses for 'hard' as applied to chairs and questions. Granted, Quine nowhere gives a clear and straightforward argument for abandoning distinctions of ontological category, but it is implicit in his discussion of Carnap's adherence to distinctions of ontological category as a means of identifying meaningless existence questions like 'Are there numbers?' There, he says that "there is no evident standard of what to count as a category, or category word."[34] Further, since many-sorted quantification is translatable into single-sorted, with sentences like 'Red is divisible by three' coming out false rather than meaningless,[35] we need only speak of "subclass questions" rather than "category questions": in other words, we do not need to puzzle over whether 'Are there numbers?' is meaningless, because we can simply determine whether our best theory of the world requires numbers as values of its single-sorted variables.[36] Better, we can confine ourselves to determining whether the predicate '. . . is a number' needs to be incorporated into our theory as true of some objects, where the objects are plurally referred to by the variables. Quine even goes as far as to assert that a predicate like '. . . is hard' applies univocally to chairs and questions,[37] though as Sommers points out this would license as meaningful the proposition 'The question I asked is harder than the chair I sat on'.[38] It is all very well for Quine to declare it false as he does,[39] but isn't it the case that if it is false that x is harder than y, then y must be either harder than x or as hard as x? But for Quine 'The chair I just sat on is as hard as the question I just asked' and 'The chair I just sat on is harder than the question I just asked' are false as well; so much for the logic of comparatives. The main point, however, is that on Quine's account the meaningfulness of such questions is founded on the idea that chairs and question are only "very unlike,"[40] not that they belong to distinct ontological categories (such as abstract and concrete).

One way of avoiding Quine's move to a single-category ontology—which is effectively a *no*-category ontology of bare objects—is to deny that '. . . exists' is univocal. That would mean giving up from the outset on the idea that existence is expressed by existential quantification and is thus to be identified with a property of concepts or functions. We would then be free to have '. . . exists' as a primitive predicate in our language and to interpret it how we will, depending on the kinds of existent or possible existent we apply it to.[41] By this I do not mean that 'exists' will not have a single general meaning, such as 'is actual', only that what it means to be actual will vary from case to case. The equivocality of 'exists' would not be taken to be akin to that of 'bank' as used of a financial house or part of a river, but akin to other highly general terms like 'true' and 'good'. There will then be no room for denying distinctions of ontological type and hence for positing bare particulars.

Another way to avoid Quine's move would be to deny the thought that predication across types must be equivocal, which is the approach Sommers takes.[42] But I think we need to understand this proposal in a way that narrows the difference between it and the first. We can say that heterotypical predication can be univocal, but only with an important gloss to the effect that the predication will not be univocal *qua* heterotypical, but only *qua* homotypical. Examinations and headaches belong to different ontological categories, but we can still say univocally that my headache lasted longer than your exam; and the reason for this is that both headaches and exams are *events* even though they are different types of entity at a lower level of classification. Again, we can speak of a flat beer and a flat landscape, where the predication is equivocal *qua* heterotypical; but also of a pleasing beer and a pleasing landscape, where the univocality is a result of beers and landscapes belonging to the same type at a higher level. A proper understanding of *analogy* will help us to distinguish purely equivocal predication such as we get with words like 'bank', and predication that is purely univocal such as 'long' applied to headaches and exams, from predication where the term applies equivocally but only in virtue of some component predication that is univocal: such is the case with 'healthy' as applied to people and diets.[43] Again, on this approach there will be no categorial reason for positing bare particulars, that is, we can keep distinctions of ontological type.

A friend of MPL, at least one of Quinean complexion, may well retort that the more traditionally minded logician has no grounds for distinguishing himself from his Fregean counterpart. For he seems to be committed to bare particulars himself given that he is surely prepared to make assertions like 'Everything she does is magic' or 'There is something in what he said'. If 'everything' and 'something' are still countenanced, the friend of TFL is in as bad (or good) a position as the friend of MPL. If the former wants to deny that sentences such as those just mentioned commit him to bare particulars, he has no reason for foisting the view on the Fregean either.

The friend of TFL, however, sees things differently. The use of highly general terms like 'exists' and 'thing' does not commit the traditional logician to bare particulars because for him they do not constitute a general referential apparatus around which all predication pivots, and hence cannot be seen as making explicit an ontic commitment (to use the Quinean jargon) to undifferentiated objects on which all features hang. For the traditional logician, 'thing', 'exist', 'object', 'entity', and the like are *just more terms*. As such, they denote precisely what more specific terms denote, only at a higher level of abstraction. When I say 'Something is mortal' or 'Some things are mortal' I am talking neither about nothing nor about something I know not what: I am talking about the very same kinds of thing I talk about when I say 'All men are mortal' or 'Some animals are mortal', namely, the things that either are or are taken by me to be mortal, whether they be humans, giraffes, or animals in general; they may even be rocks if I happen to mistake a rock for a mortal thing and say on that basis 'Something is mortal'. But by saying *Something* is mortal' I merely abstract from or generalize what it is I am talking about. When I say 'Everything she does is magic' I am saying at a more general level just what I say when I say 'Every deed she does is magic and every action she performs is magic and every speech she makes is magic . . .', where the three dots indicate a potentially infinite conjunction of kinds of thing a person can do. The expansion of a proto-MPL sentence such as

(6) For any thing x, if Georgina does x then x is magic

in terms of the infinite conjunction

(6E) For any thing x, if x is a deed and Georgina does x then x is magic, and if x is an action and Georgina performs x then x is magic, and if x is a speech and Georgina gives x then x is magic . . .

may, with a few postulates and some manipulation, look similar to the expansion in TFL, but it is a different animal. For in TFL the relation is between things done on the one hand, and deeds done, acts performed, speeches given . . . on the other. The term 'thing' in this context is a generalization over deeds, acts, speeches, and so on. In MPL, the relation is between things that are done on the one hand, and things that are deeds and are done, things that are acts and are performed, things that are speeches and are spoken, and so on, on the other. The function of 'thing' here is not as a generic (general) term embracing more specific (general) terms; it is the whole relative clause pivoting about the variables that is the general term. On the contrary, in TFL each term, 'thing', 'deed', 'speech', or whatever, functions in the same way both syntactically and semantically, to denote kinds of thing: 'thing' denotes every kind of thing, but 'speech' denotes only those kinds of thing that are speeches, and 'deed' only those kinds of thing that are deeds.

This difference between the role of 'thing' or 'object' in TFL and MPL needs to be emphasized. MPL seems to imply what might be called, following Jonathan Lowe,[44] a one-category ontology. When Quine says that what exists is 'everything', rather than 'shoes, ships, sealing wax . . .', we see already a division between things and what is predicated of them; but

he could also have answered, 'Universals, particulars, and within these categories there are substances, nonsubstances, properties, kinds, property
instances', and so on. That he does not do so reflects his belief that whether
such things exist depends on what is required by our best scientific theory
of the world,[45] and for Quine classes are just about the only other thing
such a theory is likely to require. But even if more than classes were
required, this would simply mean that more predicates were an ineliminable part of canonical notation. A multicategory ontology, on the other
hand, does not see the various ontological categories as just more predicates. To be sure, it holds that there are things that are horses, but this way
of talking is licensed only by the fact that there are *kinds* and there are
objects that fall under those kinds. There are things that are green, but
only because there are *properties* and there are objects that have those properties. There is a thing that is Socrates, but only because Socrates exists and
is a substance. 'Thing-talk' is merely an abstraction of category-talk. Even
the use of 'object' does not involve a commitment to bare particulars,
because in a multicategory ontology 'object' (and its cognates, like 'entity'
and even 'thing', suitably restricted) will have a specific use—for instance,
as a general term used to distinguish between substances and their property instances, or between particulars and universals. Objects are not kinds
of thing, as it were; they do not form a category in their own right, they
are not the featureless bearers of predication. They are the same as what
we talk about when we talk about shoes, ships, and sealing wax, or about
substances, kinds, property instances, and so on. Traditional logic does not,
therefore, have a place of privilege for objects any more than for horses or
hurricanes: 'object' is just another term, and like all terms it can go in
subject or predicate position and hence be used in logical reckoning.

In this way it can be seen that whereas MPL carries with it a certain ontic
explicitness, TFL does not. Not only does predicate logic avowedly expose
the truth conditions of a proposition in its formulae, which TFL does not—
witness their divergent treatment of definite descriptions[46]—but TFL also
eschews the very idea of building ontic commitments into syntax.
Although this may rule out the pure objective reference of the bare
pronoun-variable as found in MPL, it is perfectly consistent with the
multicategory ontology mentioned above. Such an ontology could never
be built into logical syntax—what on earth would such a logic look like?—
but what logical syntax *can* do is open a space for a theory of ontological

categories (as well as of categories in general along the lines pursued by
Sommers, for example) by means of terms. Perhaps it is not going too far
to say not only that a term logic is consistent with a theory of ontological categories, but that it even favors it. In any taxonomic tree it is terms
that are at the nodes—one need only look at the famous Porphyrian Tree.
Terms are naturally related by abstraction and specification, by classification and subclassification: their many-sortedness is an inherent feature of
their interrelationships. Traditional logic does not interfere with any of
this: it leaves taxonomy free, and it does not wait on our best scientific
theory for an interpretation of predicates—unlike MPL, which may require
only classes if Quine is right, but may require more if science says so.

The handling of negation in TFL and MPL is also a clue to the way in
which categories do or do not play a role. We recognize intuitively that
there is something different about the way in which Socrates is not black
and the way in which the number two is not black. We want to say that
although Socrates is not black he *could* have been black but that the
number two never could have been black because it is not the right sort
of thing to be black—it is not, to speak in the Aristotelian or Scholastic
way, even *in potentiality* with respect to blackness. TFL marks this distinction by means of the well-known contrast between term negation and sentence negation. Using term negation, it marks the number two's lack of
potentiality in respect of blackness by holding both 'The number two is
black' and 'The number two is nonblack' to be false, while also holding 'It
is not the case that the number two is black' to be true. Since MPL recognizes only sentence negation, it has no specific reading for 'The number
two is nonblack' but rather treats it as equivalent to 'It is not the case that
the number two is black', which it also holds to be true. (The distinction
between internal and external negation for sentences containing definite
descriptions is not the same as the contrast between sentence and term
negation, since both of the former are sentence negations; they bear on
the relation between sentence negation and existence in respect of definite descriptions, not on the lacking/failing to possess distinction.)

By eliminating term negation (or, what amounts to the same thing,
assimilating it to sentence negation), predicate logic is unable to mark categories by allowing the truth of, for instance, 'Some things are neither
black nor nonblack': with only sentential negation this comes out as logically false in MPL, even though there is more than simply an intuition

that such a proposition expresses a fundamental truth applicable to many kinds of thing. (Note that it is a contingent truth about the world that some things are neither black nor nonblack, but not a contingent fact about the kinds of thing that are neither black nor nonblack that they are neither black nor nonblack.) Our logical system should allow us to infer 'Six is not prime' from 'It is not the case that six is prime' but *not* 'Fred is not prime' from 'It is not the case that Fred is prime'; yet the quantifier-variable notation does not allow this. As far as bare things go, there is no distinction to be had between their not possessing a feature and their positively failing to possess a feature, because there is by definition nothing in their nature that could allow of such a distinction. This ontological posit is mirrored in the quantifier-variable notation of predicate logic itself. TFL, on the other hand, distinguishes between sentence negation and term negation. This is not to say that the distinction by itself allows TFL to contrast the valid and invalid inferences mentioned above, since driving the sentential minus inward is allowed, whatever the term. We can go both from

(7) $-(+X + Y)$

to

(8) $(-X - Y)$

and from

(9) $-(-X + Y)$

to

(10) $(+X - Y)$.

But then we are going to have to use a system of domain markers in order to distinguish between certain inferences, and this means an explicit recognition of category distinctions. For example, taking the ordinary domain of 'wise' to be human beings, that of 'prime' to be numbers, and taking Fred to be human, TFL will allow us to go from

(11) $-(F^*_H + W_H)$

(where * marks wild quantity) to

(12) $(F^*_H - W_H)$,

but not from

(13) $-(F^{*}_{H} + P_{N})$,

to

(14) $(F^{*}_{H} - P_{N})$.

This will reflect rules about cross-domain inferences at the level of the square of opposition, but it requires a full theory of categories, for which Sommers's work is an obvious starting point, in order to know what domain subscripting is permissible in general. We can, however, work on a case-by-case basis in specific instances of logical reckoning, as per (11)–(14).

6 Locke, Kinds, Definitions, and Bare Particulars

Geoffrey Warnock has a discussion of John Locke on substance that ought to be compulsory reading for every student of modern predicate logic.[47] In it he discusses Locke's account of substance as the bare substratum of all observable qualities, at which Locke arrives by arguing that since all we ever perceive are qualities, and since those qualities must be held together by something in order for there to be unity of object, what holds them together must by its very nature be without qualities. Leaving aside the dubious metaphysics behind the argument, what is of more direct concern is Warnock's plausible attribution to Locke of a certain logico-linguistic confusion. Locke takes the alleged fact that we perceive only qualities to be mirrored by the way in which all definition appears to be adjectival. In answer to the question 'What is an F?', we can say 'An F is a G that is . . .', but then when asked 'What is a G?' we can answer, 'A G is an H that is . . .'. But there is no logical stopping point, because completeness in definition demands that we be able, at least in principle, to eliminate every noun in definiendum position in favor of an adjectival construction.

Hence, in answer to our original question, we must be able at least in principle to say, 'An F is a thing that is G and H and I and J and . . .'. (Whether the conjunction must be finite is another matter, not to be explored here.) Since adjectival constructions require a substantive for them to qualify, the occurrence of 'thing' must be an ineliminable substantive doing genuine referential work as that on which the adjectives pivot. In answer to the question 'But what is a thing?' Warnock points out that if we are not to reject the question as meaningless—on pain of there being no meaningful definitions—we must answer that there *is* no answer, in principle, as to what a thing is. Things have no characteristics of their own by which they can be defined; we can define things only in context as things that happen to have such-and-such characteristics. The parallel with Fregean logic should be evident. In any existential generalization it is a mistake to ask, say, 'What is *x*?' or 'What is *y*?' Rather, if the question can be asked, the only legitimate answer can be '*x* is any thing'; and if the generalization is true, the only answer can be 'Whatever things satisfy the predicates'. The variables themselves, as Quine argues, are ineliminably referential terms.[48] All characterization hangs on them, but they are essentially unclothed. All singular terms can be turned into predicates, so the variables are the only referential terms.

Locke's mistake, argues Warnock, is to treat the possibility of turning any definition into one in which 'something' emerges as the only substantive as a reason for regarding 'something' as referring to a bare particular. The use of 'something', as in 'There is something behind the sofa', is not a means of making mention of an essentially characterless object that happens also to satisfy the predicate '. . . is behind the sofa'. Rather, the use of 'something' is precisely a means of *avoiding* making mention of what satisfies the predicate '. . . is behind the sofa'. 'Something' is, in Warnock's apt words, "a device for avoiding the explicit mention of anything,"[49] not for making explicit reference to we-know-not-what. Now at first sight this might seem to support the predicate logician's retort, "Exactly so! 'Something' does not refer to anything, it is just the syntactic means of avoiding explicit reference to what satisfies the predicate." This will not do. Of course we know that in MPL 'something' does not refer but is instead incorporated into the device of quantification. However, the variable *does* refer—without it, as we noted Quine saying earlier, we cannot make sense of objective reference. The variable is not a means of avoiding explicit mention of anything; on the contrary, one of the key differences between TFL and MPL is that MPL is a notation for making everything *explicit*, whereas TFL has no such ambition. MPL wears its ontic commitments on its sleeve, which is why it is explicit as to truth conditions (making, for example, what TFL treats as a presupposition concerning definite descriptions into an explicit statement of existence). The use of the variable, then, is not a means of avoiding mention of things, but of making explicit reference *to* things: those things, denoted by bare pronouns, on which hang the total characterizations of predicative constructions. In TFL, on the other hand, 'thing' is just another term, and as such it is clearly a term that avoids *specific* mention of things, that is, of things as specified, as falling under certain kinds or into certain categories. Whereas the slogan of TFL might be "Just more terms—including things," that of MPL might be "Just more predicates—apart from things."

7 Bare Particulars Exposed

This is not the place for a full critique of the notion of a bare particular.[50] The purpose of this essay has been to argue that just such a notion lies at the heart of modern predicate logic, at least as interpreted by Quine. Although not every aspect of Quine's interpretation is accepted as standard, it is difficult to see what is fundamentally wrong with those aspects that have been exposed here as underlying the commitment to bare particulars. I will end with a few major problems for the notion, and say a little more about metaphysics and logic.

First, in virtue of what can the friend of bare particulars say that there is a plurality of them rather than just some one thing—the Great Big Thing? Perhaps more accurately, what content is there to concepts of plurality and singularity in respect of bare things?[51] One might argue that the very idea of a distinction between singularity and plurality in respect of bare particulars is incoherent, since attributing either property would ipso facto involve ascribing an essential feature to something that is by definition essentially featureless. And yet MPL restricts itself to multiple bare particulars as represented by the multiple variables of the notation. By what right is such a restriction made? Mightn't one just as well, on the Quinean interpretation, see quantification over bare particulars as expressing what are no more than aspects of the Great Big Thing? Perhaps—and the suggestion is highly tentative—one might be able to introduce an "urvariable" denoting the Great Big Thing, and translate each formula of MPL into a predication of the ur-variable, the translation going via an elimination of the variables in the original formula using Quine's own method. (The inspiration for the suggestion is Sommers's treatment of sentence logic as a branch of term logic, according to which, at a fundamental level, even compound sentences are subject-predicate in form, in their case being predicable of the world as a subject: a conditional such as 'If p then q', which TFL translates as '$-p + q$', has p-worlds as its subject, and can be read as 'Every p-world is a q-world'. Moreover, since there is only one world, 'Some p-world is a q-world' [the transcription of 'p & q'] entails 'Every p-world is a q-world'. The difference, however, is that it is no part of Sommers's semantics of sentence logic that the world be anything other than the essentially featured world that supports a traditional theory of truth by correspondence.)

Suppose we could thus replace individual variables with a single ur-variable that, to use Quinean language, is the "vehicle of pure objective reference" to the Great Big Thing. Now this might seem like a triviality—if the translation can be done, what does it matter whether there are many bare things or just Something? Such a response, however, is to retreat from the ontic explicitness characteristic of MPL into either an attitude of ignorance or one of indifference to ontic explicitness altogether. As to the first attitude, it is one thing for logic to have a metaphysical color, as it were, and another for it positively to induce metaphysical ignorance. For if the best system of logic implies a profoundly ambiguous ontology whereby not even plurality or singularity is settled, we do better to look for a logic that is not so infected with obscurity. On the other hand, to retreat to indifference is to play into the hands of the traditional logician: if predicate logic does come with such obscure metaphysical baggage, and if this means it is better to eschew ontic explicitness, why not revert to a logic that has no such commitment? Needless to say, a Quinean, taking ontological relativity seriously, may well regard ontological indifference with equanimity: if MPL can be translated into notations with different ontological implications, we should simply choose the notation that is simplest, most expressive, most inferentially powerful, and most adequate to science, and if there is no clear winner we can choose any of them. To evaluate such a response would take us too far into the peculiarly Quinean thesis of ontological relativity and related epistemological ideas. Nevertheless, the traditional logician will see in this approach an invitation to compare and contrast MPL with TFL on just those scores, at the same time insisting that if there is a clear winner it cannot imply anything that conflicts with those fundamental features of reality that can rationally be discerned.

Second, there is the persistent problem of whether bare particulars have a nature. They are not supposed to have any observable features (observable in principle), though they can be extrinsically tied by a predicative relation to observable features. But their function is to individuate, that is, to ground numerical identity and difference. If this is essential to them, as it seems to be, then they must have a nature, albeit unobservable in principle. The problem here is not so much whether there can be unobservable natures, but whether we thereby have any explanation of *how* bare particulars individuate. All we apparently know about them is *that* they individuate. But if we cannot say more, how do we have a more informative explanation than if we rested content with primitive identity and difference, holding that these are ungrounded rather than grounded in bare particulars? It might be replied, "But individuation requires something to individuate"; yet this begs the question. The supporter of ungrounded identity can say that what individuates is the identity of the individuals themselves, and that to insist on something *else's* doing the individuating is not to explain why something else is required. This objection is not meant as a defense of ungrounded identity, since if the Identity of Indiscernibles were true, after all, there would be no need in the first place to invoke either ungrounded identity or bare particulars—but I do not wish to determine here whether the Identity of Indiscernibles is true. The point is simply that bare particulars—if they do any individuative work—do no more work than ungrounded identity.

Third, it is doubtful whether bare particulars do any individuative work at all, which we can see from the following dilemma. Since bare particulars have no nature (apart, let us unhappily concede, from their individuative nature), they are not essentially tied predicatively to any kind of character (to use the expression favored by Bergmann); for if they were, there would have to be something in their nature that accounted for that, for example, for the fact that some bare particulars were essentially tied predicatively to canine characters and others to feline characters. So the follower of bare particulars must allow the possibility that one or more bare particulars tied to canine characters swap with those tied to feline characters. Suppose they did. Then it would be absurd to conclude that dogs had become cats and that cats had become dogs, or in the singleton case that Fido had become Felix and Felix Fido; or that there was no numerical difference between dogs and cats, or between Felix and Fido. So we would have to hold that the identities and differences remained as they were before the swap—in which case the bare particulars would not be doing any individuative work at all, since individuation does not change when the putative individuators relocate. So they cannot be responsible for individuation.

It is no help for the bare particularist to hold that the particulars are indeed essentially tied to certain kinds of character, because even if we conceded that this was not owing to their nature we could still ask whether bare particulars *within* a character kind could swap: could the bare particulars individuating Fido and Rover swap locations?[52] If they could, they could not be doing the individuating, on the assumption that Fido and Rover would retain their identities. But if they could not, why not? It is one thing—and enough of a conceptual stretch as it is—to allow that being essentially tied to a character kind does not depend on the particular's having a nature; but are we to say that being essentially tied to a Rover-character or Fido-character also does not depend on the having of a nature by the featureless individuator? Then what does it depend on? It had better not be the identities of Rover and Fido, since these latter depend on the bare particulars; but then what else could a Fido-character or a Rover-character be if not an individual identity? Again, bare particulars do not seem to be able to do the minimum that they are supposed to.

8 Conclusion

To most modern predicate logicians it will seem quite unbelievable that Fregean logic is committed to the existence of bare particulars. To be sure, I do not claim to have demonstrated this with certainty, only to have shown that on the Quinean understanding of predicate logic it does at least appear to reflect such a commitment. If I stand back from certainty on this, it is partly because I too find it hard to believe. Like most philosophers raised on predicate logic I also find it hard to believe that it is committed to, or seems to be committed to, *any* substantive metaphysical doctrines, apart from the necessary commitment to logical entities such as functions and concepts. It were better that it had no such commitment, since logic, as suggested at the beginning of this essay, is a tool to be applied to our reasoning about being for the discovery of truths about being, not a tool capable in and of itself of providing insight into the nature of being. Traditional logic eschews this latter role, and for what it is worth traditional logicians such as Lewis Carroll had no truck with questions such as 'What is a Thing?', which he recommended treating with contempt.[53] Traditional logic is about one thing only: the connection and division of ideas, as represented by terms, for the purpose of arriving at further connections and divisions of ideas. The distinction between the logical and the extralogical in TFL is stark, certainly clearer than that in MPL if the discussion by Quine referred to above is anything to go by. The material is the terms, and the machinery is the quantifier-qualifier-valence-copula structure so elegantly distilled by Sommers into the plus-minus notation inspired by Leibniz. The TFL research program has a future, owing in large measure to the heroic efforts of both Sommers and Englebretsen. Whether it ever commands the respect of more than a small number of logicians will depend on the openness of the Fregean mainstream.

Acknowledgments

This essay was written during my tenure as a visiting scholar at the Social Philosophy and Policy Center, Bowling Green State University, Ohio. I am indebted to everyone there for providing an excellent environment in which to work. I am also grateful to Fred Sommers, George Englebretsen, and Jonathan Lowe for comments on this essay and for many insightful discussions on the subjects it concerns.

Notes

1. *Daily News*, February 25, 1905.

2. I use the word 'system' in an advisedly looser sense than that understood by modern predicate logicians.

3. "Because existence is a property of concepts, the ontological argument for the existence of God breaks down"; Frege, *Die Grundlagen der Arithmetik* s.53 (trans. Austin, *The Foundations of Arithmetic* [Oxford: Basil Blackwell, 1952]); cited in Sommers, "Intellectual Autobiography," this volume.

4. I do not claim in this essay that Quine himself, i.e. by his philosophy as a whole, is committed to bare particulars; one could easily produce slogans like "no entity without identity" that cast doubt on this. Perhaps the Quinean philosophy is unclear on this matter (would spacetime points be bare particulars?), or even inconsistent. My claim is simply that Quine's interpretation of predicate logic appears to commit *it* to bare particulars.

5. P. Geach, *Reference and Generality* (Ithaca: Cornell University Press, 1980 [1962]), p. 60.

6. Ibid., p. 62.

7. Ibid.

8. Ibid.

9. W. V. O. Quine, "Grammar, Truth, and Logic," in S. Kanger and S. Öhmar (eds.), *Philosophy and Grammar* (Dordrecht: D. Reidel, 1980), pp. 17–28, at p. 24.

10. Quine, *The Roots of Reference* (La Salle: Open Court, 1973), p. 100.

11. See, e.g., "The Variable and Its Place in Reference," in Z. van Straaten (ed.), *Philosophical Subjects: Essays Presented to P. F. Strawson* (Oxford: Clarendon Press, 1980), pp. 164–173, at p. 165.

12. Geach, "Quine's Syntactical Insights," in D. Davidson and J. Hintikka (eds.), *Words and Objections: Essays on the Work of Willard van Orman Quine* (Dordrecht: Reidel, 1969), pp. 146–157, at pp. 151ff.

13. "The Variable and Its Place in Reference," p. 166.

14. Whether this is so, of course, is debatable, as when we consider reflexive pronouns such as 'himself', 'itself', first-personal pronouns, etc.

15. "The Variable," p. 167.

16. "Grammar, Truth, and Logic," pp. 18–19.

17. Ibid., p. 18.

18. Quine, *Quiddities* (Cambridge, Mass.: Belknap Press, 1987), p. 157; there, he says that "[t]he pronoun contributes rather to structure" (unlike the predicates excepting identity). Again, on p. 238 he says the "business" of the variable "is linking and permuting."

19. As Quine pointed out in 1960, restricted quantification can be paraphrased as unrestricted and as such is a notational variant of the latter: "Variables Explained Away," in his *Methods of Logic* (Cambridge, Mass.; Harvard University Press, 1995; 2nd ed. [1966]), pp. 227–235, at p. 234. But the substantive point above is that restricted quantification, like unrestricted quantification, requires variables and can have no coherent reading apart from the variable-relative clause construction; it is not a *mere* notational variant of the unrestricted form.

20. See Quine, *Word and Object* (Cambridge, Mass.: The MIT Press, 1960), p. 179; and see also the useful brief account in A. Orenstein, "Is Existence What Existential Quantification Expresses?" in R. Barrett and R. Gibson (eds.), *Perspectives on Quine* (Oxford: Blackwell, 1990), pp. 245–270, at p. 267.

21. *Word and Object*, p. 179.

22. For a survey, see E. Bencivenga, "Free Logics," in D. Gabbay and F. Guenthner (eds.), *Handbook of Philosophical Logic*, vol. 3 (Dordrecht: Reidel, 1986), pp. 373–426.

23. See A. Orenstein, "Is Existence . . .?" for a powerful statement of the argument.

24. "Grammar, Truth, and Logic," p. 25.

25. Ibid., p. 25.

26. "The Variable and Its Place in Reference," p. 165.

27. Ibid.

28. "Grammar, Truth, and Logic," p. 25.

29. G. Englebretsen, *Something to Reckon With: The Logic of Terms* (Ottawa: University of Ottawa Press, 1996), p. 91.

30. Quine, "Reply to Strawson," in *Words and Objections*, pp. 320–327, at p. 321.

31. Quine, "On What There Is," in his *From a Logical Point of View* (New York and Evanston: Harper and Row, 1961; 2nd ed.), p. 1.

32. See, e.g., *Word and Object*, p. 131.

33. Sommers, "Predicability," in M. Black (ed.), *Philosophy in America* (Ithaca: Cornell University Press, 1965), pp. 262–281, at p. 264.

34. "Existence and Quantification," in his *Ontological Relativity and other Essays* (New York: Columbia University Press, 1969), p. 91.

35. Ibid., p. 96.

36. Quine, "Carnap's Views on Ontology," in his *Ways of Paradox and Other Essays* (Cambridge, Mass.: Harvard University Press, 1976 [revised ed.]), pp. 207ff.

37. *Word and Object*, pp. 130–131.

38. "Predicability," p. 263.

39. *Word and Object*, p. 229; *Quiddities*, pp. 191–192.

40. *Word and Object*, p. 130.

41. Sommers, *The Logic of Natural Language* (Oxford: Clarendon Press, 1982), pp. 334–336.

42. In "Predicability."

43. The concept of analogical predication could have brought out these distinctions in, for example, Sommers's "Predication and Logical Syntax," in A. Kasher (ed.), *Language in Focus* (Dordrecht: Reidel, 1976), pp. 41–53, at p. 46 ('slow' as allegedly ambiguous *simpliciter* when applied to 'man' and 'pace').

44. E. J. Lowe, "Some Formal Ontological Relations," forthcoming in *Dialectica*.

45. I use 'our' advisedly, bearing in mind Quine's insistence that ontology is a "parochial affair": see, e.g., "Reply to Strawson," p. 321.

46. Sommers, *The Logic of Natural Language*, ch. 10.

47. G. J. Warnock, *Berkeley* (London: Penguin, 1969), pp. 102–108.

48. This is not to say that variables are ineliminable per se. As Quine himself has shown, variables can be eliminated in favor of a so-called predicate functor logic— but it is precisely such a logic that looks more like a term logic than a predicate logic. See, e.g., "Algebraic Logic and Predicate Functors," in his *The Ways of Paradox and Other Essays* (Cambridge, Mass.: Harvard University Press, 1976; 2nd ed. [1966]), ch. 28.

49. *Berkeley*, p. 107.

50. For such a critique, see D. W. Mertz, "Individuation and Instance Ontology," *Australasian Journal of Philosophy* 79 (2001), pp. 45–61, but also J. P. Moreland and Timothy Pickavance, "Bare Particulars and Individuation," *Australasian Journal of Philosophy* 81 (2003), pp. 1–13, and Mertz, "Against Bare Particulars: A Response to Moreland and Pickavance," *Australasian Journal of Philosophy* 81 (2003), pp. 14–20; M. Loux, *Substance and Attribute* (Dordrecht: Reidel, 1978), ch. 8; Loux, *Metaphysics: A Contemporary Introduction* (London: Routledge, 1998), pp. 113–117; E. J. Lowe, *Kinds of Being* (Oxford: Blackwell, 1989), pp. 11–13. See also: Edwin B. Allaire, "Bare Particulars," *Philosophical Studies* 14 (1963), pp. 1–8, and "Another Look at Bare Particulars," *Philosophical Studies* 16 (1965), pp. 16–21; V. C. Chappell, "Particulars Re-Clothed," *Philosophical Studies* 15 (1964), pp. 60–64, all three of which are reprinted in part IV of S. Laurence and C. Macdonald, *Contemporary Readings in the Foundations of Metaphysics* (Oxford: Blackwell, 1998); and the classic statement by G. Bergmann in *Realism: A Critique of Brentano and Meinong* (Madison: University of Wisconsin Press, 1967).

51. As Jonathan Lowe puts it: "What, we may ask, entitles the adherent of such a view to say, in answer to the question of what there is, that there are *things*, in the plural, as opposed to just *something*?" ("Some Formal Ontological Relations"). For a Leibniz's Law–style argument that there is no numerical difference between bare particulars, see D. W. Mertz, "Individuation and Instance Ontology," p. 52.

52. Of course, even speaking of locations attributes to them a spatiotemporal nature.

53. See further the interesting discussion in G. Englebretsen, "Carrollian Things," *Jabberwocky* 13 (1984), pp. 96–100.

11   Comments and Replies

Fred Sommers

George Englebretsen

The first third of George Englebretsen's essay offers as good a popular introduction to formal category theory as one is likely to find anywhere in the literature on this important but neglected subject. The second third does the same for term functor logic (TFL).

The final third discusses my views on truth and existence. Here, as elsewhere, I have reacted negatively to the views of Frege and his admirers. Alluding to Kant's refutation of the ontological argument by pointing out that existence is not a property of what is said to exist, Frege gave his own answer to the question Kant had left over: "To what then do we refer when we speak of the existence of something?" (See the discussion in my "Intellectual Autobiography," this volume.)

According to Frege, existence is a property of concepts. One may thus interpret an affirmation of existence such as '$(\exists x)(x$ is a horse$)$' as saying of the concept *horse* (denoted by the predicate 'is a horse') that it is instantiated or nonempty. Russell had a similar conception of existence: to say that horses exist is to say of the propositional function 'x is a horse' that it is sometimes true.

As explications of existence, these 'second-order' ways of thinking about it strike me as evasive or even question-begging. It is *because* the existence of black holes is an objective feature of the world that the concept *black hole* is nonempty and the open sentence 'x is black hole' is sometimes true. To be sure, 'The existence of black holes characterizes the world' is materially equivalent to ' "x is a black hole" is sometimes true'. But when astrophysicists found that the world contains black holes, the discovery of their existence was not a discovery about some characteristics of an open sentence or a concept, but about the world. (To say that what makes 'Some celestial objects are black holes' true is the nonemptiness of the concept *black hole* is nearly circular. To say that what makes 'Some celestial objects are black holes' true is that 'x is a black hole' is sometimes true is perfectly circular.) Admittedly, we are in need of an acceptable account of how and in what way the objective existence or nonexistence of things like mangy cats or prancing unicorns characterizes the real world. Hence we must supply one.

The existence of black holes is a fact. Any truth-making fact may be construed as a fact of existence or nonexistence. If we were clear about what facts were, we would know what existence is a property of. Unfortunately, twentieth-century analytic philosophy did not produce a coherent, acceptable account of the nature of truth-making facts. On the contrary, both facts and the correspondence-to-fact theory of truth were rejected by the majority of clearheaded philosophers, so that today 'fact' is mainly used as a harmless variant of 'true statement'. Frege, C. I. Lewis, Quine, Davidson, Dummett and Putnam are all opposed to an ontology of facts.

As a realist, I reject the verdict that facts are, as Quine put it, *entia non grata*. I have, however, always accepted his view that any statement can be understood to make a positive or negative claim of existence and so may be regimented as a statement of form 'Something is (a) K' or 'Nothing is (a) K'. Thus, 'Socrates is wise' may be construed as the claim that someone is both Socrates (a 'Socratizer', if you will) and wise, and 'Every planet orbits a sun' as the claim that nothing is a planet and not a orbiter of some sun.

Each assertion makes its claim about a particular domain under consideration (DC). For example, when, looking in the drawer, I announce 'There's a hammer', I limit my claim to a DC that consists of the objects in the drawer; I assert that this little domain—the domain of the claim— is characterized by the presence of a hammer. By contrast, when I say 'There are no ghosts', the DC is the whole of the real world; the claim is that the real world is characterized by the nonexistence of ghosts. The DC of 'Some prime number is even' and 'There is no greatest prime number' is the domain of natural numbers.

A domain that contains K things is '{K}ish'. A domain that contains no J-things is 'un{J}ish'. The real world is {elk}ish but un{elf}ish. The existence of elks—a fact—is a nontrivial property of the real world, its {elk}ishness. Strictly speaking, to exist is to be a member of the domain. Elks exist; their existence, a fact that characterizes the world, but is not in the world, *obtains*. In the domain of Greek myth, the fauna are different. That DC is un{elk}ish but it is {flying horse}ish. So not everything that exists is real.

Conversely, not everything that is real exists. If the domain under consideration is the real world, then the world itself, though real, does not exist.[1] Nor do the facts that characterize the real world: the existence of elks, which is a fact that characterizes the real world, does not exist, although this fact is objectively real. By construing the existence of *K*-things ({*K*}ishness) and the nonexistence of *J*-things (un{*J*}ishness) as *mondial* attributes, that is, pertaining to the world, we take the decisive step in demystifying truth-making facts.

This idea, that existence and nonexistence are characteristics of domains, can have no applicability on the view of Frege and his followers. Speaking of tensed utterances, Frege says: "The time of utterance is part of the expression of the thought." And more generally: "The knowledge of certain conditions accompanying the utterance is needed for us to grasp the thought correctly."[2] So, for Frege, when, on January 1, 2003, I say 'There is no hammer', the "complete thought" is expressed by an eternal sentence: 'There is no hammer in this drawer [specifying its location] at time *t*'. The doctrine of propositional completeness leaves no room for the proposition understood as an existential claim made with respect to a specific domain. On my view, by contrast, 'There is no hammer' completely states the claim and the absence of the hammer is the complete fact characterizing the DC (its un{hammer}ishness). The date and place of utterance specify the DC as the venue of the claim, but they are no part of the content of what I say.

Metaphysical realists (as Putnam calls those who hold to the correspondence theory of truth) distinguish two modes of objectivity. There are the things, events, and processes in the world and their properties. There is the world itself and its properties. The world is real and so are the facts that characterize it. Focusing on the first kind of objectivity and remaining oblivious to the second, modern critics of the correspondence theory assume that the purported facts that metaphysical realists claim to be the objective correspondents of true statements must be locatable in the world. When analysis properly leads them to assert that we have no conception of such facts, they injudiciously conclude that correspondence theories are unintelligible. In arriving at this skeptical verdict, the modern critics of correspondence theory have found it easy to reject an ontology of facts by remaining oblivious to the second, mondial, mode of objectivity.

In effect, when making their arguments against correspondence, the philosophers who inveigh against facts do little more than apply Kant's doctrine that existence cannot logically be thought of as a property of anything that can be said to exist in the world. They fail to see that the proper way to think about existence and nonexistence is as properties *of* the world. Facts like {elk}ishness and un{elf}ishness, the facts to which true statements correspond, are real, nontrivial properties of, but not in, the world.

By dismissing facts as entia non grata, these philosophers have at least implicitly discredited commonsense realism.[3] Some, like Strawson and Quine, have done so inadvertently. But others like Putnam, Davidson, Dummett, and Rorty, have had realism as their specific target. Davidson, who favors a version of the coherence theory of truth, has pointed to the alleged incoherence of correspondence as a reason to renounce commonsense realism, arguing that since correspondence "cannot be made intelligible . . . it is futile either to reject or to accept the slogan that the real and the true are 'independent of our beliefs'."[4]

It is one thing to raise classical skeptical doubts about whether the real and the true are independent of our beliefs and quite another to go beyond such skepticism by asserting—as philosophers like Davidson and Rorty do—that realism is an incoherent, "futile" philosophy. The key premise of these antirealist philosophers—that the correspondence-to-fact theory of truth cannot be made intelligible—is false. Correspondence realism is a coherent, reasonable doctrine. Indeed, since it is the default commonsense position, the heavy burden of argument remains where it has always been—on the philosophers who would reject it.

Jonathan Lowe

The important issue over which Jonathan Lowe and I differ—how far one's logical language should be determined by ontological distinctions—will be clear. If modern terminism could win Lowe to its side, it would have a most valuable ally. Here are three proposed desiderata for an adequate logical language. (1) It should facilitate logical reckoning by affording adequate expressive and inferential power. (Historically, Frege's logical language achieved canonical status because it was able to express and to reckon with relational statements, which traditional term logic could not do.) (2) It should not radically depart from the syntax of the natural languages in which people do their everyday deductive reasoning. (It is this virtue that attracts us to modern versions of term logic that possess the first virtue but are natural as well.) (3) It should reflect fundamental ontological distinctions such as that between objects and concepts or particulars and universals.

Quine would stand pat with the first. I go on to endorse the second. Lowe wants us to accept the third. In arguing for the third desideratum Lowe says that logic must represent propositions in "forms that reflect the constituent structure of the possible states of affairs that we are attempting to reason about." Term logic has no atomic propositions. Lowe considers this a defect. "Suppose," he says, "that a certain possible state of affairs consists in some particular object's possessing some property, or exemplifying a certain universal. . . . Would it not then be reasonable to represent this state of affairs by a proposition that likewise contains just two constituents of formally distinct types—by, indeed, an 'atomic' proposition of the classic Frege–Russell form '*Fa*'?" He also argues that certain states have objects that are related by identity; in them he finds the justification for introducing the 'is' of identity into logical syntax.

Perhaps the main quarrel I have with Lowe is that he operates with what seems to me a vague notion of a state of affairs. Mentally noting the fact that the Morning Star is the Evening Star and seeing it as a state of affairs in which some object is identical with itself, he advocates representing it propositionally in a "perspicuous" syntax that uses a binary sign of identity. According to Lowe, the statement 'Some rabbits are gray' is made true by a state in which certain particular objects (rabbits) exemplify a universal (grayness). He recommends that such states of affairs be reflected in a logical syntax that recognizes an 'is' of instantiation, adding this 'is' to the 'is' of identity. To the objection that introducing such ontological distinctions into logical syntax needs more justification than this,[5] Lowe responds that "logic . . . cannot . . . be profitably regarded as metaphysically innocent."

How does it profit logic to give it syntactical features that do not add to its reckoning powers? Lowe does not claim that an "ontologically perspicuous" syntax confers greater inference power on a logic. In fact, such additions may make it weaker and lead to further gratuitous syntactical innovations. No one before Frege talked of an 'is' of identity. Adding the sign of identity to logic (and the newly needed axioms of identity) was forced on Frege because he had abandoned the traditional two-term syntax (in which terms are syntactically interchangeable) and introduced into his logical syntax the distinction between object words and concept words, thereby disallowing a monadic reading of 'Tully is Cicero'. Lowe defends Frege by noting (1) that he believed independently that identity is an onto-logical relation that deserved syntactic recognition and (2) that the object-word/concept-word distinction, enshrined in the '*Fa*' syntax of the atomic sentence, simply recognizes syntactically what was already evident onto-logically. "It is," says Lowe, "open to us to agree with certain of Frege's ontological insights and to concur with him on the relevance of those insights to questions of logical syntax." It is equally open to anyone to enjoy ontological insights while insisting on their irrelevance to questions of logical syntax.

One may accept Lowe's judgment that Aristotle's *Categories* is "perhaps the most important single text in the history ontology" while bearing in mind that when Aristotle went on in the *Analytics* to lay the foundations of a syllogistic logic of terms, he resolutely left the insights of the *Categories* and the *Interpretation* behind him. That he did so appalled Peter Geach, who called it "Aristotle's Fall." But it was the making of Aristotle as a logician and of logic as a formal science.

Frank Keil

A child's concept of the sky allows him to say things like 'The sky is falling'. As he matures, his concept of the sky shifts and he comes to realize that this assertion does not make categorial sense. As Gilbert Ryle would say, the sky is neither falling nor not falling; is not the sort of thing that falls or fails to fall.

Frank Keil's research showed that the formal structure of predicabilty remains invariant from childhood through adulthood. The concepts may shift their locations, but both the child and the adult locate their concepts on a hierarchical tree. On the child's tree, 'blue' and 'falls' are predicable of 'sky', 'log', and 'rain'. Later in life, 'blue' remains predicable of all three but 'falls' is located below 'blue', being predicable of 'log' and 'rain' but not of 'sky':

Child's category tree
_____

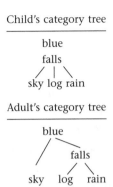

Adult's category tree
_____

Keil also showed that the tree rule (and its "M-constraint") is invariant across cultures. He credits my writings, which first proposed the tree rule, with suggesting to him the research reported in his book, and he draws a moral: when a philosopher's proposal is "sufficiently detailed as to allow precise characterizations of some aspect of knowledge, that structural description often carries with it an implicit experimental research program."

Keil notes that this kind of philosophical influence on empirical research is often unintended. It was certainly so in my case. To me, back in the 1950s and '60s, the category structure belonged broadly to logic as an a priori science. I did not think of it in terms of actual cognitive processes or developmental cognitive psychology. Keil's empirical research and findings actually surprised me. But they seemed to me to be unimpeachable, and I have since come off my a priori high horse even on so pure a topic as deductive logic. In particular, I have come round to thinking of logical competence in the way Chomsky has insisted we think about linguistic competence. An adequate logic should cast light on our deductive competence in the way an adequate grammar should cast light on our ability to learn our native language. It should, for example, explain how common deductive judgments that take many steps to prove formally in the standard logic of quantifiers and variables are instantly made by a child. Children, innocent of formal logic, instinctively judge that 'Someone who owns a colt doesn't own a horse' must be false if 'Every colt is a horse' is true. This cannot be explained by saying that they implicitly reason in a quantifier-variable notation. It is obvious that they do not reason in the logical language of MPL. Indeed, the net effect of insisting that the logical language of MPL is "canonical" is to distance formal logic from the processes of actual reasoning. In other words, the canonization of MPL has led logicians away from facing the problem of how to account for the fact that we intuitively reason so well.

I became convinced that logic must meet conditions of cognitive adequacy when I became aware that TFL is much closer to being cognitively adequate than Frege's predicate logic. Indeed, I believe that the plus/minus character of the logical constants in TFL is directly involved in our ability to reason deductively in the regimented vernacular. I hope therefore that some trained researcher, perhaps a student of Keil, will undertake the investigations that could confirm or disconfirm this conjecture. In any case, cognitive psychologists and linguists should be focusing on the phenomenon of our everyday deductive competence, taking seriously the idea that a cognitively adequate logic must not only be inferentially powerful but provide us with "laws of thought" that cast light on how we use our native language to reckon logically as well as we do.

Alan Berger

Alan Berger notes that the "semantics of predicates" differs from the "semantics of terms," arguing that the vocabulary of science is the vocabulary of terms. The late Jean van Heijenoort had similar reservations about MPL as a organon for scientific discourse. Van Heijenoort noted that the semantics of first-order logic "is based on an ontology of individuals" and is therefore unsuitable for mass terms and "stuff talk."[6] Rejecting a defensive suggestion of Quine that mass terms represent an archaic survival of a preparticular level of experience, he says: "One can even claim that stuff talk corresponds to a higher level of thought. Stuff lends itself to magnitude . . . hence to the mathematical view of the world achieved by modern physics."[7] Van Heijenoort was an orthodox Fregean and so no fan of term logic, yet he concluded his discussion by conceding that "the systematized language of Aristotelian syllogistic . . . escapes that ontology" (of individuals only).

It does indeed escape. In my article, "Predication in the Logic of Terms," I point out that TFL is free of all ontological strictures: "The semantics of TFL neither dictates nor excludes reference to any sort of thing. It is tolerant of individuals, stuff, species, abstract objects, and other kinds of things whose presence or absence may be said to characterize the world. TFL is in this sense a logic without an ontology."[8]

Berger is attracted to term logic because, unlike Jonathan Lowe, who prefers his logic with more than a dash of ontology (see my reply to him above), Berger likes his logic to be ontologically neutral. Another attraction is that Berger is committed to Kripke's main ideas about the rigidity of certain terms, and these ideas are more naturally accommodated in the vocabulary of terms.

In MPL, a term T can only appear as a constituent of a predicate of form 'is T' or 'is a T'. In TFL, the term 'tiger' may appear in subject position in a phrase like 'that tiger', or in predicate position in a phrase like 'is a tiger'. One advantage of dealing with terms and not with predicates is that terms in subject position are often "rigid designators." Logicians, persuaded by Kripke's arguments for the rigidity of certain designators in subject position, find it difficult or impossible to see rigidity in a general term like 'tiger', since its occurrence in MPL, as a constituent of 'is a tiger', is nonrigid. Berger reports Scott Soames's conclusion that we must "demot[e] the status of rigidity in Kripke's overall semantic picture" by withholding rigidity from general terms. He neatly deals with Soames's objections, by pointing out that his skeptical conclusion is a product of the insistence that 'tiger' must always appear as a constituent in predicates such as 'is a tiger'.

Taking 'the king of France' as his example of a term that can appear rigidly as subject yet nonrigidly in predicate position, Berger examines the difference between (1) 'Chirac is the present king of France' and (2) 'The present king of France is bald', noting that "in (2), as Strawson taught us, there is a presupposition that there is a present king of France," and that "this presupposition is part of an anaphoric background." On the other hand, "in (1), there is no anaphoric background." This is an excellent analysis. In effect, it treats the occurrence of the term in (2) as a pronoun harking back to something like 'France has a king'. The full context, then, is 'France has a king; he (France's king) is bald'. Since the role of a pronoun is precisely to designate the thing or things that were antecedently referred to, albeit indefinitely, all pronouns satisfy Kripke's condition for being rigid designators. According to Kripke, a rigid designator is a term that designates its referent(s) in all possible worlds in which its referent(s) exists, and fails to designate otherwise. I have not read Berger's book and do not know whether he agrees with my thesis that all definite subjects may be regarded as anaphoric, pronominal and, *therefore*, as rigid designators.

In *The Logic of Natural Language* (LNL) I argued for the terminist view that primitive predications are of the form 'Some *S* is *P*'. If primitive propositions are the vehicles of primary reference, the basic form of reference is indefinite and definite reference is not primary reference (as it is in MPL). This suggests that the following doctrine of reference is appropriate to term logic:

(1) Primary reference is indefinite reference by 'some *S*' to an *S* (or to some thing taken to be an *S*).

(2) Definite reference (by proper names, pronouns, or definite descriptions) is secondary reference, deriving its referential character anaphorically from an earlier (often tacit) indefinite reference.

The paradigm form of definite referring expression, deriving its referential character from an indefinite reference, is the pronoun. The basic form is

Some *S* is *P*; some/every *S** is *Q*

in which we move from talk about an *S* that is *P* to talk about 'the *S* in question' by means of a "proterm," *S**, whose specific role is to denote the *S* that was referred to indefinitely by the subject, 'some *S*', of the (presupposed) antecedent proposition.[9]

Unlike Kripke's modal account of rigidity, the anaphoric (pronominal) account of rigidity is nonmodal and it is the more basic one. In my view, the modal rigidity of 'the *S*' is due to its pronominal character. Berger, who is a close student of Kripke's philosophy but who also sees the virtues of the anaphoric account, could tell us more about the way the two accounts of rigidity are related.

Patrick Suppes

Patrick Suppes's account of prepositional phrases goes far beyond anything I have to offer on the subject. He is right to say that my book *The Logic of Natural Language* (LNL) does not notationally recognize a role for prepositions. LNL would transcribe 'Some missionaries lived among the heathen' as '$+M_1 + (L_{12} + H_2)$', in which 'L_{12}' represents the dyadic term 'lived among'. My later writings, however, do accord notational recognition to the prepositions that radiate out from a relational term, directing us to its relata.

To better capture the dyadic two-term analysis of a sentence like 'Paris loves Helen', I introduced pairing indices that track the term pairs implicit in the sentence. According to Leibniz, 'loves' in 'Paris loves Helen' is a Janus-faced term, 'lover$_{12}$', oriented respectively to 'Paris' and to 'Helen'. Two two-term subsentences are constituents: 'Paris is a lover' ($P^*_1 + L_1$) and 'Helen is loved' ($H^*_2 + L_2$). Transcribing 'Paris loves Helen' as '$P^*_1 + (L_{12} + H^*_2)$' ('Paris is a lover of Helen') is a perspicuous way of showing how the relational term pairs with the two nonrelational terms. Two further ways of writing 'Paris loves Helen' dyadically are:

(1) $(P^*_1 + L_{12}) + H^*_2$: Someone Paris is a lover of is Helen.

(2) $P^*_1 + (H^*_2 + L_{12})$: Paris is someone Helen is loved by.

In the transcription of 'Paris is a lover of Helen', the numerical index '2' affixed to 'L' represents the preposition 'of', directing us to 'Helen'. In the equivalent passive form 'Helen is loved by Paris' ($H^*_2 + L_{12} + P^*_1$) the index '1' represents 'by', directing us to 'Paris'. 'Some missionaries lived among the heathen' would be transcribed as '$+M_1 + L_{12} + H_2$', in which '2' attached to 'L' signifies 'among' directing us to 'the heathen'.

In LNL I took no notice of prepositions, but after I introduced the pairing markers, I occasionally remarked on the prepositional (directive) role they play. Here is one such remark: "When a term occurs 'relationally' it is often accompanied by a preposition like 'of', 'on', 'by'. . . . The terminist does not construe these as part of the term but as mere indices directing us to a term with which the indexed term is being paired. For example, '3' represents 'from' in 'T1 + B123 + C2 + H3' ('Tom bought a Cadillac from Harriet')."[10] If this interpretation of prepositions affixed to relational terms proves to be illuminating, it should also cast light on the *case* of the subject and object terms that stand for the relata.

Prepositions that direct us to and from terms with which a relational term is being paired should be distinguished from other types of preposition that do not play this directive role. In particular, they should be distinguished from most of the examples of prepositions discussed in Pat Suppes's essay. Sometimes the same prepositional word is used directively in one context and as relation in its own right in another context. Thus 'on' in 'Some students wrote on a historical figure' ($+S_1 + W_{12} + H_2$) is directive. But in 'The book is on the table' ($+B^*_1 + O_{12} + T^*_2$) (an example cited by Suppes) 'on' is itself a relational expression. Similarly, 'in' is directive in

'He put the broom in the closet' ($H^*_1 + P_{123} + B^*_2 + C^*_3$), (the numeral '3' directing us to 'C'), but in 'The broom is in the closet' ($B^*_1 + I_{12} + {}^*C_2$), 'in' is a relation.

Directive prepositions fall away under simplification. An assertion like 'June is smiling at Tom' ($J^*_1 + S_{12} + T^*_2$) entails the subsentence 'June is smiling' ($J^*_1 + S_{12}$). Modern predicate logic, which represents 'June is smiling at Tom' as 'S(j,t)' has no natural way to derive 'June is smiling'. In TFL, by contrast, the inference follows by association and simplification:

1. $J^*_1 + (S_{12} + T^*_2)$ premise (June is smiling at Tom)
2. $(J^*_1 + S_{12}) + T^*_2$ 1, association (Someone June is smiling at is Tom)
3. $J^*_1 + S_{12}$ 2, simplification (June is smiling)

In what linguists call the passive transformation and logicians call the converse, the directions are reversed, prepositions change, but equivalence is preserved. The passive transformation of (1) is '$T^*_2 + S_{12} + J^*_1$' ('Tom is smiled at by June'). MPL is at a loss to account for the entailment. But in TFL the passive equivalent is entailed by the following steps:

1. $J^*_1 + (S_{12} + T^*_2)$ premise (June is smiling at Tom)
2. $(J^*_1 + S_{12}) + T^*_2$ 1, association (Someone June is smiling at is Tom)
3. $T^*_2 + (J^*_1 + S_{12})$ 2, commutation (Tom is someone June is smiling at)
4. $T^*_2 + (S_{12} + J^*_1)$ 3, commutation (Tom is smiled at by June)

Since TFL provides us with a formal way to derive passive transformations, its concept script is in this respect superior in expressive and inferential power to MPL. Aware that his concept script was unable to account for passive transformations, Frege deemed them "of no concern to logic,"[11] treating the difference between 'Jay loves Kay' and 'Kay is loved by Jay' as of equal (nil) concern to logic as the difference between 'Jay fed the dog' and 'Jay fed the cur'. Frege's position is dictated by the patent inability of MPL's canonical notation even to express the difference between a statement and its passive transform, let alone derive the latter from the former. When we compare the merits of the two concept scripts, we deem that one superior which comprehends more transformations that really are within the "concern of logic."

Bill Purdy

Bill Purdy's essay is rich in insights and novelties, most of which I shall leave largely undiscussed as I focus on the central relation between anaphora and their antecedent backgrounds, taking particular note that this relation, properly construed (as Purdy does so construe it), helps to resolve the Liar paradox.

Purdy rightly lays down that an antecedent is a referring phrase that denotes its referent or referents independently. By contrast an anaphor "acquires its denotation by reference to its antecedent." Purdy recognizes that anaphora get their definite denotation from antecedents that are themselves indefinite. The paradigm move is from 'an S' to 'it' or 'the S'. Quine points out that 'it' and 'the lion' are interchangeable in 'I saw a lion and you saw it too'.[12] Purdy too says that "an anaphor is a third-person pronoun or a definite description" but notes that "not all definite descriptions are anaphors": when a definite description is in predicate position (as in 'John Adams was the president') it is not interchangeable with a pronoun. (This point is also made by Alan Berger in his contribution to this volume.)

It is not clear to me whether Purdy also accords anaphoric status to proper names, which, in my view, also denote what was antecedently referred to indefinitely. A proper name has an anaphoric background that originates first in indefinite reference by antecedents like 'Mrs. X has just given birth to a beautiful baby', then goes on to 'It [the baby in question] is a boy!' Later, a "special duty" anaphor, or proper name, is introduced to refer to the baby boy in question. LNL argues that all proper names have origins like this. Indeed, I argue for the claim that all definite reference is anaphoric.

One of Purdy's examples is the pronoun 'that' in 'John said Bob might lose his job. That scared Bob'. Here the pronoun could also have been the definite description 'what John said'. When someone refers to 'what John said', one must look for a sentential vehicle that expresses something John said; in so doing we treat 'what John said' as a pronoun that gets its reference from a proposition that Tom expressed.

Although Purdy pays no special attention to anaphora that refer to propositions, he acknowledges that they too are definite (pronominal) subjects. In LNL[13] I pointed out that strictly adhering to the thesis that all definite subjects are anaphors offers a ready solution to the Liar paradox. Standard solutions tend to see something semantically amiss in the Liar's use of the truth predicate. By refreshing contrast, Ryle held that what is wrong with the Liar is to be found by attending to its subject. 'What I am now saying is boring' is just as defective as 'What I am now saying is not true'. Indeed, all sentences of form 'What I am now saying is P' have definite anaphoric subjects that lack antecedents and that are, therefore, necessarily vacuous. It is like beginning a sentence with a pronoun whose reference can never be pinned down. As Ryle noted, in such utterances the futile attempt to specify the presupposed antecedent leads to a regress of "namely riders"—'What I am now saying, namely what I am now saying, namely . . .'. Englebretsen's contribution to this volume presents some of the formal arguments showing the impossibility of finding an antecedent background for a proposition that purports to refer to 'what I am now saying'. Formal arguments aside, the approach to the Liar by way of the theory of anaphora offers a ready, natural, and plausible resolution.

Steven Lindell

Lindell assures the reader: "Other than a basic understanding of first-order logic, no additional background in mathematics or physics is required to understand this essay." I found I had to read him with great care several times over before I could satisfy myself that this statement, though overly optimistic, was basically true. I do not know enough about computer science to judge the extent of its originality but I suspect that his may be an important paper.

In exploring limits imposed by spatial and physical constraints on storing and processing data, Lindell argues that information stored for purposes of symbolic manipulation may best be represented in a mathematical language of term logic whose mode of reckoning conforms closely to the mode we use when reckoning in our native language. Lindell notes, however, that "[t]he two-term syntax for statements in traditional logic provides no way to count," and he proposes to remedy this by adding numerals to the existential and universal quantifiers of a first-order logical language. I shall comment on this point.

Lindell's way of dealing with numerically quantified statements is not as efficient or as elegant as one first suggested by Lorne Szabolcsi. Szabolcsi was a student of George Englebretsen who died in a tragic accident two years ago (before he could publish his findings). Szabolcsi added to term logic the ability to count. He proposed that we interpret 'Some S is P' as 'More than zero S are P', and went on from there to reckon logically with sentences like 'More than seventeen sheep were shorn', 'At most (i.e., no more than) five Republicans will defect', and so on, and then went on to ways of reckoning with multiply quantified sentences like 'No more than three boys love more than ten girls' (where much remains to be done). I limit my remarks to monadic sentences and to numerically quantified syllogisms.

I have found it best to give sentential scope to Szabolsci's basic numerical quantifier, 'more than n', transcribing 'Some S is P' as '$+_0(S + P)$' and 'More than seventeen S are P' as '$+_{17}(S + P)$'. This notation enables us to use negative numbers as binary negative quantifiers in saying things like 'No more than eight S are P', which we may then usefully transcribe as

$-_8(S + P)$.

Other numerical locutions:

'At least n A are B' transcribes as '$+_{n-1}(A + B)$'.

'Exactly n A are B' is compound: 'At least n A are B and at most n A are B'.

Using only denials as universal forms, the locution 'No more than four cats were fed' is a natural equivalent of 'At most four cats were fed', but its logical equivalent 'All but at most four cats were not fed'[14] is unnatural. We do not naturally quantify universal sentences numerically, and we facilitate inference best by representing numerically quantified universal propositions naturally, that is, as denials of particular propositions.

A numerical schedule of the four basic categoricals then looks like this:

A	$-_0(S + (-P))$	No S is not P	Not more than 0 S are not P
E	$-_0(S + P)$	No S is P	Not more than 0 S are P
I	$+_0(S + P)$	Some S is P	More than 0 S are P
O	$+_0(S + (-P))$	Some S is not P	More than 0 S are not P

To be valid a syllogism must have the right mood. Only two moods are valid:

1. Syllogisms that have only universal statements (all have external minus signs).

2. Syllogisms that have a particular conclusion and exactly one particular premise.

The following is a valid numerical syllogism in the first mood:

No more than 3 A are B	$-_3(A + B)$
No more that 2 C are not A	$-_2(C + (-A))$
At most 5 B are not C	$-_5(B - C)$

The following is a valid syllogism in the second mood:

More than 6 A are B	$+_6(A + B)$
No more than 1 D is not C	$-_1(D + (-C))$
No more than 2 A are C	$-_2(A + C)$
More than 3 B are not D	$+_3(B + (-D))$

   To be valid, a syllogism must not only be in the right mood, but its premises (ignoring numerical subscripts or setting them at zero) must algebraically add up to its conclusion. The above syllogisms satisfy these necessary conditions for validity. However, they also have a more specific arithmetical character. To be valid the external binary quantifiers of such syllogisms must satisfy the following condition:

The sum of the numerical quantifiers of the premises must be equal to or greater than the numerical quantifier of the conclusion.

   I call this Szabolcsi's condition, having arrived at it, in straightforward fashion, from his original way of representing numerically quantified statements. Both syllogisms satisfy the Szabolcsi condition, and both are valid arguments.

   Lindell might agree that Szabolsci's way of doing numerically quantified logic is preferable to his own. In any case, an effective way of reckoning with numerically quantified statements is obviously desirable; its implementation in computer inference processing would indeed be a significant advance.

Aris Noah

Aris Noah situates himself between MPL and TFL, arguing that TFL's algebraic cancellation procedures reflect more on the oppositional nature of the logical constants than on their plus/minus character. He notes that cancellation of middles is not necessarily tied to a plus/minus reading of the constants, and he points out that plus/minus transcriptions are not very useful for doing sentential logic. I agree with him here and indeed in the logic text I coauthored with George Englebretsen (*An Invitation to Formal Reasoning*, published several years after Noah penned his contribution to this volume),[15] the methods of sentential logic are not developed on algebraic lines. Instead *ITFR* uses trees. A tree represents a normal form, DNF, and it graphically shows whether a given downward or upward path has oppositely charged literals. If all its paths are thus closed the whole tree is inconsistent. Paths left open show the entailments. Trees are a graphic way of using normal forms and oppositely charged elements to disclose the logical possibilities and impossibilities. So, as Noah strongly suggests, in sentential logic algebra is not the best way to go. (Geometry is better.)

On the other hand, TFL's algebraic transcriptions come into their own in nonsentential term logic, including inferences with relational propositions. Even here I do not claim outright that the logical words we use in everyday reasoning (words like 'some' and 'is', which I call *plus words*, and those like 'every' and not', which I call *minus words*) are cognitively reckoned with just as one reckons with the plus and minus signs of arithmetic or elementary algebra. For one thing, although logic is algebraic, its algebra differs from ninth grade algebra in being subject to the valence constraint. Noah attributes to me the view that "the DDO forms the backbone of our actual inferential cognitive process." I do strongly suspect that people, in their everyday reasoning, treat a select group of natural language constants as if they were plus and minus functors. But this is an empirical conjecture and it is so far unconfirmed. I offer it as a plausible explanation for our native logical competence; it may, for example, explain how a child, innocent of formal logic, is able instantly to infer 'No contestant correctly spelled every word' from 'Every contestant misspelled some word'.

Noah's assessments of the relative importance and powers of TFL, MPL, the Robinson resolution methods, and Quine's predicate functor logic are admirably judicious and clear. However, he omits specific consideration of our natural deductive capabilities. My claim that the algebraic, variable-free "concept script" of TFL is superior to that of MPL rests not on the claim that the former confers greater inference power on its logical calculus (both concept scripts provide about the same inference power to their respective logical calculi), but on which of the two concept scripts is more faithful to the language we use in making common, everyday deductive judgments. No one, not even Quine, uses quantifiers and variables to judge that the conjunction 'Every U.S. senator is a U.S. citizen but someone who is writing to a senator is not writing to a U.S. citizen' is an inconsistent statement. The inconsistency can indeed be formally shown by deriving a contradiction from the conjunction of '$\forall x(Sx \supset Cx)$' and '$\exists xy(Sx \ \& \ Wyx \ \& \ (\forall z(Cz \supset -Wyz)))$', but it takes a bit of doing, and no one who is not an idiot savant does it that way or does it by using the inference rules of a predicate functor logic. TFL, on the other hand, provides a simple and plausible account of how it is that we instantaneously recognize the inconsistency. Transcribing the conjunction as '$[-S + C] + [+(W + S) - (W + C)]$', it uses DDO cancellation and immediately derives '$+(W + C) - (W + C)$'— 'Someone who is writing to a citizen is not writing to a citizen'. I claim that TFL's algebraic transcriptions and processes mirror the way we actually make inferences and arrive at judgments of inconsistency in real life and real-time reckoning, and that empirical research in cognitive psychology will eventually show that I am right. Robinson resolutions are on the whole much quicker than standard MPL proofs, but they too use quantifier/variable formulations, and I would argue that TFL transcription and cancellation is miles closer to cognitive reality.

David Oderberg

Russell's theory of descriptions replaced referring expressions like 'the king' with 'definite descriptions', predicative expressions uniquely true of their referents. When Quine did the same for proper names, only the variable was left to do the job of reference. The variable, as Quine construes it, has no "sense": all it has is reference. In Quine's words, "the pronoun or variable is the vehicle of pure reference."[16]

Bereft of sense, the referring expressions in Quine's version of MPL refer to bare particulars. David Oderberg makes a compelling case for this conclusion and notes that Quine himself had all but reached it: "The pronoun is the tenable linguistic counterpart of the untenable old metaphysical notion of a bare particular." And again: "The variable is the legitimate latter-day embodiment of the incoherent old idea of a bare particular."

How legitimate is the latter-day embodiment? Its role in MPL is a formal guarantee that there is nothing logically incoherent in the idea of a bare particular. But, as Oderberg's discussion of Warnock on Locke reminds us, the idea of a bare, featureless particular is ontologically incoherent. How does the pronoun, as bound variable, meet the old animadversions against a featureless "something I know not what"? Here, Quine's idea that we commit ourselves ontologically to the sorts of things we quantify over may seem to offer some protection from utter bareness. For suppose I am quantifying over the set of natural numbers. Any given number is either factorable by 11 or not factorable by 11. And its being so seems to be a feature of numbers that things other than numbers do not possess. For it makes no sense to say of a person or an event that it is factorable by 11. If so, what I am referring to is not featureless. Here, however, Oderberg rightly calls attention to Quine's hard line on "category mistakes," pointing out that according to Quine something like 'Peter Geach is factorable by 11' is simply false and not neither true nor false. Ryle distinguished between a false but category-correct statement like '23 is factorable by 11' and a category mistake like 'Peter Geach is factorable by 11'. According to Ryle, but not to Quine, Geach is neither factorable by 11 nor does he fail to be. Quine is bound by his logical syntax to treat 'Geach is not factorable by 11' as the true negation of 'Geach is factorable by 11'. What Oderberg calls Quine's "one-category ontology" thus offers no shelter to the bare particulars that inhabit it.

Oderberg rehearses Geoffrey Warnock's acute argument directed against Locke's way of arriving at a bare particular as the featureless bearer of properties. I would argue in parallel fashion that what has a property of being red is essentially a thing that is either colored-or-colorless. A red object can lose its color and become colorless but it cannot ever fail to be either colored-or-colorless. So it is generally with things that are P; they may become "un-P" but cannot become neither-P-nor-un-P. Nothing can be divested of such essential attributes. But just this way of clothing particulars is not available to Quine. For, as Oderberg points out, he does not have an operator for term denial and must make do with sentence negation. And this economy is of a piece with his refusal to recognize distinctions of category.

At the very close of his argument, Oderberg confesses to a reluctance to ascribe to Quine the view that MPL is committed to the existence of bare particulars as the referents of its bound variables, as opposed to claiming that this is where his interpretation of MPL appears to point. I too share that reluctance. To be sure, though, Quine himself leads us to this unhappy conclusion about the nature (or lack of nature) of the things bound variables refer to. For he finds the antecedents to his pronouns in the existential quantifier, moving from 'there is a thing' to 'it is P'. That common anaphoric background offers no ground for differentiating any one thing from any other. However, when Quine talks more concretely about reference and pronominalization, he clearly recognizes that pronouns in use have a quite definite sense, which they get from their antecedents. In real life we do not move from 'some thing' to 'it' but from an indefinite description to a definite one, from, say, 'I saw a lion' to 'you also saw it [viz., the lion]' (Quine's example), "mak[ing]," says Quine, "no distinction between a pronoun such as 'it' and a singular description such as 'the lion'."[17] Oderberg points out that restricted quantification's approach to quantifiers and pronouns offer a tempting, but ultimately unsuccessful, way of recognizing that pronouns have sense as well as reference. In any case, Quine's own way with the existential quantifier systematically removes all sense from pronouns by bringing us relentlessly back to 'some thing' and 'it' as the primary form of pronominalization.

Notes

1. We do, of course, say that the world exists and speak of it as the actual world, contrasting it with other (possible) worlds. But then the domain under consideration is the totality of possible worlds.

2. Frege, *Logical Investigations*, trans. P. T. Geach and R. H. Stoothoff, ed. Geach (Oxford: Blackwell, 1977), p. 10 (see also pp. 27–28). In taking Frege as the standard bearer for the view that propositions are informationally complete, I omit consideration of assertions containing demonstrative subjects over which there is considerable dispute.

3. The rejection of metaphysical realism has left American philosophers in thrall to an unattractive pragmatism of the kind I had my fill of at Columbia, where I did graduate studies in the 1950s. It reopened the road to John Dewey's and (later) to Richard Rorty's view that knowledge is not "a matter of getting reality right, but rather . . . a matter of acquiring habits of action for coping with reality." (See my "Intellectual Autobiography," this vol., note 17.)

4. See note 16 of chap. 1, this vol.

5. After all, the truth-making state of affairs could just as well be regarded as the existence of something that is a rabbit and a gray thing. See my "Intellectual Autobiography" and my comments on Englebretsen.

6. J. van Heijenoort, "Subject and Predicate in Western Logic," *Philosophy East and West* 24 (1974): 256–268, at pp. 263, 265.

7. Ibid., p. 265.

8. "Predication in the Logic of Terms," *Notre Dame Journal of Formal Logic* 31 (1990): 106–126, at p. 123.

9. See LNL, chapter 4, passim.

10. "Predication in the Logic of Terms," p. 111.

11. See G. Frege, *Posthumous Writings*, edited by H. Hermes, F. Kambartel, and F. Kaulbach (Chicago: Univeristy of Chicago Press, 1979), p. 141.

12. Quine, *Word and Object* (Cambridge, Mass.: The MIT Press, 1960), p. 113.

13. At p. 331.

14. See Lindell's formulation, ch. 8 this vol.

15. F. Sommers and G. Englebretsen, *An Invitation to Formal Reasoning* (Aldershot: Ashgate, 2000).

16. See note 11 of chap. 10, this vol.

17. *Word and Object*, p. 113.

Works by Fred Sommers

1952: "The Passing of Privileged Uniqueness," *Journal of Philosophy* 49: 392–397.

1953: "Review: *Das 'physikalische Modell' und die 'metaphysische Wirklichkeit'; Versuch einer Metaphänomenologie*, by Erwin Nickel," *Journal of Philosophy* 50 (1953): 332–334.

1959: "The Ordinary Language Tree," *Mind* 68: 160–185.

1961: "Review: *An Introduction to Wittgenstein's* Tractatus, by G. E. M. Anscombe," *Philosophy* 36: 374–377 (with J. Jarvis).

1963: "Meaning Relations and the Analytic," *Journal of Philosophy* 60: 524–534.

1963: "Types and Ontology," *Philosophical Review* 72: 327–363. Reprinted in P. F. Strawson (ed.), *Philosophical Logic* (Oxford: Oxford University Press, 1967) and elsewhere.

1964: "Truth-Functional Counterfactuals," *Analysis* (supplement) 24: 120–126.

1964: "A Program for Coherence," *Philosophical Review* 73: 522–527.

1965: "Truth-Value Gaps: A Reply to Mr. Odegard," *Analysis* 25: 66–68.

1965: "Predicability," in M. Black (ed.), *Philosophy in America* (Ithaca: Cornell University Press), pp. 262–281.

1966: "Why Is There Something and Not Nothing?" *Analysis* 26: 177–181.

1966: "What We Can Say about God," *Judaism* 15: 61–73.

1967: "On a Fregean Dogma," in I. Lakatos (ed.), *Problems in the Philosophy of Mathematics* (Amsterdam: North-Holland), pp. 47–62.

1969: "Do We Need Identity?", *Journal of Philosophy* 66: 499–504.

1969: "On Concepts of Truth in Natural Languages," *Review of Metaphysics* 23: 259–286.

1970: "The Calculus of Terms," *Mind* 79: 1–39. Reprinted in G. Englebretsen (ed.), *The New Syllogistic* (New York: Peter Lang, 1987).

1970–1971: "Confirmation and the Natural Subject," *Philosophical Forum* 2: 245–250.

1971: "Structural Ontology," *Philosophia* 1: 21–42.

1973: "Existence and Predication," in M. Munitz (ed.), *Logic and Ontology* (New York: New York University Press), pp. 159–174.

1974: "The Logical and the Extra-Logical," *Boston Studies in the Philosophy of Science* 14: 235–252.

1975: "Distribution Matters," *Mind* 84: 27–46.

1976: "Frege or Leibniz?" in M. Schirn (ed.), *Studies on Frege* III (Stuttgart: Frommann-Holzboog), pp. 11–34.

1976: "Logical Syntax in Natural Language," in A. F. MacKay and D. D. Merrill (eds.), *Issues in the Philosophy of Language* (Proceedings of the 1972 Oberlin Colloquium in Philosophy) (New Haven and London: Yale University Press), pp. 11–41.

1976: "On Predication and Logical Syntax," in A. Kasher (ed.), *Language in Focus* (Dordrecht: D. Reidel). Special issue, *Boston Studies in the Philosophy of Science* 43: *Essays in Memory of Yehoshua Bar-Hillel*: 41–53.

1976: "Leibniz's Program for the Development of Logic," in R. S. Cohen, P. K. Feyerabend, and M. W. Wartofsky (eds.), *Essays in Memory of Imre Lakatos* (Dordrecht: D. Reidel). Special issue, *Boston Studies in the Philosophy of Science* 39: 589–615.

1978: "The Grammar of Thought," *Journal of Social and Biological Structures* 1: 39–51.

1978: "Dualism in Descartes: The Logical Ground," in M. Hooker (ed.), *Descartes* (Baltimore: Johns Hopkins University Press), pp. 223–233.

1981: "Are There Atomic Propositions?", *Midwest Studies in Philosophy* 6: 59–68.

1982: *The Logic of Natural Language* (Oxford: Clarendon Press).

1983: "Linguistic Grammar and Logical Grammar," in L. S. Cauman et al. (eds.), *How Many Questions? Essays in Honor of Sidney Morgenbesser* (Indianapolis: Hackett), pp. 180–194.

1983: "The Logic of Natural Language: A Reply to Geach," *Times Literary Supplement*, January 14.

1983: "The Logic of Natural Language: A Further Reply to Geach," *Times Literary Supplement*, February 18.

1983: "The Grammar of Thought: A Reply to Dauer," *Journal of Social and Biological Structures* 6: 37–44.

1987: "Truth and Existence," in G. Englebretsen (ed.), *The New Syllogistic* (New York: Peter Lang, 1987), pp. 299–304.

1990: "Predication in the Logic of Terms," *Notre Dame Journal of Formal Logic* 31: 106–126.

1993: "The World, the Facts, and Primary Logic," *Notre Dame Journal of Formal Logic* 34: 169–182.

1993: "'The Enemy Is Us': Objectivity and Its Philosophical Detractors," in H. Dickman (ed.), *The Imperiled Academy* (New Brunswick: Transaction Publishers), pp. 239–268.

1993: "Saying What We Think," in S. M. Cahn (ed.), *Affirmative Action and the University: A Philosophical Inquiry* (Philadelphia: Temple University Press), pp. 291–294.

1994: "Naturalism and Realism," *Midwest Studies in Philosophy* 19: 22–38.

1996: "Existence and Correspondence to Facts," in R. Poli and P. Simons (eds.), *Formal Ontology* (Dordrecht: Kluwer), pp. 131–158.

1997: "Putnam's Born-Again Realism," *Journal of Philosophy* 94: 453–471.

2000: "Term Functor Grammars," in M. Böttner and W. Thümmel (eds.), *Variable-Free Semantics* (Osnabrück: Secolo Verlag), pp. 68–89.

2000: *An Invitation to Formal Reasoning* (Aldershot: Ashgate) (with G. Englebretsen).

2002: "On the Future of Logic Instruction," *American Philosophical Association Newsletter on Teaching Philosophy* 1 (spring): 176–180.

2004: "The Holocaust and Moral Philosophy," in C. H. Sommers and F. Sommers (eds.), *Virtue and Vice in Everyday Life*, sixth edition (Belmont, Calif.: Thomson Wadsworth), pp. 150–155.

2004: *Virtue and Vice in Everyday Life*, sixth edition (Belmont, Calif.: Thomson Wadsworth) (ed. with C. Hoff Sommers).

Contributors

Fred Sommers began his academic career at Columbia University, where he taught from 1955 to 1960. He moved to Brandeis University in the early 1960s, where he held the Harry Austryn Wolfson Chair of Philosophy from 1965 until his retirement in 1993. Now Emeritus Professor, he continues to teach but devotes himself mainly to writing. Sommers was awarded a Fulbright scholarship to teach at the Hebrew University in 1961–62. He taught at the University of Tel Aviv in the spring of 1967, the University of California at Santa Barbara in the spring of 1976, and was Visiting Fellow at the Salk Institute for Biological Studies, La Jolla, California, in the winter and spring of 1970. He has lectured at Oxford, Berkeley, and Stanford, among many other places. His books include *The Logic of Natural Language* (Oxford: Clarendon Press, 1982) and (with George Englebretsen) *An Invitation to Formal Reasoning* (Aldershot: Ashgate, 2000).

Alan Berger is Professor of Philosophy at Brandeis University, and the author of *Terms and Truth: Reference Direct and Anaphoric* (MIT Press, 2002). He is the author of many articles in philosophy of language and related topics, including a number of articles critical of Quine.

George Englebretsen is a professor of logic and metaphysics at Bishop's University, Quebec. He has published and lectured extensively on Sommers's philosophy over the past thirty-five years. He is the author of *Something to Reckon With: The Logic of Terms*, and co-author with Fred Sommers of *An Invitation to Formal Reasoning*.

Frank C. Keil is Professor of Psychology and Linguistics at Yale University. He is the author of *Semantic and Conceptual Development: An Ontological Perspective; Concepts, Kinds and Cognitive Development;* and is co-editor of the *MIT Encyclopedia of the Cognitive Sciences*.

Steven Lindell is Associate Professor of Computer Science at Haverford College, Pennsylvania, where he is head of department. His research interests include logic as applied to computational complexity and database theory, and the philosophical foundations of information and computation.

E. J. Lowe is Professor of Philosophy at the University of Durham, U.K., and has published widely in many fields, including metaphysics, philosophical logic, philosophy of language, and philosophy of mind. His books include *Kinds of Being, Subjects of Experience,* and *The Possibility of Metaphysics.* He is currently working on a book entitled *The Four-Category Ontology: A Metaphysical Foundation for Natural Science.*

Aris Noah works for the Educational Testing Service, Princeton, N.J., and is the author, among other papers on Sommers's logic, of an appendix to the latter's *The Logic of Natural Language.*

David S. Oderberg is Professor of Philosophy at the University of Reading, U.K., and the author of books and articles on metaphysics, philosophical logic, and philosophy of language, among other subjects.

William C. Purdy was Senior Engineer, General Electric Co., and Associate Professor of Electrical Engineering and Computer Science, Syracuse University. He is currently Visiting Scholar, Syracuse University.

Patrick Suppes is Lucie Stern Professor of Philosophy, Emeritus, Stanford University. He has been a member of the Stanford faculty since 1950, and emeritus since 1992. Suppes is the author of many books and articles on formal logic, philosophy of science, and related topics.

Index

Anaphora. *See* Pronouns (and anaphora); Terms

Aristotle/Aristotelianism, 3–4, 6, 10, 15, 33, 34, 35, 48, 69, 85, 109, 130–131, 169, 172, 178, 184, 216

Armstrong, D., 57

Atomicity thesis, 49–50, 215

Austin, J. L., 41

Bare particulars, 6, 228–230
categories and, 194ff., 229
criticism of, 203–206
variable as latter-day version of, 193–194, 228–230
Warnock's criticism of Locke on, 201–202, 229

Berger, A., 218–220

Boole, G., 36

Carroll, L., 206

Category theory, 2–8, 26–32, 194ff.
ambiguity, rule for forcing, 30–31
Aristotle on, 3
category tree/hierarchy/ordinary language tree, 3–4
dualism and, 5–6, 31
law of category inclusion, 5, 28–29
natural predicability, 3, 35–36
and phenomenalism, 31
psychological reality of category hierarchy, 8, 32, 68–74

rule against M configurations, 28–30, 72–74, 217

Chesterton, G. K., 183

Chomsky, N., 20, 72, 217

Davidson, D., 18, 41, 212, 214

Deductive competence, 1–2, 8–9, 217–218, 228

De Morgan, A., 36

Descartes, R. (on dualism), 5–6

Descriptions, definite, 90ff., 112–113, 117, 219. *See also* Terms

Dewey, J., 18

Dictum de Omni et Nullo (DDO), 15, 172–173, 178–180, 227

Divisions of linguistic and cognitive labor, 77–80

Dummett, M., 2, 14, 52, 184, 212, 214

Englebretsen, G., 207, 211–214, 227

Essences and kinds, psychological bias toward in children and adults, 74–77

Evans, G., 114–116, 124

Existence. *See* Realism (Sommers's version of)

Facts. *See* Realism (Sommers's version of)

Feynman, R., 137

Four-category ontology, 55ff. *See also* Modern predicate logic (MPL)

Frege, G., 33, 36, 49ff., 60, 63, 85, 169,
    184, 191, 213, 214, 218, 222
and atomicity thesis (*see* Atomicity
    thesis)
disdain for natural language in logical
    reckoning, 2
and existence, 17–18, 20, 211–212
on passive transformations, 222
on saturated and unsaturated
    concepts, 185, 216

Geach, P., 35, 52, 169, 184ff., 191,
    216
Goodman, N., 7

Higginbotham, J., 92
Horwich, P., 41

Identity in TFL and MPL, 13–14,
    51–53, 63, 170, 215–216

Kant, I., 17, 211
Keil, F. C., 8, 32, 216–218
Kripke, S., 74, 86–89, 96, 219, 220

Laws of thought, 2, 8, 17
Leibniz, G. W. (inc. Leibniz's Law), 15,
    34, 36, 52, 91, 93, 207
Lewis, C. I., 212
Liar paradox, 223–224. *See also* Realism
    (Sommers's version of)
Lindell, S., 224–226
Locke, J., 201, 229. *See also* Bare
    particulars
Logic/logical syntax and ontology, ch.
    3 *passim*, 183–184, 214–216, 218
Logic and information/computation,
    ch. 8 *passim*
data storage problem, 137–140
elementary term logic (version of
    TFL), 155–167
information, mathematical
    representation of, 140–145

information, models of, 150–155
physical storage of data, 145–150
Logic and psychology, ch. 4 *passim*,
    216–218
Lowe, E. J., 197, 214–216, 219

May, R., 92, 94
Modern predicate logic (MPL)
and bare particulars, ch. 10 *passim* (*see
    also* Bare particulars)
copula, 34, 185ff., 191
deductive competence, 1–2, 8–9,
    217–218, 228
elimination of names, 191–192
existence, 17–18
and four-category ontology, 60ff.
identity, 13–14, 51–53, 215–216
multiply general sentences (contrast
    with TFL), 14–16
passive transformations, 222
predication, 10–11
quantification, 185–192, 197
relational inferences, 38
restricted quantification, 189–191
sentence negation vs. term negation,
    33, 199–201
singular and general terms treated
    differently, 34
and subject-predicate form, 49–51
translation of categorical sentences,
    184–187
variable, role of, 186, 189ff., 192ff.,
    202
Montague, R., 132
Moore, G. E., 41

Noah, A., 226–228

Oderberg, D. S., 228–230

Peirce, C. S., 36
Philosophy, implications for empirical
    research, 80–82, 217–218

Prepositions, syntax and semantics of, ch. 6 *passim*, 220–222
Pronouns (and anaphora), 16–17, ch. 7 *passim*, 223–224, 230
A-type, 117, 125
B-type, 115–116, 124
and conjunctions, 130–132
descriptions, 112–113, 117, 219
donkey anaphora, 129–130
E-type, 116–117, 124–125
Gareth Evans on, 114–116
pronouns of laziness, 187
relative pronoun/relative clause, 186–187, 192
Pronouns and reference, 186ff., 230
Purdy, W. C., 223–224
Putnam, H., 17, 18, 74, 77–78, 212, 213, 214

Quine, W. V. O., 41, 169, 170, 183, 184ff., 202, 214, 215, 218, 223, 227, 228–230
on categories, 3
elimination of names, 191–192
existence and predication, 194–196
facts, 18, 212
logical vs. nonlogical expressions, 188–189
pronouns, variables, and reference, 186ff.

Ramsey, F., 54
Realism (Sommers's version of)
de mundo beliefs, 45
existence, 17–20, 212–214
facts, 18–19, 40–47, 212–214
Liar paradox, 45–47
propositions, 45–47
truth (correspondence theory), 40–47, 213–214
Rigid designation, anaphora, and general terms, ch. 5 *passim*, 218–220

Robinson, J. (method of resolution), 169, 175–180
Rorty, R., 18, 41, 214
Russell, B., 12, 20, 36, 41, 60, 69, 85, 87, 211, 228
and atomicity thesis, 49–50
Ryle, G., 2, 5, 26, 30, 31, 69, 216

Salmon, N., 87, 89
Soames, S., 86, 88–89, 219
Sortal logic, 61–63
Strawson, P. F., 18, 35, 41, 219
Suppes, P., 8, 220–222
Szabolcsi, L., 224–226

Tarski, A., 41, 85
Term logic. *See* Traditional formal logic/term functor logic (TFL)
Terms
anaphora, 90, 97ff., 220 (*see also* Pronouns [and anaphora])
basic account of, 87
buckstoppers, 96–97
copula, 90–91
definite descriptions, 90ff., 219
general, ch. 5 *passim*
mass, 92, 218
negation of, 33, 199–201, 229
second-order, 91–93
singular, 97ff., 120
TFL account of, 96ff., 218
Traditional formal logic/term functor logic (TFL)
algebraic character of, 8ff., 171ff.
and computation, physical realization, ch. 8 *passim*, esp. 155–167
Sommers's cancellation technique compared to Robinson's method of resolution, ch. 9 *passim* (*see also* Robinson, J. [method of resolution])
central characteristics of, 169–170
copula, 34

Traditional formal logic/term functor
  logic (TFL) (cont.)
Dictum de Omni (*see* Dictum de
  Omni et Nullo [DDO])
general form of the proposition in,
  12, 97
identity, 13–14, 51–53, 98, 170
multiply general sentences, 14–16
numerical quantification, 224–226
passive transformations, 222
plus/minus notation, 171ff., 226–228
predication, 10–11, 35–36
prepositions, 220–222
reference, 220
relational sentences, 14–16, 37–39,
  170, 220–222
rules for an adequate system of logical
  reckoning, 9
sentence logic as branch of, 39–40,
  171ff., 203–204
simplicity and naturalness, as opposed
  to MPL, 8ff., 33ff., 228
singular and general terms treated
  alike, 34–36
singular terms/sentences, 13–14, 37,
  97ff., 120
and subject-predicate form, 49–51
syllogisms in, examples of, 13
syllogistic reckoning (deductive
  inference) in, 13ff., 36ff., ch. 9
  passim
syntax and semantics of, including
  pronouns, 118ff.
term negation (vs. sentence negation),
  33, 199–201, 229
terms such as 'exists' and 'thing',
  treatment of, 196–198, 218
wild quantity, 13–14, 98
Truth. *See* Realism (Sommers's version
  of)
Turing, A., 146, 150
Turing machine, 147

Universals and particulars (and four-
  category ontology), 53ff.

Van Heijenoort, J., 218
Variable (role of in predicate logic). *See*
  Modern predicate logic (MPL)

Warnock, G., 201, 229. *See also* Bare
  particulars
Whitehead, A. N., 1, 7